THE
JEWISH MOURNER'S
BOOK OF WHY

THE
JEWISH MOURNER'S
BOOK OF WHY

ALFRED J. KOLATCH

 Jonathan David Publishers, Inc.
Middle Village, New York 11379

THE JEWISH MOURNER'S BOOK OF WHY

Copyright ©1993
by
Alfred J. Kolatch

Jonathan David Publishers, Inc.
68-22 Eliot Avenue
Middle Village, New York 11379

1994 1996 1997 1995 1993
2 4 6 8 10 9 7 5 3

Library of Congress Cataloging-in-Publication Data
Kolatch, Alfred J., 1916–
    The Jewish mourner's book of why/by Alfred J. Kolatch
    Includes bibliographical references and index.
    ISBN 0-8246-0355-9
    1. Mourning customs, Jewish. I. Title
BM712.K65 1992   91-25260
296.4'45—dc20   CIP

Book design by Jennifer Vignone/TypaGrafx
Printed in the United States of America

FOR MEN AND WOMEN
OF ALL AGES
FOR WHOM
KADDISH WAS NEVER SAID

In Appreciation

Colleagues and friends of the various Jewish denominations have been good enough to read and comment on the contents of this volume in the course of its years of preparation. I am grateful to them all for giving so generously of their time and energy. I am particularly indebted to:

- My brother, Rabbi Arthur J. Kolatch, for his knowledgeable comments, particularly those relating to the practices of the Reform movement.
- Rabbi Ephraim Bennett, of Netanya, Israel, for reviewing the entire manuscript with great care, checking references, and verifying the information presented.
- Rabbi Edward Tenenbaum, of Los Angeles, California, for his helpful comments.
- Rabbi Robert Pilavin, of Spring Valley, New York, for his many useful suggestions.
- Yale Reisner, for employing his editorial eye to solve a number of stylistic problems.
- Rabbi Seymour J. Cohen, for permission to reprint his moving essay, "Kaddish in Many Places," in the Readings for the Bereaved section of this book.
- Helen Hayes, First Lady of the American Theater, for graciously granting permission to include her piece, "Precious Beyond Price," in the Readings for the Bereaved section.

- My wife, Thelma, for always being available for consultation.
- My son Jonathan for his diligent review of the entire manuscript. His keen insights contributed greatly to its improvement.
- My son David, who worked closely with me on a daily basis for more than a year and who was immensely helpful in refining much of the material to make it sharper and more understandable for the layman.
- Marvin Sekler, vice-president of Jonathan David Publishers, for his comments and advice.
- To my lifetime friend Nettie Herzog, for her careful reading of the page proofs.
- Florence Weissman and Fiorella Torre, staff members of Jonathan David Publishers, for their help in typing the manuscript and proofreading the typeset manuscript.

Contents

General Introduction

Jewish death and mourning rites are governed by two basic principles: *kevod ha-met,* respectful treatment of the dead, and *kevod he-chai,* consideration for the feelings of the living, the surviving relatives.

When Jewish law mandates that a funeral take place within twenty-four hours after a death, it is concerned with *kevod ha-met,* for to leave a body unburied for an extended period of time is considered disrespectful. And when Jewish law mandates that a person be buried in the earth rather than be cremated, its intention is also to show respect for the dead, who in Jewish tradition must be returned to the earth from which man was created.

The requirement that friends of mourners prepare the first meal to be eaten after the funeral is a manifestation of the second basic principle, *kevod he-chai,* consideration for the living. If left to their own devices, it was feared, mourners might neglect to prepare food for themselves, thus damaging their health. The intensive seven-day mourning period known as *Shiva,* which affords the bereaved an opportunity to come to terms with their loss, similarly focuses on the living rather than the deceased.

The very words and expressions for death and dying used throughout Jewish literature—from the Bible onward—reflect the Jewish desire to soften the shock and temper the trauma experienced by the mourner. Pleasant words are substituted for harsh ones, kindlier expressions for abrasive ones.

1

When Jacob died, the Bible recounts, he "drew his feet into the bed and, breathing his last, was gathered to his people." The text does not say that Jacob "died" but rather that he was "gathered to his people" (Genesis 49: 33). He joined his ancestors and was buried in the Cave of Machpelah. The same is true of King David. The Bible does not state openly that he died, but that he "slept with his fathers" (I Kings 2:10), and had been "laid to rest with his fathers" (I Kings 11:21).

The use of euphemistic language by Jewish scholars in matters relating to death is most evident in the very name of the talmudic tractate devoted exclusively to the laws of mourning. Its original title is *Evel Rabbati,* "Major Tractate on Mourning,"[1] a name used until about the tenth century. In the eleventh century Rashi introduced new terminology by referring to this tractate euphemistically as *Semachot,* meaning "Rejoicings." That name has been used ever since.

In later times softening of the word "death" is noticeable in many Hebrew and Yiddish expressions. The Hebrew word *niftar,* meaning "departed," was commonly used for one who has died, as was the Yiddish expression *Er iz avek tzum oilum ho-emes,* "He is off to the world of truth." The cemetery thus became known as *olam ha-emet,* "world of truth."

While the Rabbis of the Talmud were not nearly so sophisticated as our contemporary psychologists, psychiatrists, social workers, and many other health professionals in matters relating to death and dying, they did show unusual sensitivity to the problems of the bereaved and established meaningful laws to help ease their pain. The Sages understood that grieving openly and unabashedly is cathartic and should not be discouraged, that the release of emotions helps the mourner in the struggle to return to normalcy.

Recognizing the severity of the shock experienced by an individual upon learning of the death of a close relative, the Rabbis freed the mourner from prayer and other religious obligations until after the funeral. And they made a distinction between the bereaved's status before and after the funeral. Until the time of burial, the bereaved is called an *onen* (feminine, *onenet*), meaning "distressed one." After burial, the bereaved is referred to as an *avel* (feminine, *avela*), "grieving one."

Just as the Rabbis were sensitive to the feelings of the mourner before burial, they were also sensitive to the feeling of the mourner directly after burial. Realizing that the bereaved might require a few days to be alone after the funeral, the Rabbis suggested that, if at all possible, friends not pay condolence calls for the first three days of the seven-day mourning period *(Shiva)*.

To appreciate fully the reasons behind many of our burial and mourning practices, we must acknowledge the extent to which Jewish beliefs and practices were influenced by the outside world. We often think of Jewish communities of old as having been completely insulated from outside thinking and behavior. This is far from accurate. The Bible takes great pains to remind the Israelites not to follow the pagan practices of their neighbors, indicating that alien practices and beliefs did influence our ancestors.

Belief in ghosts and demons, widely held by many peoples among whom Jews lived over the centuries, became part of Jewish thought and is reflected in many of the Jewish customs and ceremonies relating to death, burial, and mourning. Thus, for example, attempts to mislead the "ghost" of the deceased, who may seek to harm the living, is the basis for many Jewish customs.

In this volume we shall explore and explain the reasons behind the many laws, observances, customs, and practices that apply to mourners and those who come in contact with them. Entire chapters are devoted to the laws covering the rending of garments *(Keria)* and the one-week *Shiva* period. The Rabbis consider these laws to have their roots in the Bible and they therefore demanded full compliance with them. Many of the other laws, customs, and ceremonies are discussed as well, but these are generally considered of lesser importance because they were introduced at a much later period.

The formalities of the funeral—the chapel service and the cemetery service—are discussed in great detail in this book, as are the laws pertaining to the recitation of *Kaddish,* visiting a house of mourning, and extending condolences to the bereaved. Also presented is a collection of meditations and inspirational readings that, it is hoped, will provide comfort to the mourner.

Within the body of the work, following chapter introductions, a concise summary of *traditional* observances is presented so that anyone interested in knowing precisely how the *Code of Jewish Law (Shulchan Aruch)* rules on any particular issue will find the decision unencumbered by excessive verbiage. One should be aware, however, that these laws do not always represent the accepted practice of all Jews. Not only do non-Orthodox Jews often carry out practices differently, but even within the Orthodox community practices vary, depending upon which contemporary authority one wishes to follow. These differences are set forth within the body of the work in answer to specific questions.

ALFRED J. KOLATCH

Forest Hills, New York
January 2, 1993

CHAPTER 1

From Life to Death

Introduction

Judaism teaches us that we must "choose life" (Deuteronomy 30:19). As long as a human being clings to life, no matter how precariously, tradition demands that we spare no effort to keep the person alive. To that end, we are obliged to visit the sick and pray for their recovery. We are obliged to be mindful of the manner in which we address the ill and the nature of the news we choose to share with them. Until death actually comes, we must never abandon the hope of recovery. Judaism rejects the idea of hastening death by overtly denying available medical treatment.

Immediately upon a person's demise, Jewish tradition suggests, a candle should be lighted and placed near the head of the deceased. The flickering flame reminds us that, although the soul of the individual is now without a living body to harbor it, the spirit of that life has not vanished. The religious practices applied at this point reflect the Jewish belief that every human being is to be accorded the utmost respect in death as well as in life.

This chapter examines the issues that arise when death is imminent and those that must be faced when it finally strikes. The range of such issues extends from the etiquette to be observed when visiting the sick to the issues of euthanasia, autopsy, and embalming; and from the proper way of handling the deceased to the proper conduct of mourners during the initial stage following a death.

Summary of Traditional Observances
When Death Approaches

Visiting the sick
- Visiting the sick, particularly the terminally ill, is mandated by the Rabbis, but visits should not be long so as to exhaust the patient.

Viddui
- *Viddui* means "Confession of Sins." A person on the verge of death is encouraged to confess his or her sins.

Euthanasia
- Hastening the death of an ill person is forbidden, regardless of how hopeless the condition. However, one is not required to use heroic methods to prolong the life of a patient.

When death strikes
- As soon as death is confirmed, the eyes and mouth of the deceased are closed. The arms and hands are extended; the lower jaw is bound. The body is then placed on the floor, with feet facing the door. The body is then covered with a sheet and a lighted candle is placed near the head.
- It is advisable to call one's rabbi or a funeral parlor immediately upon learning of the death of a loved one.
- The *Chevra Kadisha,* or Burial Society (see the next chapter), is called in to carry out the required formalities. The first duty of the Society is to appoint "watchers" to be with the body at all times.
- All water in the house that is in pots or other vessels is poured out onto the floor. This is not done on the Sabbath.

Autopsies
- Tampering with the body unnecessarily is forbidden.

Autopsies are permitted if required by Civil law, especially when the immediate cause of death cannot be determined or when the death is the result of an accident or a homicide. They are also permitted if another person suffering from a similar illness may be helped by what is learned from the autopsy.

Embalming
- Under normal circumstances, embalming is forbidden. It is permitted when there is a long delay before the burial can take place or when civil law demands it.

The Onen
- From the moment of death, each member of the immediate family is called an *onen,* "one who is distressed." An *onen* is not obligated to pray or carry out other religious duties and is forbidden from shaving, cutting the hair, or conducting usual business affairs.
- The laws pertaining to an *onen* apply to both men and women.
- This phase of mourning, known as the *aninut* period ends when the body is buried, at which time all of the regular laws of mourning *(avelut)* are in effect.

Why did the Rabbis stress the importance of visiting the sick?

The Rabbis of the Talmud encouraged visits to the sick, particularly the seriously ill, claiming that "he who visits the sick eliminates one-sixtieth of the ill person's pain," but he who does not visit the sick "is like one who sheds blood."[1] However, the Rabbis laid down strict rules governing *when* visits should take place. They advised that one should not visit the seriously ill during the first three hours and last three hours of the day.[2] It is during this time, the great twelfth-century scholar Moses Maimonides, himself a doctor, explained in his *Mishneh Torah,* that medical attention is most commonly given.[3]

The Rabbis also suggested that because the first three days of a serious illness are the most critical, only members of the immediate family should pay visits during this time.[4]

Why may family members violate the Sabbath to bring cheer to one who is seriously ill?

The Rabbis considered the act of visiting the sick (*bikur cholim* in Hebrew) to be a religious commandment (*mitzva*) of such magnitude that all who carry it out will share in the world-to-come.[5] They noted that if a close relative (father, mother, brother, sister, son, daughter, spouse) is seriously ill and it seems likely that a visit will cheer up the individual and improve chances for recovery, even violating the Sabbath is permitted if absolutely necessary. Preserving life is a cardinal principle of Judaism.[6]

Why must one refrain from notifying a critically ill person of a death in the family?

The Rabbis advised that we be extremely cautious in what we say to a seriously ill person. If it is suspected that notifying the ill person that a relative has died will cause great mental anguish and possibly lead to a worsening of the patient's condition, such news should not be transmitted.[7]

Other scholars go so far as to say that if a sick person inquires about a relative who has died, it is permissible to lie and say that the person is still alive.[8]

Why is a dying person never to be left alone?

Judaism is highly sensitive to the feelings of the terminally ill. Accordingly, the law[9] demands that a patient whose days are numbered not be left alone to be plagued with thoughts of death.

A second reason for the requirement that a dying person not be left alone is ascribed to a belief widespread in the Middle Ages that at the moment of death a struggle ensues between the angels and the demons (the agents of the devil), each seeking to take charge of the deceased's soul. Jews believed that the demons are denied access to the dying when a human being stands guard.[10]

Why is a candle sometimes lighted in the room of a terminally ill patient?

In the seventeenth-century classic work *Ma-avar Yabok,* which explains the customs and ceremonies in vogue at the time, the author[11] offers the probable reason for lighting a candle in the room of a person nearing death. He explains this practice, which is no longer widely observed, as a way of both warding off evil spirits (who are afraid of light) and of announcing that a human soul is about to depart this earth.

Why is a person facing imminent death encouraged to make a Confession of Sins?

The Book of Ecclesiastes (7:20) says, "There is not a righteous man upon earth who does good and does not sin." Every individual, knowingly or unknowingly, is a sinner in the course of his or her lifetime.

To expiate for sins, the Bible required that an offering be brought. The Book of Leviticus (4:1-35) describes two types of such offerings: the Sin Offering *(Korban Chatat)* and the Guilt Offering *(Korban Asham).* With the destruction of the Second Temple in 70 C.E., the sacrificial system was abandoned, and from that time on Jews were deprived of the opportunity to atone for sins through the bringing of sacrifices. To fill this void, the Rabbis introduced the idea of a deathbed confession *(Viddui* in Hebrew).[12]

One who is gravely ill is addressed as follows:

> Confess your sins. Many confessed their sins and did not die, and many who did not confess died. As a reward for your confession, you will continue to live, for anyone who confesses his sins will have a portion in the world-to-come.[13]

Traditionally, two forms of *Viddui* responses are recited by the terminally ill, depending upon the physical condition of the patient.

The shorter form is:

> May my death be an atonement for all the sins, iniquities, and transgressions of which I have been guilty against Thee.

The longer form is:

> I acknowledge before Thee, O Lord my God and God of my fathers, that both my cure and my death are in Thy hands. May it be Thy will to send me a perfect healing. Yet, should I die, I will accept it at Thy hand, and may my death be an atonement for all sins, iniquities, and transgressions of which I have been guilty. Grant me a place in the Garden of Eden and in the world-to-come that is reserved for righteous people.[14]

Both confessions conclude with the recital of the *Shema* (Deuteronomy 6:4):

> Hear, O Israel, the Lord is our God, the Lord is One.

Why did some Rabbis in talmudic and later times believe that death is a blessing?

According to the Midrash, the second-century scholar and scribe Rabbi Meir had a Torah scroll with a text that differed from traditional texts. The traditional text of Genesis 1:31 reads: "And God saw all that he had created, and found it *tov me'od* ["very good"]. Instead of *me'od,* the scroll of Rabbi Meir read *mot* (the unvocalized Hebrew letters can mistakenly be pronounced *mavet*), meaning "death," which translates to "death is good."

Some scholars believe that this narrative was created in order to introduce the idea that death is not bad because it affords one an opportunity to repent for one's sins and come closer to God.

An equally valid explanation of Rabbi Meir's rendition of the Genesis 1:31 text is that death is to be considered good—a blessing rather than a curse—because it frees the soul to be on its own, no longer encased in a body. The mortal body ceases to exist and the immortal soul begins to flourish.

Rabbi Meir had good reason to harbor a belief in the immortality of the soul, having lost two innocent sons while they were still very young. This story is recounted in the section of this book entitled Readings for the Bereaved.

Why did some Rabbis consider death to be an atonement for sin?

In the Talmud,[15] Rabbi Ammi asks, "Why is the account of Miriam's [sister of Moses] death recorded in the Bible [Numbers 20:1] immediately after the law governing the sacrifice of the Red Heifer, the ashes of which were used in the atonement ceremony for sinners?"

The reply is "To teach us that just as the Red Heifer afforded atonement [by the ritual use of its ashes], so does the death of righteous people become atonement [for the living, whom they leave behind after their death]."

Why did many Rabbis consider death to be the "wages of sin?"

"There is no death without sin," teaches the Talmud.[16] Many of the Rabbis believed that man was destined to live forever, but because Adam sinned when he disobeyed God and ate from the forbidden fruit of the

Garden of Eden (Genesis 3:17, 19), death came to the world.[17]

This concept, later rejected by mainstream Judaism, became a core belief of Christianity.[18]

Why did some Rabbis view death as unrelated to sinfulness?

While we find within Jewish tradition many scholars who looked upon death as punishment for sinfulness, a goodly number considered it to be part of the natural order of things.

Making the point emphatically, the Midrash[19] goes so far as to say that the Angel of Death was brought into the world on the first day of Creation, signifying that life and death are part of the same continuum.

Why is euthanasia generally forbidden in Jewish law?

Euthanasia, Greek for "beautiful death," is considered murder in both civil and Jewish law. Therefore, regardless of how severe the condition or how negative the prognosis, no effort may be made to shorten a person's life. Jewish tradition places in God's hands alone the decision of who shall live and who shall die.

While there exists no direct biblical commandment prohibiting "mercy killing," as euthanasia is popularly called, the Rabbis cite an action taken by King David as a biblical basis for their refusal to sanction it (II Samuel 1:1-16). During the great battle near Mount Gilboa, in which King Saul faced powerful Philistine troops, a young man appeared before David (who was not involved in the battle) and reported that he had seen badly wounded King Saul leaning against a spear. In intense physical pain, Saul asked that the young man be merciful and end his, the king's, life. The young man acceded to Saul's wishes. When David learned of this, he ordered the young man executed, saying, "You have taken the life of God's anointed!"

Based upon this incident, the Rabbis ruled that since all life is sacred to God, no person has the right to hasten the death of another person—king or otherwise—regardless of the motivation.

Joseph Caro, the sixteenth-century author of the *Code of Jewish Law (Shulchan Aruch)*,[20] emphasizes the point by noting that one may not remove a pillow from under a dying person's head, nor may one engage in any kind of activity that is likely to hasten an individual's death. Nature must be allowed to take its course.

In subsequent centuries, a more liberal attitude toward euthanasia was adopted by some authorities.[21]

Why do some contemporary authorities favor "passive euthanasia"?

Rabbi Nissim ben Reuven Girondi, the outstanding fourteenth-century Spanish scholar and physician known by the acronym Ran, was of the opinion[22] that there are times when one should pray for the demise of a person whose pain is intense and for whom there is no hope for recovery.

In support of this position, the Ran cited an incident described in the Talmud. When the death of Rabbi Judah the Prince (135-219), editor of the Mishna and the most outstanding scholar of the third century, was imminent, his disciples gathered at their teacher's bedside and prayed continuously for his recovery. However, one of Rabbi Judah's maidservants, (who was reputed to be a learned woman), realizing how intense was her master's suffering and how useless it would be to prolong his life, hurled an earthenware jug to the ground. The noise had its expected effect: it attracted the attention of everyone in the room and their praying ceased, whereupon Judah expired.[23]

A number of contemporary authorities, logically or not, cite the above-mentioned incident as the basis for

permitting "passive euthanasia." These scholars conclude that when a terminally ill patient is in great pain,
doctors are not obliged to keep the patient alive by
introducing artificial life-support systems, thus leaving
therapeutic intervention in the hands of God.

Taking a contrary position, the prominent Rabbi Eliezer Waldenberg of Jerusalem (born 1917) maintains
that it is not permissible for a relative to pray for the
death of an incurable family member who is suffering
greatly, because it is feared that the relative might be
motivated by self-interest, by the desire to relieve himself of the heavy burden of caring for the sick person.[24]

"Active euthanasia," which involves speeding up the
demise of the patient by artificial means, such as the injection of a drug, is considered murder by many Jewish
authorities.[25]

Why do Yemenite Jews remove sacred ob-
jects from the room of a dying person?

In recent centuries, the practice among Jews of Yemen has been to remove the *mezuza* and sacred books
from the room of a dying person who is in great pain.
The Yemenites believe that the presence of holy objects
lessens the power of the Angel of Death and impedes it
from carrying out its function. When the holy objects
are removed from the room of the dying, the Angel of
Death is able to take the life of the patient sooner, thus
terminating the individual's suffering.

Why is it sometimes said that the "kiss of
death" has been bestowed upon a person?

Moses, as well as his brother, Aaron, and sister, Miriam, like the patriarchs Abraham, Isaac, and Jacob who
preceded them, were said to have died through the "kiss
of death," meaning suddenly and smoothly.[26]

With regard to the death of Moses, the Bible (Deuteronomy 34:5) says:

> Moses, servant of the Lord, died there in the Land of Moab, by the mouth of God.

Rabbis who were of a mystical bent interpreted the words "mouth of God" literally, commenting that when Moses died, his soul refused to leave his body. God then put his mouth to the mouth of Moses and planted the kiss of death upon him. Suddenly, the soul of Moses left his body.[27]

In the Talmud,[28] Rabbi Nachman describes an easy death, without suffering, as being comparable to the "drawing of a hair out of a glass of milk."

Why are the eyes of the deceased closed immediately after death has been established?

The closing of the eyes of the deceased is an old Jewish tradition that was also practiced by the ancient Greeks and Romans. Plato, in his *Phaedo,* writes that, after Socrates died, Crito "closed his eyes and mouth."[29] The twelfth-century Spanish scholar Abraham ibn Ezra associated the custom of closing the eyes of the deceased with Joseph's closing of the eyes of his father, Jacob. In the Book of Genesis (46:4) Jacob is promised that when he dies, "Joseph's hand shall close your eyes," meaning that Jacob can rest in peace.

The sixteenth-century *Code of Jewish Law*[30] also indicates that after closing the eyes of the deceased, the arms and hands are to be extended and brought close to the body. (The Mishna[31] forbids the closing of the eyes of a corpse on the Sabbath.) The lower jaw is then brought close to the upper jaw and tied up before rigor mortis sets in. Finally, the body is placed on the floor and covered with a sheet. A lighted candle is then placed near the head.

It should be noted that the above procedures described in the *Code of Jewish Law* have generally been abandoned. Most Rabbis felt that such practices would be ridiculed by the Gentile world.[32]

Why, upon death, do some Jews follow the custom of placing the body of the deceased on the floor?

Some Orthodox Jews still practice the old custom of placing the body of the deceased on the floor approximately twenty minutes after death. The reason for doing so, according to some scholars, is based on the fact that, in locales where the climate was hot, placing a corpse on a cool floor would prevent rapid deterioration of the corpse.[33]

A second probable reason is that by placing the deceased on the floor, it brings the individual closer to the earth from which he sprang and to which he will be returned, thus fulfilling the biblical prognostication "For dust thou art and unto dust shalt thou return" (Genesis 3:19).

Why is the *Tziduk Ha-din* prayer sometimes recited at the moment of death?

In the death room, at the moment of a person's passing, it was once common for everyone present to recite the *Tziduk Ha-din* prayer.[34] This prayer was selected for recitation at this time because it contains the words *Dayan Emet,* the last two words of the blessing spoken upon rending the garment (*Keria* in Hebrew). When these words are pronounced, all present in the room rend their garments.

This practice is no longer in force and, generally, Keria is performed immediately before or after the funeral service.

Why was it once customary to keep a bucket of water in front of each Jewish home?

In medieval times, when a death would occur in a Jewish home, the container of water usually kept outside of the home to serve the needs of the family would be emptied, thereby announcing to all that a death has occurred. This served as a specific warning to a member of the priestly family (*Kohanim;* singular, *Kohen*) that he was to remain at least six feet distant from that house, as prescribed by Jewish law to ensure the ritual purity of priests.

The English expression "to kick the bucket" may derive from the old custom of pouring out water to mark a death.[35]

Why is water sometimes poured onto the floor as soon as a death occurs?

References to the pouring out of water in connection with a death are found in sources that describe life in thirteenth-century Germany and France. It was thought that Satan becomes active once a death occurs, and that if the word "death" is mentioned aloud, Satan would become aware of it and would be tempted to control the soul of the deceased. To avoid this, the pouring out of water became the means of silently communicating the news of a death.

It was also commonly believed in the Middle Ages that the ghost of the dead hovers about after a death and attacks relatives of the deceased. Water keeps the ghost at bay, for it is afraid of water and will not cross it.[36]

Traditional commentators explain that the water poured out when a death occurs was the water that families stored up and kept in jugs at the entrances to homes. This water is called *ma'yim she'uvim* ("drawn waters" in Hebrew) as opposed to *ma'yim cha'yim* ("living, natural waters") such as well water or rain water gathered in pits. The *ma'yim she'uvim,* which has been drawn through pipes (tap water, for example), must be poured out because the water is considered tainted by virtue of its proximity to the deceased.[37]

Why is a candle lit in the room where a person has just died?

Immediately upon a death, it is customary to light a candle and to place it near the head of the deceased.

While this 2,000-year-old practice is generally explained as a way of showing respect for the soul of the departed, mystics believe that the flame of the candle eases the soul's ascent to heaven.

Another explanation is that candlelight serves to keep evil spirits at a distance. To accomplish this, Kabbalists are known to surround the body with twenty-six lighted tapers, twenty-six being the numerical value of the Hebrew word *Yehova,* meaning "God."[38]

Today, however, the lighting of a candle is simply regarded as a way of memorializing the dead.

Why is a blessing not recited when a candle is lighted for the dead?

The Mishna[39] indicates that a blessing may be pronounced over a candle only when its light will be enjoyed, which is not the case when a candle is lighted to memorialize the deceased.

Why do rabbinic authorities differ on the question of using organs from a dead person for transplant purposes?

Based on Deuteronomy 21:22-23, which states that if a criminal is put to death by hanging, "his body shall not remain all night hanging on the tree, but thou shalt surely bury him that same day," the Rabbis conclude that to mistreat or mutilate the body of a deceased (known in Hebrew as *nivul ha-met*) is a violation of scriptural law.

Since it is argued that the body of a dead person is in a sense being mutilated when an organ is removed from it for transplant into the body of a living person, strong opposition to the procedure exists. Most authorities agree, however, that when a transplant is likely to save a life, such surgery is permitted. Transplant surgery that results in the saving of a life adds glory and honor to the dead (in Hebrew, *kevod ha-met*). Thus, the positive commandment of saving a life, the rabbinic authorities say, is of the highest priority, superseding even the laws of the Sabbath.[40] The talmudic principle that is applied by advocates of transplant surgery is *zeh ne'heneh ve-zeh lo chaser,* "one party is helped and the other suffers no loss."

Aside from the question of mutilation of the dead, many in the Orthodox community object to organ transplant surgery on the grounds that it results in a violation of the Jewish law requiring that all severed parts of a person be buried. An organ used for transplant purposes is obviously not buried.

The question was addressed by Rabbi Moshe Feinstein (Orthodox), who countered that when any organ from the body of a deceased is transplanted into a living person, the organ can no longer be considered an organ of the dead. It becomes part of the living body, and the law demanding the burial of all parts of a deceased does not apply.[41]

Rabbi Isaac Klein (Conservative) pointed out that a transplanted organ will eventually be buried, thus satisfying the requirement.[42]

Why is Jewish law traditionally opposed to autopsy in most cases?

Based on the firm belief that people are created in the image of God and that it would be sacrilegious to mutilate God's creation, Jewish law forbids autopsy under ordinary circumstances.[43]

Throughout the ages the Rabbis have also forbidden autopsy based on the belief that in the end of days God will resurrect the bodies of the dead, and any disfigurement of the bodies will interfere with the process.

Autopsy is also opposed because it is thought to be a violation of *kevod ha-met,* the Jewish concept demanding that the corpse of a deceased be treated with dignity.

Why was the ruling of Rabbi Ezekiel Landau on autopsy considered a landmark decision?

As stated above, most authorities agree that since man is made in the image of God, the body of a man should not be mutilated or disfigured by conducting an autopsy after death. However, a more liberal attitude toward autopsy was introduced in the eighteenth century when Rabbi Ezekiel Landau (1713-1793), the famous rabbi of Prague, responded to a questioner from London who asked if it is permissible to perform an autopsy on a Jew in order to ascertain the cause of death, in the hope that what is learned might save the lives of others.

Rabbi Landau ruled that an autopsy may be performed if there is reason to believe that what doctors will learn as a result of the procedure might be helpful in curing a *particular* patient who is at hand and is in dire need of help.[44] Rabbi Moses Sofer (1763-1839), the esteemed authority from Pressburg (later called Bratislava) concurred.[45]

Why is there no definitive present-day Jewish view on autopsy?

Although all contemporary authorities would agree that autopsy is permitted when civil law demands it, as when a death is the result of a homicide, many are also inclined to permit the procedure if scientific knowledge will be enhanced as a result, possibly leading to the saving of lives. This view, however, was not shared by the two Chief Rabbis of Israel and their 356 colleagues, who in 1966 declared that "autopsies in any form are prohibited by Torah law."

Of the various Jewish denominations, the Reform movement takes the most liberal position on autopsy. That view was first expressed by Jacob Z. Lauterbach in the 1924 *Central Conference of American Rabbis Yearbook*.[46] He said that in our times communication is so rapid that a discovery made by one physician is conveyed around the world almost simultaneously, and the opportunity to gather new scientific information should not depend upon there being an immediate beneficiary, as Ezekiel Landau and Moses Sofer insisted. (See the previous answer.) The Reform view is that the decision for or against autopsy should rest solely with the family.

Why do authorities agree that carte blanche not be given hospitals to perform autopsies?

A problem that for years has plagued rabbinic and medical authorities is how to satisfy the requirements of medical schools and medical researchers if anatomical dissections and post-mortem examinations are prohibited. How can scientists learn more about disease if autopsies are forbidden? How can medical students receive proper training if Jewish law *(halacha)* forbids needless handling of the body of the deceased?

To meet the demands of the scientific community in Israel, an agreement permitting autopsy within certain detailed guidelines was entered into between the Chief Rabbinate of Israel and Hadassah University Hospital.[47]

Among the important features of their agreement is the requirement that, in keeping with the principle of "honoring the dead" *(kevod ha-met),* those performing the autopsy must agree to return all parts of the body for proper burial after their studies have been concluded.

It should be noted that current Israeli law limits the freedom of doctors to perform autopsies (and organ transplants) by requiring that they respect the wishes of family members in this regard.

Why has autopsy been permitted when a deceased has so willed it?

Rabbi Yaacov Ettlinger, of Altona, Germany, one of the illustrious rabbinic authorities of the second half of the nineteenth century, declared in a responsum[48] that a dissection may be performed without being in violation of Jewish law if such was the expressed wish of the deceased, made in the interest of enhancing research so that one day others might be cured. Such autopsies are not to be considered desecration of the dead.

Not all authorities agree with this view, contending that man has no proprietary right even over his own body and that violating a body in any manner, for any purpose, is an offense to God. Accordingly, a person has no right to will that his body be tampered with for any reason.[49]

Why did the Rabbis of the Talmud object to embalming?

Embalming—preserving the remains of the deceased by draining off the blood from the body and discarding it—was once practiced by Jews. The procedure was common among Egyptians and, in fact, in the Bible (Genesis 50:2-3 and 50:26) both Jacob and his son Joseph were embalmed when they died in Egypt.

The practice was still carried out in Second Temple times, as we learn from the writings of the first-century historian Josephus. In describing the death of Aristobulus II, King of Judea (67-63 B.C.E.), Josephus writes:[50]

> His dead body also lay for a good while embalmed in honey till Anthony afterwards sent it to Judea and caused him to be buried in the royal sepulchre.

The Rabbis of the Talmud, however, objected to embalming for two reasons. First, they considered it to be disrespectful to the dead and banned the practice unless there is sufficient reason to do otherwise. Second, they felt that embalming retards the swift decomposition of the body, thereby delaying its return to the earth whence it came.

Why do contemporary Jewish authorities sometimes permit embalming?

Embalming is generally permitted today whenever government regulations require it and whenever the body cannot be buried within three days. For three days, refrigeration of the body is adequate to retard deterioration, but when burial is delayed because the body must be transported to another city, injection of embalming fluids is necessary to slow down deterioration and to obfuscate foul odors.

Jewish authorities are careful to warn that the blood and the organs removed during the embalming process must be saved in a container and ultimately be buried in the coffin together with the corpse.[51]

Why is a mourner sometimes called an *onen*?

Immediately upon the passing of a close relative (father, mother, son, daughter, brother, sister, or spouse) the mourner is referred to as an *onen* (feminine, *onenet*; plural, *onenim* and *onenot*), Hebrew for "one who is distressed." This initial period of distress, called *aninut* in Hebrew, comes to an end when burial is completed.[52] After the *aninut* period, the mourner is referred to as an *avel,* which is the general term for mourner.

Why is a mourner not to be comforted immediately after suffering the loss of a loved one?

The Rabbis of the Talmud[53] cautioned: "Do not comfort a person while his dead lies before him," that is, while the person is an *onen.* During this early stage following the loss of a loved one, the mourner is in a state of shock, and the Rabbis felt that the mourner would not be able to accept consolation readily, and might even be offended if approached with words of comfort at this time.

Why is an *onen* not obligated to pray?

The Rabbis compared the *onen,* the distressed person, to an inebriated person—one not in full control of his faculties, one guided by impulse rather than by reason. Because the mind of the *onen* is preoccupied with funeral arrangements and is not attuned to prayer or to the carrying out of positive religious commandments *(mitzvot),* the Rabbis ruled that on all days except the Sabbath the *onen* is not required to pray or to participate in religious activity of any kind.[54] The donning of phylacteries *(tefilin)* is specifically prohibited.[55]

In his *Guide to Jewish Religious Practice*[56] (Conservative) Rabbi Isaac Klein considers this ruling outmoded, arguing that "today, when organized groups or commercial firms take care of burial needs and the participation of the family is minimal," an *onen* should be encouraged to pray so as to derive the solace and comfort that prayer and the performance of religious duties bring the individual.

It is interesting to note that during the existence of the First and Second Temples—from the days of Solomon (about 1000 B.C.E.) until the Roman occupation of Palestine in 70 C.E.—a mourner was not permitted to bring a Peace Offering *(Korban Shelamim),* sometimes called a Sacrifice of Well-being, even if circumstances would have called for it. A Peace Offering was brought as an expression of gratitude for deliverance from danger or misfortune, and since an *onen* is not in a mood to express thanks for anything, he was banned from bringing a Peace Offering.

The Talmud[57] declares: "An *onen* does not offer sacrifices, for one offers Peace Offerings only at times when one is untroubled, but not at a time when one is an *onen.*" And Rabbi Simeon underscores this by adding that when one brings sacrifices, he is to "rejoice before the Lord," and one who has just lost a loved one is not in a joyful mood.

Why is an *onen* not counted as part of a religious quorum?

Since an *onen,* a person whose loved one has not yet been buried, is not obligated to pray or carry out the positive religious obligations incumbent upon the average Jew, the mourner at this stage is considered to be *outside* the religious community and therefore may not be counted as one of the ten adults who constitute a religious quorum *(minyan).*

Why may an *onen* carry out religious duties and engage in prayer on the Sabbath?

Because the Sabbath is considered to be a day of peace and joy, all forms of public mourning are forbidden on this day. Therefore, on the Sabbath the *onen* is required to carry out all religious duties normally incumbent upon a Jew.[58] The Talmud[59] points out that in Judea, to indicate that mourning was not to be observed on the Sabbath, it was customary to greet mourners with the word *shalom,* "peace," a greeting that is forbidden on other days of mourning.

CHAPTER 2

Preparing the Deceased for Burial

Introduction

First established in the Middle Ages, the Burial Society is possibly the most prestigious organization within Jewish life. It is also perhaps the least known, the least publicized, and surely the least glamorous. The Society consists of Jewish volunteers—members of a particular synagogue or members of the community at large—who prepare the dead for burial and sometimes even manage the administration of the local cemetery. Those who volunteer for this service are regarded as among the most selfless, most dedicated people in the Jewish fold.

Whereas Ashkenazim call the Burial Society by the Hebrew name *Chevra Kadisha,* meaning "Holy Society," Sephardim use a variety of terms that are indicative of the noble nature of the work to which the men and women of the group have dedicated themselves. Syrian Jews call the *Chevra Kadisha* by the name *Chevra Rodfei Zedek,* "Society of Pursuers of Justice." The Spanish-Portuguese community calls the group *Hebra Chased Va-emet* [sic], "Society of Lovingkindness and Truth." Moroccans call it by a variety of names, including *Chevrat Gomlei Chasadim,* "Society of Providers of Lovingkindness," *Chevrat Chesed Ve-emet,* and *Chevrat Rabbi Shimon bar Yocha'i,* "Society of Rabbi Shimon bar Yocha'i." Rabbi Shimon, the legendary charismatic mystic,

26

is buried atop Mount Meron in northern Israel. Each year on Lag B'Omer, which is the anniversary of Rabbi Shimon's death, thousands of his followers make a pilgrimage to Mount Meron.

The two guiding principles that govern the activities of the Burial Societies are the same as those that govern all Jewish death and mourning rites. First, that proper respect and reverence be shown the dead, referred to in the Talmud[1] as *yekara di-shichva*. And, second, that due respect be accorded the bereaved, referred to in the Talmud as *yekara de-cha'yay*.[2] These terms are Aramaic, which was the vernacular of the Jews in the talmudic and post-talmudic periods. The Hebrew term for the Aramaic *yekara di-shichva* is *kevod ha-met* ("honor of the dead"); and for *yekara de-cha'yay, kevod he-chai* ("honor of the living").

This chapter explores the various duties of the Chevra Kadisha and explains the manner in which their responsibilities are carried out.

Summary of Traditional Observances in Preparing the Deceased for Burial

The Chevra Kadisha
- The Chevra Kadisha (Burial Society), a committee of local Jews, is responsible for preparing the deceased for burial.
- Separate groups attend to men and women.

Dressing the deceased
- The deceased is dressed in simple, inexpensive white shrouds without pockets. Street clothes are not used. The *talit* (prayershawl) of the individual is draped over the body after one of the fringes *(tzitziot)* has been cut off.

The Coffin
- The deceased is placed in a simple pine coffin, which is not opened unless there is a need to identify the body. Except for earth from Israel, nothing is placed inside the coffin.
- Holes are sometimes drilled in the bottom of the coffin.

The "Watchers"
- From the time the coffin is closed until the funeral service takes place, one or two "watchers" are always present in the room with the body. During this time they recite selections from the Book of Psalms.

Why is the Burial Society an important institution in Jewish life?

Preparing the deceased for burial in a dignified manner is of the highest priority in Judaism.

When Jewish communities were close-knit, each town or village, and often each individual synagogue, had its own Burial Society. Commonly called the *Chevra Kadisha* (see chapter introduction), the institution was comprised of men and women who consecrated themselves without remuneration to the holy task of preparing the dead for burial.

Although the Jewish community is no longer as cohesive as it once was, the Chevra Kadisha still functions, either under the aegis of one or more of the synagogues in a community or under the auspices of a funeral parlor. After the funeral director has arranged for the attending physician to certify a death, and after the body has been transported to the chapel, the Burial Society is called in by the rabbi or the funeral director to attend to the corpse and prepare it for burial.

On rare occasions, particularly when the funeral is held in the home and burial is to be in a distant place, the Chevra Kadisha performs its functions in the home of the deceased.

Why is a "guardian" designated by the Chevra Kadisha to keep watch over the corpse?

In Jewish tradition, a human being is equated with a Torah scroll. Just as the scroll must be treated reverentially not only when being read in the synagogue but also when resting in the ark, so must a person be treated with respect once his or her life has ended. This is in accordance with the talmudic principle referred to in Hebrew as *kevod ha-met* (see chapter introduction).

One way of showing respect is to guard the body of the deceased. It is the Chevra Kadisha that assumes this responsibility by appointing one individual to stay with the body at all times. The person so designated is called the *shomer* (feminine, *shomeret*), meaning "watcher" or "guardian." The person on duty stays with the body and recites Psalm 23, Psalm 91, or selected verses from Psalm 119. Particular verses from Psalm 119 are selected so that the first letter of each verse, when put side by side, spell out the name of the deceased. [4]

Note that it is also customary not to leave a seriously ill person alone during the last moments of life. See page 8 for further discussion.

Why is the corpse thoroughly cleansed before being dressed for burial?

Jewish tradition insists that just as the body is washed when it emerges from the mother's womb, so at death must it be thoroughly cleansed in order that it may be returned to God in a state of purity.

A second explanation for the cleansing requirement is that just as the Priests (Kohanim) in Temple times had to thoroughly cleanse themselves before donning white garments to perform sacrificial duties, so must the deceased be thoroughly cleansed before being dressed in white shrouds.

It is the function of members of the Chevra Kadisha to wash the corpse thoroughly from head to toe. This cleansing procedure carried out by members of the Burial Society is called *tohora* (sometimes mistakenly spelled *tahara*), Hebrew for "purification." Separate groups conduct the purification procedure for men and women. [5]

Using twenty-four quarts of water, the Burial Society must make sure not to neglect any of the orifices or the spaces between fingers and toes. The nails must be pared and the hair groomed, but cosmetics may not be used. During the washing procedure, the body of the deceased is not to be placed face down, for this is considered disrespectful. [6] After washing, the corpse is dressed in shrouds and placed in the coffin.

Among the Falashas of Ethiopia, the practice was for four men from the village to come to wash the body. These individuals, as well as those who carry the corpse, were considered unclean, and for seven days thereafter they had to live outside the village. On the third day they sprinkled themselves with water, and on the seventh day they washed their bodies and clothes, shaved their heads, and returned to the community. [7]

Why is it sometimes permissible for non-Jews to prepare a Jewish corpse for burial?

While Jewish tradition demands that Jews, particularly observant ones, perform the cleansing of the body of the deceased before burial, in cases where Jews are not available to do this, Gentiles may perform the function, with a Jew supervising the activity. [8]

Why is lime sprinkled on the body of the deceased?

In some Jewish communities, such as the one in Yemen, it is customary to sprinkle lime on the body of the deceased to hasten decomposition.

Why were the dead once buried in ordinary street clothes?

There is no evidence in the Bible that in early times the dead were buried in shrouds, as is the practice today. The witch of Endor (I Samuel 28:14) saw the prophet Samuel arise from the grave clad in a robe, which the Midrash, [9] reminding us that Samuel's mother had made a robe for him when he was a boy (I Samuel 2:19), assumes was his normal, everyday clothing.

Later, the practice of burying the dead in street clothing was associated with the concept of the Messiah. It was believed that if buried in street garb, the deceased would be ready for resurrection. (See Chapter Twelve for a full discussion of resurrection.) Accordingly, a fourth-century Babylonian-born scholar, Rabbi Jeremiah, left the following instructions to be carried out upon his death:

> Clothe me in white hemmed garments...
> place my staff in my hand and my sandals
> on my feet, and lay me by a road so that
> when I am summoned [at the time of the
> resurrection of the dead], I may be ready. [10]

Why was the practice of burying scholars and wealthy persons in expensive garments discontinued?

In early talmudic times, it was customary for wealthy persons to bury their dead in costly garments. This was practiced until the first century, when Rabbi Gamaliel I, grandson of Hillel, insisted that it be discontinued because it was unfair to those who could not afford fancy clothing, and furthermore, because it was wasteful. Gamaliel proposed that everyone, rich and poor alike, be buried in inexpensive linen garments as a sign that all human beings are equal in the sight of God.[11]

Rabbi Judah the Prince, the outstanding scholar and wealthy religious leader of the second century, followed the view of Gamaliel and left instructions that he be buried in a simple linen shirt.[12]

Some authorities did not agree that all persons had to be buried in simple, inexpensive garb. If done in good taste and in keeping with the lifestyle of the deceased, it was argued, burial in elegant garments was not to be viewed as sinful.[13] Nonetheless, the accepted tradition is for all Jews to be dressed in inexpensive garb.

The Talmud[14] adds insight into the reason why burial garments are to be simple and inexpensive. It explains that at one time the expense of burying the dead became so prohibitive that many poor folks just abandoned the dead so that the community would assume the responsibility.

Why did shrouds replace street clothing as burial garments?

In talmudic and post-talmudic times, the concept of resurrection and the afterlife became increasingly popular among Jews, and it was believed that by wearing loose, unknotted garments—rather than normal street clothing—one would be better prepared for the resurrection.[16]

It is not until the seventeenth century that we find the first allusion to the practice of dressing the dead in unknotted clothes—that is, in shrouds. This reference appears in the classic work *Ma-avar Yabok,* by the Italian mystic Aaron Berechya of Modena (died 1639), which, in addition to laws of mourning, contains laws and prayers pertaining to the sick and terminally ill.

In time, the use of shrouds became a strongly entrenched practice in Jewish life. Today, even secular Jews are averse to the idea of burying relatives in elaborate clothing, which they consider a non-Jewish practice. In his book *Patrimony,* the noted author Philip Roth, who is not an observant Jew, remarked how incensed he was when the mortician asked him to pick out a suit in which to bury his father. "A suit!" said Roth. "He's not going to the office! No! No suit! It's senseless." Roth wanted his father to be buried in shrouds, just as his father's parents and their ancestors had been buried.[17]

Why is inexpensive white fabric traditionally used to make shrouds?

Traditionally, shrouds are made of inexpensive muslin, flax (linen), or cotton. White was selected because it is the symbol of purity and forgiveness. This symbolism dates back to the time of the prophet Isaiah, who said (Isaiah 1:18):

> Though your sins be like crimson,
> They can turn snow-white.
> Be they red as dyed wool,
> They can become [white] like fleece.

Not all talmudic and post-talmudic scholars have felt bound by the custom of using only white for shrouds, and over the years black, red, and other colors have also been used. Rabbi Yochanan, the third-century talmudist, was one of those who did not feel bound by the "white" tradition. He left these instructions before his death: "Do not bury me in white or black shrouds, but in colored ones."[18]

Yochanan assumed that white was chosen for those destined for heaven and black for those destined for hell. Not being sure of his final destination, Yochanan did not want to offend the righteous in heaven or the wicked in hell, so he requested burial in neutral-colored shrouds.[19]

From the sixteenth century on, white has been the accepted color for shrouds.[20]

Why is there confusion over precisely what is meant by "shrouds"?

In common parlance, the Hebrew term for shrouds, *tachrichim* (literally, "wrappings"), is used to refer to the large white cloth in which the entire body of the deceased is wrapped before being placed in the coffin. (Sephardim refer to *tachrichim* as *cortar mortaza*, "cloth cut for the dead.") Actually, the word *tachrichim* refers to all seven garments[21] in which the deceased is dressed by the members of the Burial Society:

- Trousers *(michnas'ayim),* which extend from the abdomen to the soles of the feet and are generally sewn across the bottom of each leg. The trousers are put on the corpse by two members of the Chevra Kadisha and are loosely tied around the waist and ankles. The ties around the waist are twisted, without forming knots, to form the Hebrew letter *shin,* the first letter of *Shaddai* (God).

- A slipover blouse with sleeves *(ketonet),* which is tied at the neck to form the letter *shin,* the first letter of one of God's names.

- A coat *(kittel),* which may be either an open-front or a slipover garment. If the deceased had worn a *kittel* during his lifetime (such as at the High Holiday services or at the Passover *seder*), that particular garment is used, but all fastening devices must first be removed. Like the *ketonet,* the *kittel* is tied at the neck to form the letter *shin.*

- A sash *(avnet),* which is wrapped around the *kittel* three times at the waist and is tied by the same manner as the *ketonet.*

- A prayershawl *(talit),* usually the one worn by the

deceased in his lifetime. If the deceased did not own a prayershawl, the Burial Society provides one. Usually, one of the fringes of the *talit* is cut off, thereby rendering it invalid (see page 37), and the ornamental neckband *(atara)* is removed (see page 38). The *talit* is draped over the *kittel*.[22]

- A headcovering *(mitznefet)*, resembling a hood, which is drawn over the entire head and neck until it reaches the *ketonet.*
- A large sheet *(sovev)*, in which the entire dressed corpse is wrapped.

The above seven shrouds are used for men. In dressing women, a *talit,* and often the *mitznefet,* is not used. The basic requirement for men and women is that three of the seven shrouds be used.[23] The number and type of garments that constitute the *tachrichim* are not uniform in all communities.[24]

Why, although forbidden in other garments, may shrouds be made of mixed fibers?

The Bible (Leviticus 19:19 and Deuteronomy 22:11) prohibits the wearing of garments made from a mixture of wool (animal) and linen or cotton (vegetable) fibers, Such a mixture is called *shaatnez* in Hebrew.

Shrouds for the deceased may be made of *shaatnez* because the dead are free of all commandments, and laws that apply to the living are not applicable to the dead.[25] The Jerusalem Talmud[26] says: "When a person dies, he is freed from carrying out the commandments," meaning that the living do not have the responsibility of seeing to it that what is done for the dead is in compliance with the law that applies to the living.[27]

On the question of why the *shaatnez* legislation was introduced, Nachmanides disagreed with Rashi. Rashi was of the opinion that there is no rational explanation for this law, while Nachmanides was of the view that "it was designed to preserve the integrity of creation." He concludes that behind the law is an insistence upon the integrity of each species.[28]

Why is the thread that is used to sew shrouds not knotted?

Just as the ties of the shrouds are not knotted (see page 34), the thread used to sew shrouds is not knotted, but the reason relates to the living rather than to the dead.

This practice is based on an ancient superstition that knots, or really anything that ties or binds, can debilitate people and adversely affect their ability to perform properly. The Book of Daniel (5:12,16) emphasizes the power of the knot by stating that the ability to loosen knots is considered to be among the great feats performed by magicians.

It is interesting to note that, based on the same superstition, it was once common practice to loosen the hair of a bride and thus remove all knots.[29]

Why is a *kittel* sometimes called a *sargenes*?

The *kittel,* mentioned above, is the Yiddish name for one of the garments in which the deceased is dressed for burial. It refers also to the long white robe worn by men on various occasions when conducting or attending a religious service. Individuals wear the *kittel* when leading the Passover *seder* service and when attending Rosh *Hashana* and Yom Kippur services. Rabbis, cantors, and other officiants also don such a garment at High Holiday and other holiday services when special penitential prayers are recited.[30]

In some communities, the burial *kittel* is called a *sargenes,* which is probably related to the German *Sarg,* meaning "coffin." However, some linguists see a relationship between *sargenes* and the word "serge," a strong, twilled fabric with a diagonal rib.

It is interesting to note that, in the Talmud,[31] Rashi identifies the commonly worn upper garment called *levu-*

sha as *serok* or *siruk,* an Old French word which may be related to the Latin *serica,* from which the word "serge" is derived.

Why do shrouds have no pockets?

Many early societies—the Egyptians, for example—believed that the deceased are able to take wordly possessions with them to the next world. In preparation for a new life, they filled their tombs with precious stones, utensils, and provisions. Even today, in cultures such as that of the Apache Indians, this same practice is followed.

Jews did not share the view that wordly possessions could be taken to the world-to-come by the deceased. Although not specifically prescribed by early Jewish law, since the seventeenth century it has been customary to make shrouds pocketless as an expression of this belief. The Ethics of the Fathers states: "In the hour of man's departures from this world, neither silver nor gold nor precious stones nor pearls accompany him, only Torah and good deeds."[32]

Why is one of the fringes of the prayershawl in which a person is buried generally cut off?

Before draping a deceased with the *talit,* one of the four fringes (*tzitziot;* singular, *tzitzit*) is generally cut off so as to make the prayershawl invalid (*pasul*).[33] This symbolic expression denotes that in death one is no longer bound by Jewish law. The commandment pertaining to *tzitziot* (Numbers 15:37-41) demands that a Jew should "look at them and remember all the commandments of the Lord." The deceased can obviously no longer fulfill this commandment, and making the *talit* invalid reflects this reality.

Some noted authorities, including the eighteenth-century scholar Rabbi Joel Sirkes (the Bach), contend that one need not cut off a fringe to render the *talit* defective. It is sufficient to tuck one of the fringes into a corner pocket of the prayershawl, thus hiding it from view, or to tie all four fringes of the *talit* together, thereby rendering it unfit for normal use.[34]

Why is the ornamental neckband removed from the prayershawl that is used for burial?

The *atara* (neckband, or more literally, "crown") is removed from the prayershawl before burial to symbolize that the "crown" that graced the *talit* of the deceased during life has served its function and must now be retired.

Why are the dead generally not dressed with shoes?

In Jewish law, there is no objection to dressing the deceased with foot coverings so long as they are made of simple linen or cotton materials.[35] Today, however, most Jews are dressed for burial in shrouds that cover the feet. It is neither practical nor necessary to use footwear of any kind.

Why did the Rabbis insist that the fingers of a corpse be straightened out before burial?

In the Middle Ages it was commonly believed among Jews and others that the gesture created by closing the fist after inserting the thumb between the middle and index finger is a sign of defiance that was feared by demons, an act that rendered them helpless to attack the deceased. (Applying the gesture was called "to fig" because the shape of the fist resembled a fig.) The Rabbis disapproved of Jews copying this "heathen" custom and insisted that the fingers of a deceased be straightened out before burial.[36]

Some scholars associate the practice of extending the fingers of a corpse with a midrashic interpretation of Rabbi Meir. He said:

When a person enters this world, his hands are clenched, as if to say, "The whole world is mine; I shall inherit it." But when he departs this world, his hands are spread open, as if to say, "I have taken nothing from the world."[37]

Why are ashes, earth, or pieces of pottery sometimes placed on the eyelids of the deceased?

The *Code of Jewish Law*[38] requires only that the eyes of the deceased be closed, but some Jews follow the practice of also placing ashes, earth from the Holy Land, or fragments of pottery (called *sherblach* in Yiddish) on the eyelids to symbolize the thought expressed in the Book of Genesis (3:19), "For dust you are and unto dust you shall return." Others relate the practice to the verse in the Book of Psalms (103:14), "He [God] is mindful that we are but dust."

As the eyelids are covered, members of the *Chevra Kadisha* recite words from the Book of Numbers (4:20) in which God instructs Moses and Aaron to say to the Priests, "Let them [the Kohathites] not draw near to see the sanctuary being dismantled, lest they die." The responsibility for setting up and then covering the holy vessels belonged to the family of Aaron. None of the other priestly families were permitted to gaze upon the sacred objects of the sanctuary even for a moment, for this was tantamount to looking at God.

In Judeo-Spanish communities it is customary for sons to place earth from the Holy Land on the eyelids of parents.[39]

Why does Jewish tradition demand that coffins be made out of wood rather than metal?

The third-century Palestinian scholar Rabbi Levi was of the opinion that the origin of the custom of using coffins made entirely of wood can be traced to the Garden of Eden. He said that the fact that Adam and Eve were hiding among the trees when God called to them (Genesis 3:8) "was a sign for his descendants that they would be placed in wooden coffins."[40]

Use of metal caskets, which are slow to decompose, is discouraged in Jewish law because that would make the biblical commandment "Unto dust shalt thou return" (Genesis 3:19), difficult to fulfill. In addition, wood is preferred over metal because the latter is a symbol of war. Burying a loved one in a metal coffin would conflict with the concept of "resting in peace." For the same reason, wooden pegs rather than nails are used when constructing a coffin.

Finally, the use of wood—preferably unpolished wood —for coffins is seen by the Talmud[41] as a reminder that ostentatious funerals are to be frowned upon, that Jewish tradition favors modesty and simplicity in its treatment of the dead.

Why are coffins commonly fashioned from raw pine wood?

The kind of wood used to make coffins is of little consequence, but over the years inexpensive soft woods, especially pine, have been preferred because they decompose more rapidly than other woods. Nowadays, funeral directors sometimes exert undue pressure on families to purchase expensive padded and lined wood caskets as a symbol of their love for the deceased. This is contrary to Jewish tradition.

Why is earth from the Land of Israel sometimes placed in the coffin?

Because earth from the Land of Israel is considered to have atoning powers,[42] burial societies in many communities adopted the custom of placing a bag of earth from Israel under deceased's head, or of sprinkling some of the earth over the body. Both procedures are intended to symbolize that no matter where on this planet one lives or dies, the individual remains connected to the Land of Israel. Many Jews still believe, as did the Rabbis of the Talmud, that the resurrection of the dead will take place in the Holy Land, and that those who merit it but live outside of Palestine will roll underground to the Holy Land to be resurrected. In Hebrew, this concept is called *gilgul mechilot,* which means "rolling through underground passages." As a kind of "homing device" and in order to ease the journey, the Rabbis said, earth from Israel should be placed in the coffin.[43]

Why are holes sometimes drilled in the bottom of the casket?

Many authorities feel that the statement in the Book of Genesis (3:19), "Unto dust shalt thou return," is best fulfilled by drilling holes in the bottom of the casket. Air and moisture are better able to penetrate the box, thereby hastening decomposition of the corpse and enabling the remains to rejoin mother earth more quickly. Talmudic scholars, including Rabbi Judah the Prince *(Yehuda Ha-nasi),* leader of first-century Jewry, specifically requested that holes be drilled in their coffins.

Rabbi Hezekiah of the fourth century instructed: "Let my coffin be perforated so that [my body] will make better contact with the earth [and thus decompose more readily]."[44]

Why did the Rabbis discourage the practice of burying the dead along with valuables?

The pagan custom of burying valuable personal effects in a coffin along with the corpse—whether as a way of honoring the dead or providing for the soul in its afterlife or with the intent of hiding the valuables in order to retrieve them later—was discouraged by the Rabbis of the Talmud. To counteract the practice, they issued a ruling prohibiting man from touching anything that has made contact with a coffin.[45]

Why is the coffin not opened for viewing once it has been closed by the Burial Society?

Once the Chevra Kadisha has completed its work and has sealed the coffin, the casket is not opened again for viewing. The concept of a "wake," which is common among Christians, is alien to Jews.

The opening of the coffin is permitted—and even then only momentarily—when the funeral director, in order to avoid a mix-up, requests that a member of the family identify the body before the chapel or synagogue service begins.

Why is an earthenware jug sometimes broken by members of the Burial Society?

In some Sephardic communities, when leaving the funeral home after having completed the task of preparing the body for burial, the members of the Burial Society break an earthenware jug. This action symbolizes the fragility of man's life. Some authorities suggest that the jug is broken to frighten off evil spirits, who cannot tolerate noise.

Why are members of the Chevra Kadisha highly respected in the Jewish community?

The small group of dedicated men and women volunteers who comprise the Chevra Kadisha are heartily praised for assuming the religious obligation of burying the dead with dignity and in accordance with Jewish law and tradition.

It has been suggested that their mandate was first stated in the Book of Psalms (85:11-12):

> Faithfulness and truth meet,
> Justice and peace kiss.
> Truth springs up from the earth,
> Justice looks down from heaven.

In this verse, the words "faithfulness" and "justice"

have been interpreted as referring to the activities of the Burial Society.

When the members of the Chevra Kadisha perform their important task faithfully, it may be said that "truth springs up from the earth," bringing heaven and earth into harmony. Through their noble deeds, these individuals are emulating God, as was once noted in the Talmud:

> As He clothes the naked, so
>   you should clothe the naked.
> As He visits the sick, so should
>   you visit the sick.
> As He comforts mourners, so should
>   you comfort mourners.
> As He buries the dead, so should
>   you bury the dead.

CHAPTER 3

———◆———

Rending the Garment

Introduction

When a death occurs, Jewish law requires that a garment be rent as a sign of mourning. This ritual is referred to as *Keria,* which literally means "tearing." Precisely when, where, how, and by whom this procedure is carried out is the subject matter of this chapter.

Aside from the Talmud, a goodly number of codes and other works over the centuries have dealt with the subject of rending a garment. What is noteworthy about these classical treatises is that many *begin* their discussion of the laws of mourning with a section on Keria, an indication of the importance ascribed to this aspect of the mourning protocol.

Although there are exceptions, the rending of a garment generally takes place immediately before the chapel service begins. It is usually performed by the officiating rabbi, who leads the family in the recitation of a special Keria blessing, sometimes referred to as the "Righteous Judge *[Da'yan Ha'emet]*" blessing, the exact wording of which can be found in the body of this chapter. Although Keria traditionally is performed on the mourner's garment, today a ribbon is usually used in its place. In whatever way the act is carried out, its essential purpose is unchanged: namely, to give public expression to the inner pain and anguish being felt by the mourner.

This chapter explores the variety of laws and procedures involved in executing the requirement to rend a garment. The next chapter delves even more deeply into the subject and addresses questions that explain *when* the rending should be performed.

Summary of Traditional Observances Relating to Keria

Who is required to perform Keria
- All members of the immediate family—parents, children, siblings, and spouse—are required to rend a garment. Included are children above Bar and Bat Mitzva age. For minors, the procedure is optional, as it is for in-laws and other relatives.
- If a child is too young to comprehend the significance of the loss of a family member, the child's garment is not torn. Some authorities, however, maintain that in such cases a small tear should be made in the child's garment. The same rule applies to the mentally ill.

When and where Keria is performed
- Keria may be performed immediately upon receiving news of a death, at the chapel before the funeral service, at the cemetery before burial, or in the house of Shiva immediately upon returning from the cemetery.

How and by whom Keria is performed
- The individual may tear his or her own garment, or another individual (the rabbi or funeral director) may make the tear. Often the tear is started by making a cut with a knife. It is then extended by hand.
- Keria for a parent is done on the mourner's left side; for others, on the right side.

Which garments are rent

- The type of garment normally worn indoors is rent. For men, this includes jackets, vests, and sweaters; for women, blouses and dresses. Outer garments, such as overcoats, are not rent.

- A necktie or a ribbon that is pinned to the mourner's garment may be rent. Not all authorities permit the use of a ribbon.

- If one is wearing an expensive garment, he or she may change to less expensive clothing. This applies to Keria for all relatives, including parents.

Keria posture and blessing

- When Keria is performed, mourners stand and pronounce the *Baruch Dayan Ha-emet* blessing.

Keria cancelled

- Except for parents, Keria is not performed if more than thirty days have passed since burial. For parents, the requirement is never cancelled.

Keria for infants

- Keria is not performed when mourning infants who have not lived a full thirty days.

Sabbath and holidays

- Keria is never performed on the Sabbath or festivals, but may be performed on the Intermediate Days of Passover and Sukkot.

- Rent garments are not worn on the Sabbath or on holidays.

Keria deferred or delayed

- For those mourning relatives except parents, if for any reason Keria was not performed at the time of death or burial, it must be done at any time within the Shiva week. After the Shiva week, it is not performed at all. For parents, Keria is performed whenever one learns of the death, regardless of how much time has elapsed.

- If a bride or groom suffered a loss during the first week after their wedding, they wait until the honeymoon week is over before rending a garment.

Repairing garments

- Garments rent for parents may never be fully mended. However, after thirty days they my be basted and worn again. Garments rent for relatives other than parents may be basted after Shiva and permanently mended after Sheloshim.

Changing clothes

- When a person mourning a parent changes into a different garment during Shiva, a tear must be made in the new garment. This is not necessary for those mourning other relatives.

Why is the phrase "tearing Keria" redundant?

Since *Keria* means "tearing," the phrase "to tear *Keria*" is redundant. The same redundancy is used by Sephardim when they employ the Spanish-Hebrew expression *cortar Keria,* in which *cortar* means "to cut."

The correct expression is "to perform Keria," which means to perform the act of tearing (a garment).

Why was the practice of tearing a garment instituted?

Rending a garment is performed as an expression of grief following the loss of a relative. The first recorded instance of this practice can be found in the Book of Genesis (37:34). There, we are told that when Jacob learned that his son Joseph had been killed, Jacob immediately tore his own garment. David[1] did likewise upon learning of the deaths of Saul and Jonathan. And, in the Book of Job (1:20), the title character is described as tearing his garment upon learning of the death of his children.

The Talmud[2] ascribes the basis of the Keria law to the incident described in Leviticus 10, wherein Nadav and Avihu, two of the four sons of Aaron, met an untimely death because they had brought an unauthorized sacrifice on the altar. Moses then told Aaron and Elazar and Ittamar, the other two sons of Aaron, "Do not bare your heads and do not rend your clothes [that is, do not carry out the mourning rites]" (10:6). Nadav and Avihu were unworthy of being mourned and hence their relatives were not to rend garments in mourning for them. This implied that relatives in general *are* obligated to mourn the loss of relatives by rending a garment.

Some scholars consider the rite of Keria to have been introduced as a substitute for the pagan practice of gashing one's flesh and shaving off the hair on one's head (Deuteronomy 14:1).[3]

Why did Jewish law once require that everyone present in the death-room at the moment of death rend a garment?

The Talmud[4] prescribes that everyone who witnesses a death must rend a garment immediately. The Rabbis considered a human life to be equal in value to Judaism's most holy object: the *Sefer Torah,* the Torah scroll. And, they reasoned, just as everyone who witnesses the burning of a Torah scroll is required by law to tear a garment to symbolize the serious personal loss, so is everyone who witnesses the expiration of life required to tear a garment. The gender of the deceased and the relationship of the deceased to those present are both irrelevant. In all cases it was considered incumbent upon everyone present at the time of death to perform Keria.[5]

In time, this requirement was modified to include only immediate relatives present in the death-room at the time of death. The change was effected because authorities feared that if the original regulation were allowed to stand, visitors would be discouraged from visiting the terminally ill out of concern that if a death were to occur in their presence, they would be obligated to tear their garments. Sick people would thus be denied the comfort visitors can offer. [6]

Why, at one time, was Keria not required if a mourner was wearing black?

In ancient times, when it was customary for a Jewish mourner to wear black as an expression of bereavement over the loss of a loved one, the Rabbis felt it unnecessary for the mourner to repeat that expression by tearing a garment. Later authorities, however, disagreed and insisted that the mourner rend the garment regardless of its color. [7]

Why are mourners obligated to tear a garment only for members of the immediate family?

Keria is performed for seven primary relatives: father, mother, son, daughter, brother, sister, and spouse. Of these, only the spouse is not a blood relation. In other words, one must rend a garment for all decedents for whom one is obligated to observe Shiva, the traditional seven days of mourning. [8] See page 150 for an explanation of the Shiva requirement for relatives.

Why did Reform Jews once discourage the practice of rending a garment?

In the middle of the nineteenth century, Rabbi Isaac Mayer Wise, the prominent leader of American Reform Judaism, and his followers discouraged the rite of rending a garment as a sign of mourning. In support of his position, Rabbi Wise cited a verse from the prophet Joel

(11:13): "Tear your hearts and not your garments."[9]

In recent years Reform rabbis have reintroduced the Keria ceremony.[10] *Gates of Mitzvah,* a guide to Reform practice, indicates that the choice of rending a garment or cutting a black ribbon "is left to the discretion of the family and rabbi."

Why do distant relatives sometimes rend their garments?

When a close bond has existed with the deceased, distant relatives, including relations through marriage, sometimes feel impelled to tear a garment as an expression of grief. Although there is no law requiring this of distant relatives, there is also no regulation prohibiting it. However, if the parent of a person desiring to perform Keria for a distant relative expresses an objection, it is customary for the child not to do so.

Why does the Talmud prescribe that a male bare his breast when mourning a father or mother?

The Rabbis of the Talmud[11] ruled: "For all other dead he [the mourner] need not bare his breast, but in mourning his father and mother he should bare his breast."

In Jewish tradition, the heart is considered the seat of wisdom and love. In early times, when mourning the death of a parent, males exposed the flesh above the heart to demonstrate the depth of the loss. To accomplish this end, the normal tear made in the garment was extended an additional two and one-half inches until the bare flesh above the heart was exposed. For the sake of modesty, this was not required of women.

Why is a garment sometimes torn on the left side and at other times on the right side?

In reference to precisely where the tear must be made on the garment, the *Code of Jewish Law,*[12] written in the sixteenth century, simply states that "the tear must be made by all mourners [who are members of the immediate family]." In later years, however, for parents it became established practice to rend the left side of the garment, at the neckline, as a token of special respect and "to expose the heart." The right side is rent for other relatives—namely, son, daughter, brother, sister, and spouse.[13]

Because the practice of making a tear on the left side is not mandated in Jewish law, if one inadvertently tears the right side of the garment for a parent, the Keria is considered valid and need not be repeated.

Why is there disagreement over how many rents need be made by a mourner if both parents die at the same time?

The talmudic tractate Mourning[14] gives the following general rule: If one's father and mother die at the same time, a single rent should be made in the mourner's garment. However, the scholar Ben Tema, apparently believing that full love and respect should be shown each parent individually, said that a separate tear in the garment should be made for each.

Subsequent works, such as Joseph Caro's *Code of Jewish Law,* rule that only one tear need be made for both parents.[15]

If two close relatives other than parents die on the same day, mourners are required to make only one tear in a garment, and they recite only one blessing. The single tear is considered sufficient to remind the mourner of both losses.[16]

Why is a second tear sometimes made in a mourner's garment during the week of Shiva?

If a mourner has already performed Keria for a relative—parent or otherwise—and a second relative dies within the week of Shiva, the mourner has two options: (1) the original tear may be extended by three or four inches (one *tefach*) or (2) a new tear may be made three fingerwidths *(etzaba'ot)* from the first.[17]

If the second death occurs after the Shiva period for the first death has ended, the tear in the old garment need be extended only a fraction of an inch.[18]

The above rules apply only if Keria is being performed on a garment. If a ribbon is used for Keria, a second ribbon is used in all of the instances described.

Why is Keria not performed for a child who has lived thirty days or less?

In Jewish law, insofar as Keria and other mourning rites are concerned, a child is not considered a full-fledged person until he has completed his thirtieth day of life.[19] Keria, therefore, is not performed. (See pages 96, 133, and 142 for a further discussion of mourning rites for infants.)

Why is Keria sometimes performed after family members have begun to sit Shiva?

There are instances where a family member learns of the death of a loved one after burial has been completed and Shiva has begun. In cases where the person learns of the death within the first three days of the Shiva period, the person is required to rend a garment and recite the Keria blessing. However, if the news reaches the individual from the fourth day on, the garment is torn but the blessing is not recited. The above applies to all relatives other than parents. For parents, the obligation to perform Keria and recite the blessing is always in effect. See the next answer.

Why is Keria for most relatives not performed if the mourner learns of the death thirty days or more after burial?

The Rabbis point out that the rending of a garment carries significance only if it is performed when the grief is intense.[20] If thirty days have elapsed and Keria is not been performed, the law does not demand that the ritual be carried out—except in the case of the death of a parent. A child must tear a garment whenever he or she learns of a parent's death, because grief over the loss of a parent is always intensely felt.[21]

Why is one required to rend a garment upon learning of the death of a great scholar or teacher?

Jewish law states that upon learning of the death of a great scholar or a respected teacher, one is required to tear a garment. A teacher, says the Talmud, is like a parent: "All are his near kin and must rend their clothes on his account."[22] Henry Brooke Adams (1838-1918), in his *Education of Henry Adams,* makes a cogent comment in this regard: "A teacher affects eternity; he can never tell where his influence stops."

Why may a divorced person rend a garment for a former spouse?

A person is not obligated to perform Keria for a former spouse, but he or she may do so. This is considered proper because at one time all persons—even those not related—would tear a garment if present in a room when a person expired (see page 48).

An individual might choose to rend a garment for a former spouse if children continue to live with the surviving parent and the parent wishes to provide emotional support for the children during their time of intense grief.

Why are authorities of the opinion that only a vertical tear satisfies the legal requirement of rending a garment?

According to most authorities, the tear made in a garment for Keria must be vertical. A horizontal tear does not satisfy the law of Keria because the rent may appear to have been made accidentally rather than as a deliberate mourning symbol.[23]

Why is it considered improper to make a tear longer than four inches?

The Rabbis ruled[24] that the proper length of the rent made for Keria is one *tefach*, about the width of the average palm (three to four inches). To make a longer tear might cause unnecessary damage to the garment and would thus be in violation of the biblical law of *bal tashchit*, wanton waste and unnecessary destruction.[25]

Why do some mourners avoid wearing new garments to the funerals of loved ones?

Many relatives, aware of the fact that an outer garment will be torn for Keria during the funeral service, make a point of donning an old garment rather than a new one. As mentioned above, the Rabbis were intent on avoiding waste and therefore felt that mourners should not wear good clothes on which Keria would have to be performed.

The talmudic principle that serves as the basis for this ruling is *Ha-Torah chasa al mamonam shel Yisrael,* "The Torah is concerned about the [loss of] money of Israel." [26]

Why are ribbons usually used for Keria?

Although strict observance demands that a tear be made in the garment worn by the mourner, the fact that the rent often makes an otherwise serviceable garment useless has led to the custom of pinning onto the garment a black ribbon.

Justification for this now commonplace practice is based on the *bal tashchit* principle referred to above. Those who use ribbons for Keria explain that the rite is basically an expression of grief, and the same emotions are felt whether the tear is made in a ribbon or a garment.

However, many Orthodox Jews consider the use of ribbons to be in violation of Jewish law. Orthodox authority Rabbi Yekutiel Greenwald[27] recommends that if a ribbon has been used for Keria, a new (second) tear must be performed on a regular garment before the Shiva period is over, although the Keria blessing need not be repeated. Rabbis of the Spanish-Portuguese community refuse to perform Keria on a ribbon.

Reform as well as many traditional Jews find the use of ribbons for Keria perfectly acceptable. In fact, the Committee on Jewish Law and Standards of the Rabbinical Assembly (Conservative) expressly permits the use of ribbons.

Why may Keria not be performed on a garment that is not the property of the mourner?

The *Code of Jewish Law* states that the garment upon which a mourner performs Keria must legally belong to the mourner, even if only temporarily. Thus, if one borrows a garment to visit a very sick parent, the parent dies during the visit, and the distraught mourner then performs Keria on the garment, the Keria is considered valid. This is so because it is assumed that the lender was aware of the fact that the patient might die at any moment and that Keria would have to be performed. In this situation it is assumed that the lender temporarily transferred ownership to the borrower. The borrower, however, must compensate the lender for the cost of repairs and for the loss in value.[28]

Stated generally, the rule is that Keria may not be performed on a borrowed garment unless the owner of the garment has actually agreed, or would have agreed if aware of the circumstances, to have the garment used for the purpose of Keria.[29] Thus, if Keria is performed on a stolen garment or a garment borrowed without permission, the Keria is considered invalid and must be repeated on a garment actually belonging to the mourner.[30]

Why is a modified form of Keria performed on the garment of a minor?

In Jewish law, a minor is generally thought to be one who has not reached maturity (Bar or Bat Mitzva age) and is therefore not fully bound by the religious commandments to which adults are subject. However, in the matter of rending a garment for a deceased family member, a minor is defined by authorities as one who has not yet begun his or her Jewish education.

The Rabbis ruled that the garment of a child who has not yet begun Jewish studies should only be torn slightly as a symbol of anguish—just enough so that others, seeing the rent, will empathize with the young mourner. For a child who has already begun Jewish studies, the normal adult Keria procedure is followed.[31]

Why are the severely mentally disabled not required to perform Keria?

From the outset, Keria was intended as a conscious act reflecting inner pain and anguish. Each individual was required to tear his or her own garment. Since the severely mentally ill and retarded are not always fully aware of what is happening, they are not required to comply with the laws of Keria and other mourning rites.

In the case of a loss of a parent, should a mentally disabled person return to normalcy at some future date, the person is required to perform Keria at that time.[32]

Why is a newlywed not required to rend a garment during the first week after the wedding?

In Jewish law, nothing may intrude upon the celebration of a marriage, and nothing may intrude upon the joy of the occasion. Although a bride or groom feels intense grief upon hearing of the death of a member of the immediate family, he or she is not permitted to assume the role of mourner until after the honeymoon period, the seven days following the marriage. Keria is therefore delayed for a week, or until the bride and groom return from their honeymoon, at which time Shiva begins.

Why is it now customary for someone other than the mourner to make the tear in his or her garment?

While the Talmud and the *Code of Jewish Law*[33] specify that a mourner should make the actual tear in his or her own garment, later authorities expressed the view that a stranger should make the tear so as to minimize the mourner's suffering and anguish (in Hebrew, *agmat nefesh*).[34] The stranger may be the officiating rabbi, the chapel attendant, or anyone else.

In cases where the tear is made in the actual garment (rather than a ribbon), it is customary for the stranger to begin the tear by making a small cut with a knife at the neckline or lapel of the garment. The mourner then extends the cut manually by tearing downward to a depth of three to four inches (one *tefach*).

Why is it customary among some Jews to permit only women to perform Keria on other women?

Generally, the officiating rabbi or some other male performs the Keria on all mourners. In Orthodox circles, however, where it is considered an act of immodesty for a man to touch a woman, a knowledgeable woman who is able to lead the mourners in the Keria prayer performs the rite on other women.

Why does the Talmud forbid the use of a knife when performing Keria for a parent?

The Talmud[35] says, "For all other dead the mourner may rend his clothes with a knife, but for a father or mother a knife may not be used." For a parent, a tear must be made entirely by hand.[36]

The Rabbis reasoned that because performing Keria completely by hand, without the use of a knife, is so much more difficult, it will increase the sensitivity of the mourner to his predicament. Later authorities have ruled that if it is too difficult to perform Keria for a parent manually, a knife may be used to start the rent.

It should be noted that today, the talmudic law notwithstanding, Keria is often begun with a knife, regardless of the relationship of the deceased to the mourner.

Why is the Keria generally performed in the funeral chapel?

Whereas at one time it was customary for a person to tear a garment and recite the blessing if he or she was present at the time of death (see page 48) or immediately upon learning of the death, it became more practical to wait for all mourners to assemble in one place so that a rabbi or a knowledgeable person could monitor the procedure. That place is usually the funeral chapel.[37]

Why do mourners stand when Keria is performed?

The Rabbis[38] require that mourners be in a standing position when the Keria rite is performed, whether by the mourner himself, the officiating rabbi, or the chapel attendant. They consider this to be biblically mandated, citing the posture assumed by Job upon hearing of the death of his family members: "Job stood up and tore his clothes" (Job 1:20). Some Rabbis associate the requirement of standing with the story of II Samuel 13:31, wherein David, upon learning that his son Amnon had been killed, "rose and tore his garments."

According to later authorities,[39] if a mourner does not stand when Keria is performed, the rite must be repeated. (This does not apply to mourners who are ill.) Some authorities are of the opinion that before the second tear is made, the mourner must recite only the last three words of the Keria blessing, *Baruch Da'yan Ha-emet.*[40]

Why is it customary for each mourner to recite the Keria blessing individually?

Although the Rabbis generally favor having a leader recite public prayers in behalf of the assembled, with all responding "Amen," they favor each mourner reciting the Keria blessing individually. Rabbi Yechiel Tuktzinsky, author of *Gesher Ha-cha'yim,*[41] explains that it is important for each mourner to speak the blessing individually because, by so doing, the mourner is showing acceptance of God's harsh decision and proving that he or she harbors no resentment toward the Almighty.

When mourners are unfamiliar with the Hebrew blessing, the rabbi or another knowledgeable person recites the words and the mourner repeats them. If family members agree, one mourner may recite the Keria blessing for everybody. By responding "Amen," the other mourners fulfill their religious obligation.

Why is the "Righteous Judge" blessing pronounced when Keria is performed?

The blessing recited by the mourner before Keria is performed affirms the mourner's unwavering faith in God as the truthful and righteous Judge, despite the personal loss just suffered.

The "Righteous Judge" (*Da'yan Ha-emet* in Hebrew) blessing, which each mourner pronounces aloud, is:

בָּרוּךְ אַתָּה יהוה, אֱלֹהֵינוּ מֶלֶךְ הָעוֹלָם, דַּיַּן הָאֱמֶת.

Baruch ata Adonai, Elohenu Melech ha-olam,

Da'yan Ha-emet.
Praised be Thou, O Lord our God, King of the universe, who is a Righteous [true] Judge.

Thus, the mourner affirms that God is not to be held responsible for the present misfortune and that the mourner accepts his lot as part of the natural order of the world.

Why do most Sephardim perform Keria after burial has taken place?

Scholars have sought a reason for the popular Sephardic practice of performing Keria in the Shiva home *after* the burial. Often, a member of the Chevra Kadisha awaits the arrival of the mourners to assist in the fulfillment of the Keria requirement.[42] The only exception is the Spanish-Portuguese community, which follows the Ashkenazic practice.[43]

One reason for the Sephardic practice may be that the mourner is considered an *onen* ("person in distress," see page 23) until the body has been buried, and an *onen* is not obligated to pray or recite blessings. Once the mourner leaves the cemetery and the Shiva period begins, a new stage of mourning has begun, and at this point the mourner may recite the *Da'yan Ha-emet* blessing.

It is also reasonable to assume that since among most Sephardim it is customary for women not to attend funerals, the best time for rending the garment is after the funeral, when the whole family assembles in the Shiva house.

Why may Keria not be performed on the Sabbath and holidays?

Since tearing of any kind is one of the thirty-nine types of work (*melachot* in Hebrew) that were banned on the Sabbath and holidays by the Rabbis of the Talmud,[44] Keria is forbidden on these days.

Why do some authorities prohibit Keria on the Intermediate Days of Passover and Sukkot?

If a person dies on the first or second day of Passover or Sukkot and is buried on one of the Intermediate Days of the holiday (Chol Ha-moed), Keria is performed after the entire holiday is over.

There are, however, varying opinions among authorities as to when Keria is to be performed for a person who dies on Chol Ha-moed. This depends on how one characterizes the Intermediate Days. The Mishna[44] states that Chol Ha-moed is to be regarded as an ordinary weekday and that Keria therefore may be performed. A second view is that Chol Ha-moed is a holiday, albeit a half-holiday, and that Keria should not be performed. A third view is that one may rend a garment on Chol Ha-moed only for a parent, but not for other relatives, for whom the garment is to be rent after the holiday is over. This is the common practice today.[46]

Why has one fulfilled the Keria obligation even if he had mistakenly performed it on the Sabbath or a festival?

If, out of sheer ignorance, a mourner violates the law by rending a garment on the Sabbath or a festival, the Keria requirement is considered to have been fulfilled, because the purpose of the Keria is to express grief,[47] and that has been accomplished.

It should be noted that although Keria is not to be performed on the Sabbath or festival, the *Da'yan Ha-emet* blessing itself is recited when one is notified of a death on those days.[48]

Why are Keria garments never worn outside the home on the Sabbath?

Because the Sabbath is a day of joy, all manifestations of mourning are prohibited outside the home. Hence, the rent garment is not worn. On the Sabbath that falls during the Shiva period, mourners are required to wear their usual special Sabbath attire when appearing in public. The same dress code applies to holidays.

Why are there different regulations governing the repair of rent garments?

The Rabbis of the Talmud weighed the emotional impact of the loss of parents versus that of other immediate family members. The loss of parents was considered more grievous.

To accentuate the intensity of anguish experienced when a parent dies, the Talmud[49] ruled that a garment torn in mourning for a parent should never be permanently mended. However, to minimize the financial loss, after thirty days (Sheloshim) the garment may be basted and worn again.

Should an individual mourning a parent decide to change the rent garment during Shiva, a slight tear must be made in the new garment. This garment, too, may not be permanently mended, although it may be basted.

For relatives other than parents, the rent garment may be basted after Shiva and permanently mended after Sheloshim.[50]

Why, when basting a tear in a garment, are the stitches sometimes made in an irregular fashion?

When basting a rent garment, irregular, zigzag stitching is used to symbolize the disorder and unevenness that has overtaken the life of the mourner. After thirty days, the irregular stitching in garments rent for relatives other than parents may be replaced with permanent stitching. As stated above, garments rent for parents are never permanently mended.[51]

CHAPTER 4

The Chapel Service

Introduction

The Rabbis of old were asked: What has God been doing since He finished the creation of the world? How has He been occupying His time?

High on the list of activities attributed to God by the Rabbis was involvement with the burial of the dead.[1] This was the Rabbis' way of saying that there is no greater kindness one human being can show another than to favor the individual with a dignified and proper burial. Showing reverence for the dead in this way, they said, is the ultimate expression of caring. It is a uniquely selfless act, since it is obvious that the recipient cannot reward the donor for the kindness shown.

The Bible emphasizes that even the body of a stranger found lying unattended on the roadside is to be accorded a proper burial. Caring for such a corpse—referred to in Hebrew as a *met mitzva*—was considered of the highest priority by the Rabbis. Even a High Priest, who was never permitted to come into contact with a deceased unless it was a member of his immediate family, was commanded to become personally involved in the ritual of burying the unattended dead (Leviticus 21:1-4).[2]

In the Jewish tradition, the dead are accorded the same respect as that due a living person. All of the instructions left by the deceased are honored so long as they do not contravene Jewish law.

In her essay "The Lord Was His," Deborah Lipstadt,

a writer and professor of history and comparative religion, describes how she honored the instructions left by her father. One request was highly unusual. He asked that his funeral service "close with the singing of *Adon Olam* [the hymn sung at the close of most Sabbath, holiday, and weekday services] according to the Portuguese melody." These wishes were carried out.[3]

The importance of showing reverence for the dead has become ingrained in the consciousness of Jews and is reflected in some of the procedures of the chapel and cemetery funeral services. This chapter and the one that follows highlight the care and love that must be lavished upon the deceased as they are memorialized and eulogized in the chapel and then carried to their final resting place.

Summary of Traditional Observances Pertaining to the Chapel Service

Speedy funerals
  • Wherever possible, the funeral service should take place within twenty-four hours after a death.

When funerals are held
  • Funerals are must often held in the daytime, but never on the Sabbath or Yom Kippur. They may be held on holidays. If the funeral takes place on the first day of a holiday, all labor must be done by non-Jews.

Where funerals are held
  • Funerals are generally held in a funeral parlor or a synagogue. They may also be held in the home of the deceased or in the cemetery chapel.

Flowers at funerals
- Jewish custom discourages the sending of flowers, but this is not forbidden by Jewish law.

Viewing the body
- Once the coffin is closed by the Burial Society, it is not reopened for viewing by the public. The "wake" is a purely Christian custom.

Eulogies
- Eulogies are not delivered on Friday afternoon or on the eve of a holiday if the hour is late. They are not delivered for "intentional" suicides.

Family members at funerals
- Mourners who are sitting Shiva for a loved one are not to attend a funeral for a distant relative or friend during the first three days of Shiva. They may, however, attend the funeral of an immediate family member.
- After the third day of Shiva (part of the third day is equal to a whole day), a mourner may attend the funeral of any family member.
- A bride and groom on their honeymoon are not required to attend a funeral, even for parents.

Kohanim at funerals
- Kohanim (Priests) are only permitted to attend funerals of immediate relatives. Women members of a priestly family are not bound by this rule.

Why does Jewish law require speedy burial?

Jewish law demands that the deceased be buried promptly, within twenty-four hours, unless there are extenuating circumstances, such as the need to await the arrival of close relatives from distant places.[4] The basis for the prompt burial practice is a passage from the Book of Deuteronomy (21:23):

> You must not permit his corpse to remain impaled on the stake overnight; you must bury him the same day. For an impaled body is an affront to God; you shall not defile the land that the Lord your God is giving you to possess.

It was considered an affront to God to allow a human being, created in His image, to remain exposed to the mercy of the elements and not be accorded a dignified, speedy burial. Although the passage refers to burial of a criminal who had been executed by order of the court, prompt burial was extended to include all deceased.

Some scholars have pointed out that it was once widely believed that for as long as the dead is unburied the ghost (spirit) of the deceased can be exceedingly harmful to mourners, especially to those who were disrespectful to the deceased. It therefore became common practice to bury the dead promptly.[5]

Why is it sometimes permissible to delay a funeral?

When it is important to await the arrival of very close relatives, when a government regulation so dictates, or when a strike occurs and burials cannot take place, funerals may be delayed—but never for more than three days. To keep the body unburied for a longer time dishonors the dead (referred to in Hebrew, as *nivul ha-met*).[6]

If extenuating circumstances demand a delay longer than three days, the procedure is to hold the chapel service and then to take the body to the cemetery, where it is stored in a vault until burial can take place. In such an instance, the body is embalmed to prevent early decay and malodor.

Why are funerals generally not held at night?

Although nighttime funerals are not in any way prohibited by Jewish law, they never became the norm. This is based on the Deuteronomic law (21:23) which states, "You must bury him [on] the same *day*." The Rabbis took the word "day" literally and encouraged daytime funerals.[7]

In medieval times funerals were held after dark, but the practice was later rejected, mainly owing to the belief in demonology that was shared by many Rabbis of the Talmud.

According to the talmudic scholar Rabbi Yochanan, "One may not greet anyone at night [when he cannot be certain that he is a fellow human being] for fear he may be a demon."[8] The tractate Chagiga[9] says, "Our Rabbis taught: 'He who goes out alone at night or spends the night in a cemetery is a fool [because demons are active at night].'"

Modern biblical scholars, such as Dr. Julian Morgenstern, clearly connect the avoidance of nighttime funerals to demonology. In his *Rites of Birth, Marriage, and Death Among the Semites,* Morgenstern writes: "Evil spirits are generally thought by the Semites, ancient and modern, to be dangerous at night. With the rising of the sun, their power wanes or departs completely."

In general, nighttime funerals are generally avoided today. There are exceptions, however, such as in the Mea She'arim section of Jerusalem, where funerals are sometimes held after dark.[11]

Why are Friday funeral services usually brief?

The Talmud[12] says, "On Sabbath eve one should hasten the burial and not prolong the funeral." Consequently, when a funeral takes place after noon on a Friday (or before a holiday), the funeral service is curtailed so that the family will have sufficient time to go home and begin sitting Shiva before sunset. To shorten the service, some of the usual prayers are not recited, and the eulogy itself is abbreviated or completely omitted.

Why are funerals never held on the Sabbath or on Yom Kippur?

On the Sabbath and Yom Kippur, the holiest days in the Jewish calendar, the performing of any sort of work is strictly prohibited.[13] This includes activities involved in burying the dead. While it is true that Jewish law requires speedy burial, the Rabbis believed that postponing interment until the day following the Sabbath or Yom Kippur would not constitute a violation of the law.

Why are funerals sometimes held on major holidays?

Although funerals may not take place on the Sabbath or on Yom Kippur, they may be held on Passover, Shavuot, Sukkot, and Rosh Hashana. In addition to the requirement that the deceased be buried as soon as possible, the holding over of the dead for an extra day before burial would necessitate the use of spices and perfumes to remove unpleasant odors. This was a non-Jewish practice, and a basic rule of Jewish life was to avoid imitating non-Jewish practices.

The *Code of Jewish Law*[14] states that if a burial must take place on the first day of a holiday, the digging of the grave and other burial activities must be done by non-Jews. If the burial is to take place on the second day of a holiday, Jews may perform the work. But this leniency applies only to those involved in making funeral arrangements and those *required* to be present at the burial.

The Rabbis cautioned that the principle of burying the dead promptly must not be violated, and a funeral may not be postponed to the second day of a holiday for the singular purpose of allowing a Jew to dig the grave of a loved one, which is considered a meritorious act. On the first day of a holiday Jews are not permitted to perform work, and thus may not dig a grave. In actual practice non-Jews are usually employed as gravediggers.

Why do some communities today discourage holding funerals on major holidays?

Concerned that friends of the family of the deceased would wish to attend funeral services held on a holiday and thus might violate Jewish law by traveling on that day, not all communities permit burials on major holidays. In London, England, for example, the Burial Society (see Chapter Two for a detailed discussion of the nature of this institution) ruled as follows: "It is an accepted custom in the Anglo-Jewish community not to arrange any funerals either on the first or second day of a holiday."[15]

Why, in earlier centuries, were funerals held exclusively in cemeteries?

When Jews lived in small towns, the entire funeral service was conducted in the cemetery. The deceased was carried in a coffin from the home to the cemetery, which was on the outskirts of the town, not far from the homes of the populace.

When cities grew and cemeteries were located further and further away from population centers, not all who wished to be present at each funeral could manage to reach the cemetery. It therefore became customary—although not required by Jewish law—to hold an additional service in the home of the deceased.

Why are funeral services sometimes held in the synagogue?

As previously stated, in early times a home funeral service was sometimes held in addition to the cemetery service. The eleventh-century scholar Rashi said that an exception could be made in the case of a great scholar or community leader. For him, the home funeral service could be replaced by a synagogue service so that large numbers of people could attend.[16]

The sixteenth-century *Code of Jewish Law,* in speaking of synagogue funerals, comments that if the deceased was a worthy community leader—rabbi or layman—it was the practice in some communities to bring the body into the synagogue for the funeral service and eulogy. But the line between the deserving and undeserving could not be clearly drawn, and the practice led to much confusion, as wealthy families sometimes demanded a synagogue service for a less than deserving relative. Consequently, synagogue funeral services were reserved for pious persons and esteemed scholars.

Over the centuries, many scholars have opposed the idea of bringing a coffin into the synagogue. This attitude was based on the verse in the Book of Psalms (115:17), "The dead cannot praise the Lord." To bring a deceased, who obviously can no longer pray, into the synagogue would constitute an affront to the dead *(nivul ha-met).*

Today, almost all funerals are held in funeral chapels, largely for the convenience of having the funeral director take care of the many necessary details. However, funerals are sometimes conducted in the home of the deceased or in the synagogue if it suits the family and the congregation.

Some congregations in the United States have adopted a policy of holding the funerals of all their members in the synagogue so as to accord everyone the same degree of respect.[18]

Why are Jewish funerals sometimes conducted in non-Jewish funeral chapels?

Some Jewish communities are too small to support a Jewish funeral chapel, so funerals are often conducted in the synagogue. Where that is not feasible, it is permissible to hold funerals in non-Jewish chapels if all Christological symbols are removed.

Why are Jewish funerals kept very simple?

In talmudic times, funeral costs escalated and many families simply abandoned their dead. This led Rabbi Gamaliel[19] to rule that ostentatious funerals were not in keeping with the spirit of Judaism. Simplicity is to govern all aspects of burial, and rich and poor must be accorded equal treatment. A simple, wooden pine coffin is recommended for all burials, and simple white shrouds are the designated attire.

Why are people discouraged from sending flowers to Jewish funerals and houses of mourning?

According to the Talmud,[20] diverse kinds of fragrant spices were used at funerals (and even laid on the burial plot) in order to offset the odor of a decaying body. But when the practice of sending flowers to funerals became commonplace among non-Jews, who kept their dead for longer periods before burial, Jewish law discouraged the custom to establish a distinction between Jewish and non-Jewish practice.

For this same reason, Jews were discouraged from sending flowers to the chapel or to the house of mourning and were encouraged instead to make charitable contributions.

Why is Jewish tradition opposed to exposing the body of the deceased before or during a funeral?

In early talmudic times, some two thousand years ago, and for a period of time thereafter, it was customary for the faces of the deceased to be left uncovered, in full view of the public. Often, the faces of the poor turned black because their families could not afford to have the corpses treated with spices and embalming fluids that would retard discoloration and deterioration. Consequently, to spare the poor embarrassment, the Rabbis ruled that the faces of all dead should be covered.[21]

Viewing the remains of a decedent before burial is a recent American custom. The practice was not widespread in Europe, except for the lying-in-state of royalty and other notables. Jewish tradition regards viewing a corpse as incompatible with the Jewish requirement of showing proper respect for the dead (kevod ha-met).

Why is the coffin of a Jew draped with a cloth?

There is no specific law regarding this practice, which probably began as a local custom and then grew in popularity. The cloth covering may have been introduced to soften the harsh appearance of an unadorned pine coffin.

Covering the coffin may also be seen as a way of demonstrating respect for the dead. Just as the Torah scroll must be covered when not in use as a sign of respect, so should the coffin containing a deceased be covered until it is lowered into the ground.

The cloth used to cover the casket of a Jew is usually black, the color of mourning in Jewish tradition. For decorative purposes, the Star of David is generally embroidered on the cloth. The cloth is removed before burial.

Why was the delivery of eulogies encouraged by the ancient Rabbis?

The first eulogy of record in Jewish sources was delivered by David when King Saul and Saul's son Jonathan died. Among the striking words spoken by David are these (II Samuel 1:19):

> Your glory, O Israel,
> Lies slain on your heights;
> How have the mighty fallen!

The Rabbis of the Talmud and those who later codified the law believed that the delivery of a eulogy (*hesped* in Hebrew) is important, not only to honor the dead by lavishing praise upon them, but secondarily to bring tears to the eyes of the mourners,[22] thus helping them to express their grief.

A prominent sixteenth-century preacher reminds us that eulogies for scholars were delivered not only at funerals but also on the last day of Shiva, on the thirtieth day after the death, and at the end of the year. For very prominent scholars it was not unusual for a eulogy to be delivered each day during Shiva.[23]

The noted Orthodox authority Rabbi Joseph B. Soloveitchik said: "The *halakha* [Jewish law] did not like to see the dead interred in silent indifference. It wanted to hear the shriek of despair and to see the hot tear washing away human cruelty and toughness."[24]

Why should family members be prepared to submit information to the rabbi for use in a eulogy?

Since the officiating rabbi is not always intimately acquainted with the deceased, it is important that mourners take time to jot down the virtues of their loved one and to convey the information to the rabbi as soon as possible. In addition, the following information should be supplied: the full Hebrew and English name of the deceased, his or her age, the names of members of the immediate family, names or organizations with which the deceased was affiliated, any offices he or she held, unusual qualities possessed by the individual, and any other noteworthy fact or incident worthy of mention in a eulogy. One of the purposes of a eulogy is to elicit a sense of pride among family members, so no pertinent information should be withheld.

Why do chapel services conducted by different rabbis often differ in form and content?

There is no official chapel funeral service prescribed by Jewish law, and we therefore find little uniformity in the content of chapel services or in the manner in which they are conducted.

The structure of the chapel service as well as the prayers selected for recitation are the individual choice of the officiating rabbi. Generally, the chapel service consists of the reading aloud of one or two selections from the Book of Psalms, followed by a eulogy. The *El Malay Rachamim* prayer is then recited or chanted by the rabbi or cantor. The service generally concludes with the reading of the Twenty-third Psalm.

Why are eulogies sometimes not delivered at funerals?

Since one of the purposes of a eulogy is to intensify grief and bring tears to the eyes of mourners, it is considered improper to deliver a eulogy on a Friday afternoon or on the eve of a Jewish holiday, for this is when one must prepare for the joyous day that is to follow. Eulogies are also often omitted at funerals held on the day following one of the Pilgrim Festivals (Sukkot, Passover, Shavuot), which is traceable to the times when the pilgrims were returning home from their journey to Jerusalem and were still in a joyous state.[25]

This practice is not always observed, especially when the funeral is held early in the day and the mourners and others in attendance will have ample time to reach their homes and prepare for the Sabbath or festival. An exception is often made for distinguished leaders and scholars[26] and even for laymen whose families insist that a eulogy be delivered.

Why are eulogies that exaggerate the virtues of the deceased prohibited?

The Talmud[27] and *Code of Jewish Law*[28] condemn the delivery of eulogies that are untruthful or that exaggerate the virtues and achievements of the deceased. The Rabbis did not condemn eulogies that embellish slightly on the truth, but they objected vigorously to outright distortion. The tractate Berachot[29] says: "Just as the dead are held responsible for their sins, so are funeral orators held accountable for delivering dishonest eulogies."

But the Rabbis were more lenient with regard to exaggerated eulogies for the sons of the wealthy and for sons of scholars. Out of deference to their parents, exaggerated eulogies were permitted, but a warning was issued against delivering eulogies that are "woven out of nothing."[30]

Why are eulogies not delivered for suicides?

Since honest words of praise cannot be spoken for those who have taken their own lives, the Talmud[31] and *Code of Jewish Law*[32] forbid eulogizing suicides. Exceptions are sometimes made for a suicide whose irrational action may have been the result of undue duress.

Why may a eulogy be delivered even if it is contrary to the instructions of the deceased?

The Rabbis of the Talmud believed that a great injustice is done the memory of the deceased when a eulogy is not delivered.[33] However, based upon the principle that one may not give away that which is not his, rabbinic authorities are in general agreement that certain requests made by an individual prior to death may be ignored. Despite this rabbinic view, the prevalent practice is that if a person requests that his funeral service be simple—specifically, that no eulogy be delivered—the request is to be honored because the eulogy is delivered primarily to praise the deceased.[34]

Why is a convert to Judaism sometimes permitted to deliver a eulogy at the funeral of a non-Jewish parent?

The convert, as any other Jew, is required to abide by the fifth commandment, which demands that one always show respect for parents. Thus, the convert is permitted to deliver a eulogy for a non-Jewish parent so long as the funeral service is not held in a church. A church funeral is considered to be a religious service, and participation in such a service is prohibited by Jewish law.

Why do mourners sometimes follow the hearse for a block or two immediately after the funeral service has been held at the chapel or synagogue?

Halva'yat ha-met ("escorting the dead") is an old Jewish practice that is encouraged as a way of showing proper respect for the deceased. The Rabbis of the Talmud[35] considered the observance of this custom so important that all who adhere to it, they said, will be rewarded in the world-to-come. And the Rabbis even went so far as to allow students to suspend their Torah studies in order to accompany the dead to their final resting place.[36]

In earlier centuries, particularly in the Middle Ages, there were communities in which it was customary for mourners to lead the procession after the funeral service. They were followed by those carrying the bier, after which other relatives and friends joined.

Later, it became customary for the coffin to leave the chapel first and for one to walk in front of it. This was predicated on the belief that "spirits roam the universe to find out what has been decreed about the living, and should they see a condemned sinner before their attention is absorbed by the coffin and its occupant, they pounce upon him."[37]

Today, the custom of escorting the dead is fulfilled, especially among some Orthodox Jews, by walking behind the hearse for a block or two after the chapel or synagogue service.

In this connection, it should be noted that there are a variety of local customs in Sephardic communities. Among Jewish Kurds, for example, sons of the deceased do not follow the coffin, but remain in the courtyard of their house. Among the Jews of Libya, sons do not stand close to the coffin. After it is taken into the cemetery, they wait on the outside, and that is where they recite the Kaddish after the burial service.

Why do non-Jews sometimes act as pallbearers?

Although Jewish law does not prohibit non-Jews from acting as pallbearers, it is traditional for only family members and close Jewish friends to carry the deceased to their final resting place. At funerals of Jewish public figures, non-Jews are often accorded the honor of acting as pallbearers.

Why do funeral processions occasionally stop in front of a synagogue?

Following a home or chapel funeral service, it is customary in some communities for the funeral cortege to pause in front of the doors of the synagogue that the deceased had frequented. Mourners leave their cars and stand in front of the synagogue entrance to listen to the recitation of the *El Malay Rachamim* prayer (see page 82) or to a brief eulogy. The coffin is not brought into the synagogue, nor is it generally removed from the hearse, but the doors of the hearse are opened.

This custom, believed to have been introduced in some unidentified community during the Middle Ages, was undoubtedly based upon the desire to accord respect to a learned individual or a communal leader. None of the codes of Jewish law or the classic books dealing with Jewish customs refer to the practice, which is only occasionally observed today.

Why was it once required that mourners bare an arm during the funeral procession?

As a sign of mourning in talmudic times, it was customary that one expose an arm during the funeral procession.[38] The type of cape commonly worn in those days by Jews as well as non-Jews covered more of the left arm and shoulder than the right. When the left arm was uncovered, this signified that the person was in mourning.

The Talmud[39] records that when the righteous King Hezekiah of Judah died, 36,000 warriors with bare shoulders marched in the funeral procession to do him honor.

Why was the requirement pertaining to the baring of an arm by mourners modified?

The requirement that mourners bare an arm during the funeral procession was discontinued when the practice was carried to the extreme and non-Jews began to mock Jewish mourners. The Talmud gives the following example of how the practice was exaggerated:

When Rabbi Eliezer, the teacher of Rabbi Akiba, died, the Talmud[40] tells us that Akiba bared both arms and beat his breast, drawing blood." He then cried out, using the words that the prophet Elisha used when his teacher, Elijah, died (II Kings 2:12): "Oh, father, father!

Israel's chariots and horsemen." Then Akiba added, "A vast number of coins [knowledge] do I have, but I have no money-changer [teacher] to sort them." Akiba lamented the passing of his teacher, who had always been there to help him sort out and put into focus the vast amount of learning that he had accumulated.

Because of behavior such as that described above, the Rabbis relaxed the requirement of baring an arm and ruled:[41] "For all other dead the mourner need not bare his arm; for his father and mother he should do so. But even for his father and mother he need not do so if he does not wish to."

Today, the practice of baring an arm has been completely abandoned, except in Yemen, where sons of the deceased, arms and shoulders uncovered, follow the coffin. (Other mourners follow the bier wearing black *talitot* [plural of *talit*].)

Why are funerals for a parent sometimes more protracted than those for others?

The Talmud[42] says: "For all relatives, one should not make the funeral elaborate. In the case of a father and mother, however, he should make an elaborate funeral and not hasten the burial, for whoever takes pains with [laying to rest] his father and mother is praiseworthy."

The Siftay Kohen commentary on the *Shulchan A-ruch*[43] explains that one must grieve deeply over the loss of a parent, and the funeral should therefore not be hurried.

Why may Kohanim (Priests) generally not attend Jewish funerals?

The prohibition against Priests (Kohanim), one of the three classes of Jews, attending funerals is based on biblical law (Leviticus 21:1 and Numbers 19:1-16), which forbids members of the priestly family from coming in contact with, or being in an enclosure (*ohel* in Hebrew) with, a Jewish corpse. When not in an enclosure, the Kohen is required to stay a minimum distance of six feet (four cubits) from a Jewish corpse. (More than six feet is considered outside the domain of the deceased.) These restrictions date back to ancient times, when Priests were obligated to be in a constant state of purity so that they would be ready to offer sacrifices in the Temple. Despite the disappearance of the sacrificial system, this tradition has been retained.

An exception to the above is made in the case of the death of an immediate relative of a Kohen, because, like every other Jew, the priest is obligated to bury his own dead.

The Kohen's immediate family consists of mother, father, son, daughter, brother, unmarried sister, and wife. The first six are mandated in the Bible (Leviticus 21:1-3). The wife was added to this category by the Rabbis at a later time. Also considered a member of the Priest's immediate family are a brother or unmarried sister from the same mother but a different father, and a married sister be it from the same mother or same father.[44]

Because of the restrictions against a Kohen coming into contact with the dead who are not of his immediate family, traditional rabbis who are Kohanim will not officiate at funerals or unveilings. However, many non-Orthodox rabbis who are Kohanim do not follow these proscriptions because they believe that the laws of ritual purity applied only as long as there was hope that the Temple and the sacrificial system might be restored. This hope, they feel, is no longer viable. They also question the accuracy of a Kohen's lineage. Reform rabbis, in particular, reject the validity of a hereditary priesthood and do not practice ceremonies, such as the *Pidyon Haben* ("Redemption of the Firstborn Son"), that center about the Kohen.

Why do some Kohanim (Priests) attend the funerals of non-Jews but not of fellow Jews?

The ban against a Kohen being present in an enclosed area together with a deceased applied only to a corpse of a Jew, not that of a gentile. Only by coming into physical contact with a gentile corpse did a Priest become impure (*tamay* in Hebrew).[45]

For this reason many rabbis today permit a Kohen to attend the funeral of a non-Jew and to visit a non-Jewish cemetery. However, there is a strong body of opinion that disapproves of this, believing that it is best to be more stringent in these matters. They maintain that the same restrictions that apply to the Kohen with regard to being in proximity to a Jewish corpse should apply to a non-Jewish corpse.[46]

Why may female members of a priestly family attend funerals?

Although male members of a priestly family may not attend funerals or come within six feet of a corpse, female members of a priestly family are not bound by this rule. The priesthood is transmitted only through the male line.

Moses Maimonides, in his *Mishneh Torah,* says, "The daughters of Aaron [from whom all priestly families stem] were not warned to be careful about defiling themselves through contact with the dead, for it is written [Leviticus 21:1]: 'Speak to the Priests, the *sons* of Aaron....'"[47]

The fact that in Leviticus no reference is made to the *daughters* of Aaron is considered proof that female members of a priestly family are not subject to the same laws of defilement as are male members. Another explanation is that since female members of the priestly family did not perform Temple duties, the question of defilement by virtue of being in the presence of the dead was nonexistent.

Why are funerals denied those who have been executed for committing a murder?

Murder is so repugnant a crime that Jewish law requires that an executed murderer be buried unceremoniously. Normal funeral rites are denied, and the criminal's family is excused from observing the mourning rites. In fact, the Talmud[48] says that mourners should make a concerted effort to find the judge and witnesses who convicted their relative, and say to them: "We bear you no ill will, for you have rendered a true judgment."

Because capital punishment is considered so abhorrent, in Jewish tradition members of the court who imposed the penalty were advised to fast on the day the execution is carried out.[49]

Why is the *Kaddish* not recited during the chapel funeral service?

The *Kaddish* is recited by mourners for the first time at the burial site. This prayer of praise to God is not recited during the funeral chapel service because mourners at that point are still considered *onenim* (singular, *onen,* meaning "one who is distressed") and an *onen* is not required to recite prayers. (See page 23 for more discussion on the *onen.* See Chapter Six, beginning on page 119, for a full discussion of the *Kaddish.)*

Why is the *El Malay Rachamim* prayer recited at the funeral service?

The *El Malay Rachamim* prayer—or simply the *Malay,* as it is popularly called—is recited at both the chapel and cemetery funeral services as well as on other occasions when an individual is memorialized. In congregations that hold a *Yizkor* service, the service concludes with a rendition of the *Malay* by the cantor.

El Malay Rachamim, which means "O God, Full of

Mercy," is recited in order to evoke tender memories of the dead and to emphasize the unbroken bond that continues to exist between the living and the dead. This unbroken bond is referred to in Hebrew as *tzeror ha-chayim,* "bundle of life." The Hebrew expression appears for the first time in I Samuel 25:29. Whenever the *Malay* is recited, congregants rise. All are touched by its haunting melody.

In some synagogues it is customary after the Torah reading to recite the *Malay* in behalf of the deceased whose *Yahrzeits* will be observed during the coming week. Occasionally, it is also recited in memory of a deceased parent of the bride or bridegroom after the signing of the marriage contract *(ketuba)* before a wedding.

Rabbi Mordecai Breisch (born 1896) of Zurich, in response to a question concerning the propriety of reciting the *Malay* to memorialize the parents of a bride and groom at a wedding, notes that customs differ in various European localities and that it was not customary in his town.[50]

Why do Sephardim recite a prayer called the *Hashkaba* at the chapel service?

At the chapel service, rather than recite the *El Malay* prayer, Sephardim traditionally recite the *Hashkaba,* the "Rest in Peace" prayer. The word *Hashkaba* is from a Hebrew root meaning "to lie down."

For males, the prayer begins with the words *Tov shem mi-shemen tov,* "A good name is more precious than the choicest oil" (Ecclesiastes 7:1). For women, the prayer opens with words from of the Book of Proverbs (31:10), *Eshet cha'yil mi yimtza!* "A woman of valor, who can find!"

Among Syrian Jews, the *Hashkaba* is recited each morning and evening during the Shiva week prayer service.[51]

Why is the Twenty-third Psalm recited at funerals?

The Twenty-third Psalm, which begins with the familiar words "The Lord is my Shepherd, I shall not want," is widely used at funeral services (and unveilings) because it expresses unbridled faith in God's judgment despite the tragedy being faced. It encourages mourners to be strong and fearless because God, the Good Shepherd, stands beside them and leads them.

Added to this assurance of a sheltering presence, the soothing imagery set forth in such terms as "green pastures" and "still waters" has a calming, comforting effect upon the bereaved. The expressions of quiet beauty make it easier for those who are grieving intensely to accept the finality of the moment.

CHAPTER 5

The Cemetery Service

Introduction

The basic Hebrew term for cemetery is *Bet Kevarot,* meaning "House of Graves."[1] But in keeping with an ancient Jewish tradition, abrasive terminology and harsh appellations such as this one are often softened and even eliminated (see General Introduction). Instead of *Bet Kevarot,* a cemetery is sometimes referred to euphemistically as *Bet Olam* ("Eternal House"), *Bet Cha'yim* ("House of the Living"), or *Bet Avot* ("House of the Fathers [Ancestors]"). In the Book of Job (30:23) a cemetery is called "The House Assigned for All the Living," and in the Midrash[2] the Aramaic form, *Bet Almin,* is used.

The poet Henry Wadsworth Longfellow reminded us of a very unusual and appealing term for cemetery: "I like that ancient Saxon phrase that called the burial ground 'God's Acre,'" he wrote. This designation has had much appeal for Jews as well, for in Jewish tradition the burial ground is accorded the highest degree of respect. This was once reflected in the advice given to Nebuchadnezzar of Babylonia by his lieutenants. He was looking for a place to set up camp in anticipation of his conquest of Palestine. "There are no better or neater places than Jewish cemeteries," the lieutenants advised. "Their graveyards are better than your palaces."[3]

* * *

While not all contemporary authorities are comfortable with the revelation that many of the laws, customs and ceremonies that revolve about the burial service are associated with ancient superstitions stemming from the world of demonology, this is an incontrovertible fact that must be acknowledged if we are to understand the reasons behind many cemetery procedures and practices.

When the Rabbis of the Talmud[4] said that "three persons need protection ['against evil spirits' is added by Rashi]—a sick person, a bridegroom, and a bride, "they meant it literally. And, when the Talmud[5] states that "a man is forbidden to stand in his neighbor's field at a time when its fruit is at the peak of ripeness [lest it might be damaged by the evil eye]," Rashi warned that this proscription is to be taken literally.

The origins of many burial practices can only be satisfactorily explained in terms of the belief that there is an ongoing battle being waged by humans against demons and evil spirits. Foremost among these practices is the recitation of Psalm 91, which begins with the words *Yoshev b'seter Elyon,* "O, you who dwell in the shelter of the Most High." This lyric poem, which came to be known as the Antidemonic Psalm, is recited as the coffin is carried from the hearse to the grave. Seven stops are often made during the procession. When the grave is filled with earth, mourners use the back of the shovel to drop earth onto the coffin. When the burial is over, two lines are formed by those in attendance so that the mourners may pass through securely. As this chapter explains, these and other burial practices have their origin in superstition and demonology. They are best understood as we view them through the eyes of the Rabbis of earlier centuries who created them.

Summary of Traditional Observances Pertaining to the Cemetery Service

Cremation
- Cremation is contrary to Jewish law. However, no law prohibits burial of the ashes of cremation in a Jewish cemetery, although many Orthodox rabbis forbid the practice.

Non-Jewish cemeteries
- When there is no Jewish cemetery in a town, the community may purchase a designated area in a general cemetery in which to bury their dead.

Coffins
- Coffins must be made of inexpensive soft wood. The use of ornate metal coffins is not in keeping with Jewish practice.

Mausoleums
- Burial in a mausoleum is permissible only if the coffin is placed in the earth itself and the mausoleum is built around the grave. Above-ground burial is prohibited.

Pallbearers
- Family members and friends should serve as pallbearers. Traditionally, non-Jews may not carry the casket to the grave, although many rabbis today do not object to such a practice.

Burial of sacred articles and books
- Worn-out Torah scrolls and other religious books and articles are buried in a grave next to a pious individual.

Headcovering
- Jewish tradition demands that visitors to a cemetery keep their heads covered.

Kaddish

- Traditionally, a special Kaddish known as *Kaddish De-itchadeta* is recited at the burial service.

Special cemetery areas

- Suicides and executed criminals are buried in designated areas of the cemetery. Apostates are also interred in such areas.

Burial of Kohanim

- Kohanim (Priests) are often buried near the cemetery perimeter so that family members may visit their graves.

Widows and widowers

- A widow or widower who remarries may be buried next to his or her first spouse, unless the second spouse objects.

Divorced persons

- Divorced persons may be buried next to each other.

Non-Jewish spouse

- A non-Jewish spouse may not be buried in a Jewish cemetery.
- Children of a Jewish woman and a non-Jewish man may be buried in a Jewish cemetery. This includes sons of such a marriage, even if they had not been circumcised.

Filling in the grave

- The first shovelfuls of earth are thrown on the coffin by family members and friends. The shovel is pushed into the pile of earth after each use rather than being passed from hand to hand. It is customary to use the backside of the shovel. The entire grave may be filled in while the family is present, or it may be partially filled in and then covered with a green grasslike carpet. In the latter case, the service is concluded and the grave is then filled in by the cemetery crew.

Flowers
- Although there is no objection in Jewish law to placing flowers on a coffin, Jewish custom has never favored this practice.

Handwashing
- When leaving the cemetery after the burial service, or when entering the house upon returning from the cemetery, the hands are washed in the traditional manner.

Reinterment
- The remains of an individual, regardless of the state of decomposition, may be removed for reburial in a plot where other family members are buried.
- Those buried in national cemeteries may be reinterred in Jewish cemeteries.

Why did the Rabbis insist that Jewish communities establish cemeteries for the burial of their dead?

The establishment of a separate place for the burial of Jews is not mandated directly in the Bible or Talmud or in the codes of Jewish law. The Bible (Genesis 23) describes the acquisition by Abraham of a private plot to bury his wife Sarah, and the Talmud also calls for the burial in one's own family plot *(b'toch shelo).*[6]

In talmudic times, while ancestral tombs continued to be used, public burial plots had already been established.

In one reference, the Talmud suggests that a righteous man not be buried next to a sinner,[7] which would indicate that burial in communal cemeteries did take place. The sinner the Talmud speaks of is one guilty of a capital offense, which includes the worship of idols.[8] Since idolatry was prevalent among non-Jews, all heathens—and by extension all non-Jews—were placed in the same category. This is probably the rabbinic foundation for insisting that Jews be buried in their own cemeteries. Traditionally, the establishment of a burial place for Jewish dead was of the highest priority in every Jewish community, even moreso than the building of a synagogue.

Why do Orthodox rabbis sometimes permit a Jew to be buried in a non-Jewish cemetery?

Rabbi Yekutiel Greenwald, in his book on mourning,[9] mentions the case of a Jew who lived among non-Jews and who feared that when he died, he would be buried in their cemetery. The Jew therefore left word that upon his death his body was to be burned. When the man's wish became known, the Rabbis ruled that the wish was not to be honored because it is far better for a Jew to be buried among non-Jews than to be cremated. (See page 91 for more on the Jewish attitude toward cremation.)

Rabbis also permit the burial of a Jew in a non-Jewish cemetery if a Jewish community does not have a cemetery of its own. In such an instance, in order to bury its dead, the community will purchase a parcel of land within a general cemetery. The Jewish section must be delineated by a fence or some other form of demarcation, thus in effect making it a Jewish cemetery.[10]

During World War II, the law committee of the Jewish Welfare Board's Division of Religious Activities, consisting of Orthodox, Conservative, and Reform rabbis, ruled that Jewish chaplains may officiate at military funerals in national cemeteries such as Arlington, where Jewish and Christian soldiers are buried side by side.

Why do non-Orthodox rabbis sometimes permit a non-Jew to be buried in a Jewish cemetery?

Reform and Reconstructionist rabbis permit a non-Jew to be buried next to his or her Jewish mate in a Jewish cemetery if the non-Jewish partner identified positively with the Jewish community during the course of the marriage. They also will often allow the burial of close non-Jewish relatives in the family plot in a Jewish cemetery.[11]

In Conservative Judaism, some rabbis are less lenient in this regard. They require that a railing of three to four feet (ten *tefachim*) be erected on either side of the grave of the non-Jew or that space equal to the width of one grave be left on either side.[12]

The Orthodox rabbinate does not permit the burial of a non-Jew in a Jewish cemetery.

Why is a space equivalent to a minimum of six handbreadths left between graves?

In the ghettos of Europe, where burial space was limited, it was often necessary to inter bodies above those previously buried. The rule was therefore established that at least six handbreadths *(tefachim)* of space separate each corpse from the other.[13] Later, it became a requirement that at least six handbreadths be left between one grave and another.

Why is cremation considered to be in violation of Jewish law?

Although there are instances in the Bible where cremation is seemingly considered to be an acceptable practice,[14] early rabbinic authorities considered it a violation of biblical law. Their ruling is based on the statement in the Book of Genesis (3:19) in which God says to Adam, "For dust thou art, and unto dust shalt thou return." This, say the Rabbis, means that the body itself must be returned to the earth from which it was formed.

Additionally, some modern authorities consider cremation to be a pagan practice that harks back to the funeral pyre. Imitation of non-Jewish practices is forbidden in Jewish tradition.

Why do some authorities permit the ashes of cremation to be buried in a Jewish cemetery?

Most Orthodox authorities consider the burial of the ashes of cremation in a Jewish cemetery to be a violation of Jewish law. Rabbi Ben Zion Uziel (1880-1953), known as the Rishon Le-Tzion, explains that the burial of ashes of cremation in a Jewish cemetery is prohibited because a Jewish cemetery is a sacred place, and to bury ashes there would be an act of desecration.[15]

While many authorities agree with this position, some rabbinic bodies, such as London's Burial Society of the United Synagogue (Orthodox) and the Law Committee of the Rabbinical Assembly (Conservative), do permit the ashes of cremation to be buried in a Jewish cemetery. In this way, these organizations maintain, at least part of the deceased is being returned to the earth as demanded in Genesis 3:19, "...unto dust thou shalt return."

All Jewish authorities agree, however, that if a body had been accidentally incinerated, such ashes may be buried in a Jewish cemetery. The Rabbis compared the burning of a body to the burning of a Torah scroll. Just as the scroll that is burned must be buried in the ground, so must a corpse that has been burned in a fire be buried. When cremation is deliberate, traditional law forbids the burial of the ashes of a corpse in a Jewish cemetery.[16]

Why were criminals once buried in designated areas within a cemetery?

The Rabbis of the Talmud[17] ruled that a wicked person should not be buried beside a righteous one. For this reason, Jewish courts in early talmudic times set aside certain burial plots to be used exclusively for criminals who had been executed by order of the court. These dead were permitted to be reinterred in their family plots only after a year had passed and the bodies had decomposed, with only bones remaining.[18]

Why do some Jews wish to be buried in Israel?

In talmudic (and later) times, many Rabbis believed that the resurrection of the dead *(techiyat ha-metim)* would take place only in the Holy Land, and that only those buried there would be revived in the end of days. Rabbi Anan commented: "Whoever is buried in the Land of Israel is deemed to be buried under the altar [and there is no more prestigious place in the world]."[19]

Other Rabbis, while agreeing that the resurrection would occur in the Holy Land, did not agree that those buried in the Diaspora would be denied resurrection. They believed that the bodies of the pious dead buried outside of Israel would roll underground through tunnels burrowed by God. And when the bodies arrive in Israel, they will be reunited with their souls.[20] This concept is known as *gilgul mechilot* (literally, "rolling through underground passages").

Why may a Kohen (Priest) attend the funeral of a Gentile but not of a fellow Jew?

The Bible states (Numbers 19:11) that all Israelites become ritually impure *(tamay* in Hebrew) if they touch a corpse, whether the deceased is a Jew or a non-Jew. A Kohen, however, had special responsibilities and therefore had to measure up to a higher standard. He became impure not only when he touched a corpse but even when he entered an enclosure (*ohel* in Hebrew) that contained a Jewish corpse. When not in an enclosure, the Kohen was also required to stay a minimum distance of six feet from a Jewish corpse. (More than six feet is considered outside the domain of the deceased.) This rule did not apply if a *Kohen* simply entered an enclosed area where there was a Gentile corpse. Only by actually touching a Gentile corpse did a Kohen become impure.[21]

For the above reasons a Kohen today may attend the funeral of a non-Jew, and he may visit a non-Jewish cemetery. He may not, however, attend the funeral of a Jew when it is held in an enclosed area, unless that Jew is a member of his immediate family: mother, father, son, daughter, brother, unmarried sister, and wife. The first six are mandated in Leviticus 21:2, the seventh by a ruling of the Rabbis of the Talmud.

A traditional rabbi who is a Kohen may not officiate at a funeral held in any enclosed area. If he wishes to be present at the funeral, he must wait outside the building. The rabbi-Kohen may visit the cemetery because it is not in an enclosure, but he must distance himself at least six feet from all graves.

Non-Orthodox rabbis who are Kohanim generally do not follow these proscriptions because they believe that the laws of ritual purity and impurity were only applicable as long as there was hope that the Temple and the sacrificial system might be restored, the possibility of which is remote.

Why is a Kohen (Priest) usually buried next to the walkway of a cemetery?

As stated in the previous answer, a Kohen becomes impure by touching or coming into close proximity to a corpse. Because according to the Jewish law a Kohen must distance himself a minimum of six feet (four *amot*) from a Jewish corpse, a deceased Kohen must be buried next to a walkway that is at least twelve feet wide. Or he may be buried at the edge of the cemetery, making it possible for relatives who are also Kohanim to visit the grave without violating the law.[23]

Why are the female members of the family of a Kohen permitted to attend funerals?

Moses Maimonides, in his *Mishneh Torah,* says, "The daughters of Aaron [from whom all priestly families stem] were not warned to be careful about defiling themselves through contact with the dead, for it is written in the Bible [Leviticus 21:1]: 'Speak to the Priests, the sons of Aaron...'"[24] The fact that no reference is made to the daughters of Aaron is proof that female members of a priestly family are not subject to the same laws of defilement as are the male members of the family, undoubtedly because women were not required to perform in the Temple. They may, therefore, attend funerals and visit cemeteries like every other Jew.

Why may an apostate be buried in a Jewish cemetery?

In Jewish law, a Jew who has forsaken Judaism is still a Jew and has every right to be buried in a Jewish cemetery. The third-century Palestinian scholar Rabbi Abba ben Zavda explained: "Even when Jews sin, they continue to be regarded as Jews." He amplified upon this, saying: "A myrtle, though it stands among reeds, is still a myrtle and continues to be so called."[25]

Although this means that an apostate never ceases to be a Jew and has every legal right to be buried in a Jewish cemetery, the act of apostasy is repugnant to the apostate's fellow Jews. Therefore, burial of the apostate in a grave close to other Jews is generally discouraged. Often, a special section of a cemetery is reserved for apostates.

Not all Jewish communities, however, follow this custom. The Spanish-Portuguese community in New York, for example, does not designate a special area in their cemetery for the burial of apostates.[26]

Why are some suicides buried apart from their fellow Jews?

Those who commit suicide under duress are buried in a Jewish cemetery like any other Jewish dead. However, those who were known to be fully aware of their actions are buried at a distance of at least six feet (four *amot*) from other graves. In some traditional cemeteries a special section close to the perimeter is reserved for the burial of suicides.

Among the Falashas of Ethiopia, suicides were traditionally not buried in the Jewish cemetery. They were usually buried at a site close to the place where the suicide act was committed.[27]

Why are infants not accorded the same burial rites as adults?

The Rabbis of the Talmud[28] considered a child who has not lived thirty full days to be in the same category as an unborn fetus and hence not a viable person. For this reason they ruled that one need not mourn an infant that lived less than thirty days, and that the family need not even stand in a row to accept condolences after the informal burial service has been completed. For infants over the age of thirty days, all mourning rites are to be observed. It is for this same reason that the Pidyon Haben ("Redemption of the Firstborn Son") ceremony is held only after the child has lived thirty full days.[29]

Why are infant males circumcised at the time of burial?

As stated above, regular funeral services and mourning rites are not observed for a child who has not lived a full thirty days. According to Jewish law, a male infant who survived less than eight days is taken directly to the cemetery, where he is circumcised and given a Hebrew name before burial[30] This practice, rarely observed by modern Jews, was introduced in geonic times (after 500 C.E.), when it was generally believed that uncircumcised Jews would have no share in the world-to-come.

In *A Guide to Religious Jewish Practice*,[31] Rabbi Isaac Klein (Conservative) notes that Maimonides makes no mention of this circumcision custom, suggesting that it need not be observed.

Why, in matters of burial, is more consideration given to a man's first wife than to his second wife?

Most rabbinic authorities agree that a man who has remarried after the death of his first wife should continue his loyalty to his first wife because the strong bond established in a first marriage is not automatically dissolved with the passing of a mate. The Talmud says that a man's first wife is his true love, and that when she dies during his lifetime, it is as though the Temple had been destroyed in his lifetime.[32]

For this reason, a widower who remarries may be buried next to his first wife, especially if there are children from the marriage. When the second wife dies, she may also be buried next to her husband if that was her expressed wish. However, if the second wife had been married previously and she had children from that marriage, custom would indicate that she be buried next to her first husband.[33]

Some authorities believe that as a matter of course a widower who has remarried need not necessarily be buried beside his first wife. Each case must be judged individually, they maintain, bearing in mind the effect upon children and other family members.[34]

None of this, of course, applies to a divorced couple.

Why do many Sephardic burial customs differ from those of Ashkenazim?

All Jews were greatly influenced by the cultures of the peoples among[35] whom they lived. Quite naturally, then, Sephardic burial and mourning practices are markedly different from those of Ashkenazim.

In *A Treasury of Sephardic Laws and Customs,* Rabbi Herbert C. Dobrinsky points out that:

- Among Syrian Jews, men and women are buried in separate sections within the same cemetery. Sons may go to the cemetery for the burial of a mother, but sons may not be present at the burial of a father. Women do not go to the cemetery.[36]
- Among Moroccans, women are banned from being present at a burial. Only sons attend the actual interment of a parent. Among Moroccan Jews living in America, these rules have been relaxed.[37]
- Among the Jews of Greece, Turkey, and other Balkan states, until recently women have been barred from attending a burial. In some communities a father was not allowed to be present at the interment of a child, nor was a child permitted to attend the burial of his father.[38]

It should be noted that while it is quite evident that many Sephardic practices are clearly based on superstition, their precise origin is difficult, if not impossible, to ascertain.

Why was it customary in some Jewish communities for women to abstain from attending burial services?

This practice, which was prevalent among Sephardim (see the previous answer), is based on an ancient belief that women, even more than men, attract demons and spirits. The Talmud recounts that the third-century

Palestinian scholar Rabbi Joshua ben Levi was once warned by the Angel of Death never to stand near women returning from a funeral "because I [the Angel of Death] go before them dancing with sword in hand, and with permission to kill."[39]

In his sixteenth-century *Code of Jewish Law,* Joseph Caro, a Sephardic Jew born in Toledo, Spain, is quite explicit in warning women not to frequent cemeteries,[40] undoubtedly because many people believed that the Angel of Death and Satan would be attracted by them.[41] The seventeenth-century Ashkenazic commentator Shabbetai ben Meir Ha-Kohen (popularly known as the Shach, an abbreviated form of the name of his commentary , Siftay Kohen) issues a similar warning: "Women should not go to the cemetery because they would bring misfortune to the world."

Gradually, the superstition that women attract evil spirits lost its adherents, and today, in most Sephardic and Ashkenazic communities, women are permitted to attend burials.

Why is it not permissible to bring religious articles into a cemetery?

The *Code of Jewish Law* prohibits the bringing of a Torah scroll into a cemetery. It also prohibits the wearing of *tefilin* (phylacteries) in a cemetery and engaging in formal prayer there.[42] (In talmudic times *tefilin* were worn by men all day long, not only when engaged in prayer.)

These prohibitions are based on the interpretation of the verse in Proverbs (17:5), "He who mocks the poor *[lo'eg le-rash]* blasphemes God." (In Jewish literature, a poor man is equated with a dead man. Hence, those lying in their graves are sometimes referred to as "the poor ones.") Tradition considers it a mockery of the dead to come into a cemetery with religious articles, which the deceased can no longer use and enjoy.[43]

Rabbi Abraham Palaggi (1809-1899), of Izmir, Turkey, extends the concept of not doing anything in a cemetery that would "mock the dead" by declaring in a responsum that it is forbidden to use snuff in a cemetery.

Why are coffins sometimes not used in Jewish burials?

Although the Book of Genesis (50:26) refers to Joseph as being "put in a coffin in Egypt," this Egyptian custom was not practiced by the early Israelites. In fact, when Joseph's father dies and is buried in Canaan (Genesis 50:13), no mention is made of placing him in a coffin.

The Talmud[44] reminds us that in the early centuries of the Common Era coffins were not used by Jews. It was customary to place deceased rich persons on a *dargesh,* a tall, richly ornamented, stately bed. The poor were brought out for burial on a simple bier or wooden platform. When it became apparent that the poor felt humiliated by the simple burial accorded their relatives, it was ruled that all the deceased should be brought out on a simple bier.

This ruling was not strictly adhered to, and by the Middle Ages a variety of customs prevailed. In France, coffins were used; in Spain, they were not. In the sixteenth century, the Kabbalists considered it important that the dead body make direct contact with the earth, and coffins were not used. The corpse was placed in a body bag and carried to the grave on a wooden platform. A bed of interwoven reeds, prepared in advance, was first placed on the floor of the grave, and the corpse was laid on the mat.

Burial without a coffin is still practiced by many Orthodox Jews in Israel and by many Sephardim outside of Israel, particularly in Greece, Turkey, and other Balkan states.

In Western countries the law generally demands that the deceased be buried in coffins.[45]

Why do some Jews march around the coffin seven times?

Among some Sephardim, it is customary to take the coffin into the cemetery chapel before burial and for mourners then to march around the coffin seven times while reciting special prayers known as *Rodeamentos* in Spanish (*Hakafot Ha-met* in Hebrew; "Processions Around the Dead" in English).

The concept of encirclement as a protection against evil spirits is popular in Jewish tradition. It was once widely believed that demons follow the dead to the grave but that they can be warded off by forming a protective circle around the body of the deceased. Demons are able to operate only in the public domain, and the circle creates a private area within which they are rendered ineffective.

The famous preacher Elijah Ha-Kohen (1645-1729), of Izmir, Turkey, a mystic who initially believed Shabbetai Zevi's messianic claims, notes that it was customary to throw pieces of all kinds of metal, primarily iron, in every direction each time an encirclement took place. The clanging noise, it was believed, scared off demons intent upon causing harm to the deceased.[47]

Some Sephardim perform the ritual of encirclement when the coffin is placed on top of the grave, just before it is lowered into the ground.

Why do most Jews keep their heads covered during the funeral service?

In biblical times one sign of mourning was to cover the head and face. This is how King David expressed his grief upon learning of the death of his son Absalom (II Samuel 19:5). The custom continued to be observed in talmudic times. The Talmud notes that when the third-century Palestinian scholar Bar Kappara mourned the passing of his teacher Yehuda Ha-nasi, he covered his head.[48]

When a funeral service is in progress in the chapel or cemetery, the head is kept covered because prayers are being recited. However, it has become a strong Jewish custom to keep the head covered even when a service is not in progress, just as is done in most synagogues. Although a cemetery is not considered to have the sanctity of a synagogue, Moses Sofer (1762-1839), the Hungarian legal authority, responded to a question on the subject by saying that just as one may not sleep in a synagogue, so one may not sleep in a cemetery: the two must be accorded equal respect.

Why is escorting the dead to their final resting place considered "the ultimate kindness"?

The Talmud[49] considers escorting the dead (especially outstanding scholars) to their final resting place to be an act worthy of great praise. Escorting the dead is considered one of the most meritorious deeds an individual can perform in his or her lifetime and one of the best investments a person can make to achieve immortality. It is referred to in Hebrew as *chesed shel emet,* "the ultimate kindness," for it is done out of pure motive, without the expectation of a reward.[50]

The Talmud[51] admonishes that no one allow a funeral cortege to pass by without joining in the procession. Such inaction would be in violation of the law that cautions against "mocking the poor [the dead]," for he who does so blasphemes God (Proverbs 17:5).

Why do some funeral directors insist that cemetery workers carry the coffin from the hearse to the grave site?

At an Orthodox Jewish funeral, only Jewish male relatives and friends of the deceased may serve as pallbearers, whereas at non-Orthodox funerals non-Jews are permitted to be pallbearers as well. The pallbearers carry the coffin from the hearse to the grave site and are followed by a procession of mourners.

Some funeral directors today insist that all who come to the cemetery to attend the burial remain in their cars near the cemetery administration building while the hearse pulls ahead and parks near the burial site. Cemetery workers then carry the coffin and place it on top of the open grave, to be lowered later, during the service. The family and friends then drive up to the walkway nearest the grave site. They then join the procession to the grave.

Funeral directors contend that this procedure, aside from being a more practical and efficient way of conducting the burial, is less painful for mourners. In addition, they point out, insurance rates would be higher if nonprofessionals were permitted to carry the coffin, and this cost increase would have to be passed on to the family of the deceased. Another consideration is that those not used to carrying heavy objects might drop the coffin, causing the lid to open and the corpse to be exposed and thus dishonored.

Why does the procession from the hearse to the grave pause periodically?

Traditionally, Psalm 91 is read by the rabbi as he leads the procession that follows the coffin to the grave. The rabbi usually walks in front of the coffin and the mourners follow behind it. When verse 11, consisting of seven Hebrew words (the English translation of the verse is "For He will order His angels to guard you wherever you go"), is recited, seven stops are usually made, one after each Hebrew word, although in some traditions only three stops are made. (The numbers seven and three are both significant in Jewish tradition.)[52] Each stop is sometimes explained as an opportunity for the bereaved to express hesitation and reluctance to take leave of their departed.

A second common explanation, offered by the Rabbis of the Talmud,[53] is that the seven stops reflect the seven times the Hebrew word *hevel,* "vanity," is mentioned in the Book of Ecclesiastes (1:2); "Vanity of vanities," said Kohelet, "vanity of vanities, all is vanity." (Actually the word "vanity," *hevel,* is mentioned only five times: three times in the singular and twice in the plural. But each plural is counted for two singular forms, making a total of seven.)

A third popular explanation for making seven stops during the procession from hearse to grave is that they reflect the seven stages through which a person passes in a lifetime. These are outlined in the Midrash:[54]

- At age one, he is fondled and kissed by all.
- At ages two and three, he is like a pig, sticking his hands in filth.
- At age ten, he skips like a kid.
- At twenty, he is like a neighing horse, preening his person and longing for a wife.
- Having married, he is like an ass (struggling for a living).
- When he has children, he battles like a dog to provide food for their needs.
- When he grows old, he is bent like an ape (and begins to lose the characteristics of a human).

Modern scholars generally believe that the origin of the custom of pausing during a procession has roots in the belief that the stopping and starting will cause the evil spirits that follow the dead to the grave to become confused and disoriented, uncertain over the whereabouts of the deceased. This view is in keeping with the attitude of many early authorities. One such authority, the Gaon Sar Shalom, ninth-century head of the great academy in Sura, Babylonia, explained that in his day processions paused seven times in order to shake off evil spirits that clung close to those who attented a funeral. With each stop, one of the spirits would disappear.

Scholars in subsequent centuries (Rashi in the eleventh and Moses Isserles in the sixteenth) repeated this explanation of the practice of halting the procession on the way to (and also from) the grave, noting that with each pause the evil spirits lose their effectiveness.[55]

Rashi offered one additional explanation: namely, that the purpose of halting the procession is to allow a final opportunity, for those who wish to do so, to eulogize the dead.[56]

The custom of halting during the procession is not observed on days when the *Tachanun* prayer is omitted from the daily prayer service. These include the day before a holiday (except for Chanuka) and Friday afternoons. See page 180 for more on *Tachanun*.[57]

Why is Psalm 91 usually recited during the procession from the hearse to the grave?

Psalm 91, beginning with the words "O you who dwell in the shelter of the Most High [*Yoshev b'seter Elyon*]," is sometimes referred to as *Shir Shel Pega'im,* "Psalm of Afflictions," because it lists catastrophes that can befall those who do not have faith in God but who will be saved if they trust in Him.

It was generally believed that the recitation of Psalm 91 could counteract the evil intentions of demons and harmful spirits that are unusually active at the time of burial, and this selection has therefore also become known as the Antidemonic Psalm.

The Midrash ascribes the authorship of Psalm 91 to Moses, contending that it was first uttered by him when ascending Mount Sinai to receive the two Tablets of the Law. Fearful of harmful spirits, Moses recited this Psalm to announce that God was his fortress and protector. He was using the power of God's name to ward off demons that might be intent upon frustrating his mission.

Not only is Psalm 91 recited at burials and when private grave visits are made, but in the past it was recited by some Jews even before going to sleep. In a responsum, the noted scholar Rabbi Israel Isserlein (c.1450-1500) makes reference to the statement of a contemporary, Rabbi Jacob Weil: "When I prepare for my afternoon nap, I recite the Antidemonic Psalm, for all sleep is dangerous because of demons."[59]

Professor Julian Morgenstern[60] notes that it was once customary at funerals to recite the first nine verses of Psalm 91 together with Psalm 3, and both together were called *Shir Shel Pega'im.* He also notes that in funerals of the Greek Orthodox Church in Constantinople Psalm 91 is part of the ritual.

During Operation Desert Storm, in 1991, when Iraq began launching SCUD ballistic missiles against Saudi Arabia and Israel, Major Kathleen Murray, a registered nurse from Madeira, Florida, who ran an Air Force medical facility, reported that soldiers in bunkers read Psalm 91, with special emphasis on verses 5 and 6:

> You need not fear the terror by night,
> Nor the arrow that flies by day,
> Nor the pestilence that stalks in the darkness,
> Nor the destruction that ravages at noon.

Why is it sometimes permissible to place coffins in concrete or plexiglass liners?

Funeral parlors, anxious to increase sales, sometimes suggest to mourners that a concrete or plexiglass liner be placed in the grave as a protective measure. However, use of a grave liner is in clear violation of Jewish law, which requires that there be no airtight, nondecaying barrier between the corpse and the earth, thus enabling the body to decompose quickly and return to the earth from which it came (Genesis 2:7). Wooden coffins disintegrate within a relatively short period of time.

In areas where the earth shifts easily or where the earth might be contaminated and state law requires that a liner be placed in the grave, Jewish law accedes to the government regulation.

Why is the coffin covered with earth immediately after is it placed in the ground?

The custom of immediately covering the coffin with earth is connected with the medieval concept that the ghost of the deceased, still in the coffin with the body, might want to leave and harm some of the living relatives. By immediately covering the casket with earth, the ghost is unable to escape.

Another reason offered for the practice is that at one time corpses were stolen so that medical students would have cadavers on which to practice. By covering the coffin immediately, the corpse was provided greater protection.

A more meaningful, modern explanation is that the piling of earth on the coffin in the presence of the mourners emphasizes the irrevocability of death.

Before the earth is shoveled onto the coffin, it is traditional for those present to pronounce the following words: *Al mekoma yavo (tavo) be-shalom,* "May he (she) rest in peace."

Why do mourners drops shovelfuls (usually three) of earth onto the coffin?

It is the responsibility of relatives to bury their dead, and their dropping shovelfuls of earth onto the coffin is symbolic of fulfilling that responsibility. In cases where members of the family are visibly upset by the piercing sound of earth landing on the casket, rabbis will not insist that all family members carry out the practice.

Rabbi Maurice Lamm, author of *The Jewish Way in Death and Mourning,* considers the "heart-rending thud of earth on the casket" to be psychologically beneficial because it signals finality and "helps the mourner overcome the illusion that his relative still lives."

There is a tradition among some Jews of German extraction to drop three handfuls of earth on the coffin.

Why is the backside of the shovel used to fill in the grave?

The reason mourners use the back side of the shovel when beginning to fill in the grave is obscure. The practice probably started as local custom and may have been instituted to indicate a difference (*shinui* in talmudic parlance) between ordinary shoveling (the purpose of which is to dig or fill in a hole) and the shoveling of earth to bury a loved one.

Using the backside of the shovel is a practice particularly common among the Sephardim of Greece, Turkey, and other parts of the old Ottoman Empire.

Why is the shovel that is used to fill in the grave not passed from person to person?

As pointed out above, once the coffin has been lowered into the ground, it is customary for some of those present—men and occasionally women—to take turns dropping earth onto the coffin. When one individual is finished, the shovel is pushed into the mound of earth alongside the grave instead of being handed directly to the next person. The next mourner then picks up the shovel and repeats the procedure. In some Sephardic communities, such as those in Turkey and Greece, the custom is for individuals to simply throw the shovel onto the ground after using it.

The practice of not passing the shovel directly from hand to hand has been explained as a way of saying that we do not wish to pass sorrow from one person to another.

Why do some authorities say that the mourning period does not officially begin until the grave has been completely filled with earth?

In ancient times, when bodies were buried in caves, the mourning period officially began when the mouth of the cave was covered with a rock. When caves were no longer used and bodies were buried in the earth, authorities disagreed as to whether mourning was to begin at the moment the corpse was laid in the ground and covered with some earth or when the entire grave was filled with earth. The disagreement stemmed from the interpretation given the words *yisatem ha-golel,* which literally means "to seal [or cover] with a rock." This phrase is used in the Talmud to indicate that burial has been completed and mourning has begun.

The great scholar Rashi (eleventh century) believed that the word *golel* refers to the cover (lid) of the coffin, implying that once the corpse is placed in the coffin and the cover closed, mourning begins. His grandson, Rabbenu Tam (twelfth century), argues that just as the stone in early times covered the cave opening completely, so must the coffin be lowered into the grave and covered completely with earth before mourning begins.

Nachmanides, the famous thirteenth-century authority, agreed with Rashi, but later scholars have largely sided with Rabbenu Tam, and so it has become traditional for the grave to be filled to the top before the mourning period officially begins.

Why has the partial filling-in of a grave become acceptable to many traditionalists?

Although traditional Jews favor the filling in of a grave to the very top before the family leaves the burial site, in extenuating circumstances, such as when the family is extremely distraught or when the hour is late and the Sabbath or holiday is to begin that evening, the coffin itself is only partially covered with earth in the presence of the family. The burial service is concluded, and after the mourners have left the grave site, the cemetery crew fills in the grave completely.

Non-Orthodox rabbis, siding with Rashi (see the previous answer), believe it proper, if the family concurs, to have only several token shovelfuls of earth dropped onto the coffin, after which a grasslike carpet is stretched out over the grave and the family leaves.

Why are coffins generally not adorned with flowers?

Although there is no objection in Jewish law to covering a coffin with flowers or greenery, Jewish custom has never favored the practice.

Rashi, the eleventh-century French scholar, points out that there existed a custom "to place myrtle branches on a coffin to honor the dead."[62] However, because adorning a coffin in this manner was considered a non-Jewish practice, Jews were discouraged from following it.

A second reason for the custom of not adorning coffins is that in Jewish tradition all people, rich and poor, are equal in death.[63] Just as the burial garments of both the rich and the poor are to be simple white shrouds, so are the graves of both rich and poor to be simple and unadorned.

It should be noted that in Israel today people do bring flowers to the cemetery.

Why is the *Tziduk Ha-din* prayer traditionally recited at funerals?

As the coffin is carried from the hearse to the grave, in addition to the commonly recited Psalm 90, beginning with the words *Tefila le-Moshe* ("A Prayer for Moses"), and Psalm 91, beginning with the words *Yoshev b'seter Elyon* ("He who dwells in the Shelter of the Most High"), the *Tziduk Ha-din* prayer is also recited. The Hebrew words *tziduk ha-din* mean "justification of God's pronouncement," implying acceptance of God's decree that which took a loved one from our midst.

Of talmudic origin, the *Tziduk Ha-din* prayer dates back to the years of Roman persecution in the second century C.E. when Jews, led by Bar Kochba, failed in an attempt to retake Palestine from Roman control. Three martyrs of that period—Rabbi Chanina ben Teradyon, his wife, and his daughter—died with words from the biblical books of Deuteronomy and Jeremiah on their lips. Through these words they expressed their undying faith in God and His administration of justice.[64]

Rabbi Chanina spoke first, reciting a verse from the Book of Deuteronomy (32:4): "The Rock [God]. His deeds are perfect, all His ways are just." Chanina's wife continued: "A God of faithfulness, lacking in wrongdoing, just and right is He."

And their daughter concluded with words from Jeremiah (32:19): "Great in counsel and mighty in deed [is God] whose eyes see all the ways of men, to repay every one in accordance with his conduct, and according to the fruit of his deeds."

These verses were amplified upon in the course of time and became the *Tziduk Ha-din* prayer as we know it today.

The prayer opens with verse 32:4 from the Book of Deuteronomy and includes selections from the Talmud and later rabbinic writings expressing the same theme—namely, justification of God's judgment.

Moses Maimonides ascribed great importance to the *Tziduk Ha-din* prayer when he noted that its essence—our acceptance of God's decree—is a fundamental principle of the Jewish faith. Christianity made the concept central to their faith through the popular prayer ascribed to Jesus: "Thy will [not ours] be done."

Moses Isserles, in the *Code of Jewish Law,*[65] indicates that in most communities it is customary to recite the *Tziduk Ha-din* and *Kaddish* only for a child who has attained the age of one year. The commentator Be'er Hetev disagrees, noting that in most congregations these prayers are said for a child who has lived for more than a full month.

In addition to being recited at the burial service, the *Tziduk Ha-din* is also recited by individuals paying a graveside visit on various occasions.

Why is the *Tziduk Ha-din* sometimes not recited at funerals?

Traditionally, the *Tziduk Ha-din* prayer is not recited at funerals on days when the *Tachanun* penitential prayer is omitted from the synagogue service. The *Tachanun* is not recited on joyous or sorrowful days, including Friday afternoons, the afternoon of the day preceding a holiday (except for Chanuka), Rosh Chodesh (the beginning of a new month), the entire month of Nissan (when Passover falls), Lag B'Omer, from the beginning of Sivan through the Shavuot holiday, Tisha B'Av, the Fifteenth of Av, on the morning before Rosh Hashana, from the morning before Yom Kippur through the Sukkot festival, the fourteenth and fifteenth of Adar (Purim) in normal and leap years, and the Fifteenth of Shvat (Chamisha Asar Bi-Shvat).

On these days, Psalm 16, which opens with the words *Michtam le-David,* is often substituted for the *Tziduk Ha-din* by traditional Jews.[66]

The non-Orthodox, by and large, do not refrain from reciting the *Tziduk Ha-din* prayer on the above days.

Why is *Kaddish* recited for the first time at the cemetery?

As explained in Chapter Four, *Kaddish* may not be recited by mourners until the body has been made ready for burial and transported to the cemetery. This is so because, as an *onen* (see page 23), the mourner is not obligated to pray from the time of death until the time of burial.

In Israel, the *Kaddish* is customarily recited before the coffin is lowered into the ground, whereas in the Diaspora it generally is recited after the actual burial.[67] Since the *Kaddish* and *Tziduk Ha-din* prayers express the same sentiment, on days when the *Tziduk Ha-din* prayer is omitted from the burial service, the *Kaddish* is omitted as well.

See Chapter Six for a discussion of the type of *Kaddish* that is recited at the cemetery as well as for other pertinent regulations.[68]

Why, after the burial, do those attending the service form two lines through which the mourners pass?

In order to give those present at a funeral the opportunity to offer words of condolence to the mourners, two rows through which the mourners pass are formed after the burial is completed. At one time, it was customary for the mourners to form the two rows and for those in attendance to file between them[69] because it was easier to extend condolences when the mourners were stationary.

However, when two families in Jerusalem began to fight bitterly over who shall have the privilege of being first to walk past the mourners, the Rabbis decided that henceforth the comforters would form the two lines and the mourners would pass between them.[70]

Talmudic scholars believe that this arrangement, which is the current practice, also serves to protect the mourners from attack by demons who, it was believed, lurk in the cemetery.[71]

Why is the expression "May the Lord comfort you together with all the mourners of Zion and Jerusalem" commonly used to console mourners?

The Rabbis, in trying to formulate words of comfort that could be used to ease the distress of mourners, adopted sentiments expressed by the prophets Isaiah and Jeremiah.[72] Both of these prophets had been trying to bring hope to subjugated, grieving Jews who had been driven from their homes in Palestine and were now in Babylonian Exile.

Isaiah, when looking forward to a reestablished Jewish homeland, said (51:3):

> Truly the Lord has comforted Zion...He made her like a Garden of Eden...Gladness and joy shall abide there....

Jeremiah, having in mind personal resurrection in the hereafter as well as a reconstituted Jewish state, says (31: 11-12):

> They shall come and shout on the heights of Zion,
> Radiant over the bounty of the Lord...
> I will turn their mourning into joy,
> I will comfort them in their grief.

The Rabbis took these sentiments of the prophets and formulated the following expression to be used to offer comfort to mourners: *Ha-Makom ye'nachem otcha* [plural, *etchem*] *be-toch she'ar avaylay Tziyon vi-Yerushala'yim,* "May the Lord comfort you together with all the mourners of Zion and Jerusalem."

This expression of consolation is used today by Ashkenazim not only when comforting mourners after the burial, but also when paying a condolence call. Sephardim use a different expression to comfort mourners. They say, *Min ha-Shama'yim te-nuchamu,* "May Heaven comfort you."

Why do some Jews take up a clump of grass and throw it behind them after the burial?

After the burial service, it is customary for those present to take up a clump of grass and toss it behind them. This practice, unknown among Jews before the eleventh century, was first noted by the twelfth-century scholar

Rabbi Eliezer ben Nathan, who assumed that the origin of the custom is based on three biblical verses (Psalms 103:14, Psalms 72:16, and Job 2:12) that speak of grass and earth as symbols of sorrow and resurrection.[73]

Other scholars, among them the sixteenth-century Greek authority Rabbi Binyamin Ze'ev of Arta, have connected the practice to a reference in the Book of Isaiah (26:19) that speaks of the resurrection of the dead and the renewal of life. Rabbi Ze'ev notes that taking up the clump of grass is not only a reminder that the dead will one day rise up as the grass, but also suggests that man, who came from earth, must return to earth. (The Hebrew name for the first man, Adam, means "earth," for he came from the earth [Genesis 2:7].[74]

The custom of tossing a clump of grass over one's shoulder is given serious attention in the sixteenth-century *Code of Jewish Law,* where it is linked to the activity of demons and spirits. In his notes, Moses Isserles refers to the unusual custom of mourners, after tossing the clump of grass, to walk, pause, and sit seven times because evil spirits follow mourners leaving a burial site. Spirits, it was believed, flee when persons remain stationary. Isserles observed that in the sixteenth century the custom in Eastern Europe, primarily Poland, was for Jews to pause and sit only three times, not seven.[75]

Why did rabbinic authorities once ban the custom of throwing a clump of grass?

Scholars point out[76] that the custom of throwing a clump of grass was borrowed by Jews from their Christian neighbors, primarily in Germany and France. Gentiles considered the practice particularly effective in driving off evil spirits, which tend to follow mourners leaving the cemetery after burying their dead.

When Christians began claiming that Jews were employing this custom as an act of sorcery directed against them, the practice was discontinued. Rabbi Moses ben

Yechiel was able to persuade Church authorities that the throwing of a clod of grass was a harmless activity.[77] Nonetheless, the custom was never completely abandoned. When practiced today, it is often accompanied by a recitation of the verse, "He [God] is mindful that we are but dust" (Psalms 103:14).

Why is a charity box circulated at the conclusion of the burial service?

This practice is associated with a verse in the Book of Proverbs (11:4), "Wealth is of no help on the day of tragedy, but righteousness [charity] saves from death." At the conclusion of the burial service, it has become customary, primarily among Sephardim, for the rabbi to pronounce the words *Tzedaka tatzil mi-mavet,* "Charity saves from death," and for all present to deposit coins in a charity box that is passed around.

Why do some authorities consider it improper to visit the graves of other persons when attending a funeral?

There is no absolute basis in Jewish law for the belief that it is improper to visit other graves while at the cemetery to attend a funeral. Nevertheless, the belief persists, and the following reasons have been given:

- One may not perform religious duties in wholesale fashion.[78]
- To visit other graves detracts from the attention and respect due the deceased. It is also an affront to the immediate family.
- Distraught mourners who wander off to visit other graves might inadvertently step on graves that block their way.
- Evil spirits lurk about cemeteries at times of burial. It is therefore wise for all mourners to leave the cemetery together as quickly as possible.

Why do most authorities insist that everyone present at a burial wash their hands after leaving the grave site?

The handwashing custom became part of Jewish practice immediately after the talmudic period, and by the Middle Ages it was widely accepted. In fact, some Jews washed not only the hands, but the eyes and face as well.

The esteemed Babylonian authority Hai Gaon (939-1039), head of the academy of Pumpedita, believed that it is not necessary to wash hands after a cemetery visit, but conceded that "where it is a local custom, there is no objection."[79] However, most later authorities considered it an important rite that should be adhered to.

Rabbi Jacob Levi Mollin, the fourteenth-century authority on Jewish customs and ceremonies, explains[80] that the reason for washing the hands after frequenting a cemetery is to remove "the spirit of uncleanness that dwells in the cemetery" because of the demons that were believed to congregate there.[81]

The sixteenth-century Greek authority Rabbi Binyamin Ze'ev of Arta considers the act of handwashing to have been an expression of atonement. Just as in Deuteronomy (19:6) the elders washed their hands as an expression of innocence, so is the washing of hands upon leaving a cemetery a way of saying that "we are not responsible for this death."[82]

Today, most traditional Jews wash their hands upon leaving the cemetery after the burial or before entering the Shiva home. A jug of water is generally placed at the entrance of the home for that purpose.

After washing the hands, some Jews recite a verse from the Book of Isaiah (25:8):

> He will erase death forever.
> My Lord, God, will wipe the tears away
> from all faces,
> And will put an end to the reproach
> of His people over all the earth.
> For it is the Lord who has spoken.

Why is the cup used for handwashing not passed directly from person to person?

Just as a shovel is not passed from hand to hand when a grave is filled (see page 108), so is the cup used for handwashing after a burial not passed directly from one mourner to another. Instead, each individual places the cup on the ground for the next person to pick up, thus satisfying the folk-belief that sorrow should not be passed from hand to hand.

CHAPTER 6

—◆—

Kaddish

Introduction

The *Kaddish,* which is sometimes referred to as the Great Doxology of Jewish liturgy, is a paean to God that is unsurpassed in Jewish literature. Even Jews who are indifferent to many aspects of religious observance deem it a sacred duty to recite the Kaddish in memory of a departed mother, father, or other relative.

In a 1951 essay entitled *My Father Moved,* Max Lerner describes his emotions upon learning of the death of his father at the age of eighty-seven. The elder Lerner was an ordinary, gentle, hardworking man who had led a roller-coaster life. He had been involved in a variety of occupations, including that of Hebrew teacher, and although he had not achieved great success in his professional life, he was respected and loved by his family.

As Max Lerner viewed the shrunken, wasted body of his dying father, he was struck by the helplessness of man and "the crazy tragic absurdity of the whole human condition."

But, Lerner relates, when along with the other mourners he recited the "thunderous syllables of the great Kaddish, *Yit-gadal ve-yit-kadash shmay rabba,* ['Glorified and sanctified be God's great name'] the absurdity became a little less absurd. Even the most rational of us," Lerner concludes, "must admit that there is a healing power in the ritual words when you face what reason cannot fathom."[1]

The late Supreme Court Justice Felix Frankfurter (1882-1965) visited the synagogue for the last time when he was a youth and never returned, declaring himself an absolute agnostic. Yet, before he died, Frankfurter left instructions that the Kaddish be recited at his grave by Louis Henkin, a devoted colleague well versed in Judaism. Justice Frankfurter explained that this was the only way to inform the world that he was leaving this life as a Jew.

The Mourners' Kaddish has, in many ways, become the thread that links Jews to their faith and binds the generations to each other.

Summary of Traditional Observances Relating to the Kaddish

For whom Kaddish is recited
- Kaddish is recited for anyone for whom a mourner sits Shiva: a parent, child, sibling, and spouse. One may also elect to say Kaddish for other relatives and even friends. It is customary not to say Kaddish for others while one's parents are alive.
- Adopted children are encouraged to say Kaddish for adoptive parents, but are not required to do so.
- Most authorities agree that one need not heed the request of a parent that Kaddish not be said for him.

Minyan requirement
- The Kaddish may be recited at a public prayer service only if a *minyan* (religious quorum) is present.

For how long recited
- For parents, Kaddish is recited for eleven months, and for other relatives for thirty days.
- A mourner who does not learn of the death of a par-

ent until long after the burial is obligated to recite Kaddish only until the end of the eleventh month after burial.

Women and Kaddish
- Although only sons are obligated to say Kaddish for parents, most authorities permit women to do so if they so wish.

Minors and Kaddish
- Boys under Bar Mitzva age are obligated to say Kaddish for parents. Most authorities permit girls under Bat Mitzva age to do so if they wish.

Second death in the family
- If a mourner is saying Kaddish for a parent and another family member dies during those eleven months, the mourner says Kaddish for one additional month (a total of twelve months).

Kaddish during High Holiday period
- The text of the Kaddish is slightly modified during the Days of Awe, the ten-day period from Rosh Hashana through Yom Kippur.

Why was the Kaddish introduced?

The Kaddish, which in essence is a sanctification of God's name (the word *Kaddish* derives from the Hebrew word *kadosh,* meaning "holy"), was not originally intended as a prayer for mourners. Although the origin of the prayer is obscure, most scholars believe that it was introduced in Temple times to be recited primarily after a Torah study session or a scholarly discourse.

This original form of the Kaddish—or Great Doxology, as it may be called—has come to be known as *Kad-*

dish of the Rabbis, Rabbis' Kaddish, or *Scholars' Kaddish* (in Hebrew, *Kaddish De-rabbanan*). The main thrust of the prayer is clearly indicated in its opening words, *Yit-gadal ve-yit-kadash shmay rabba,* "Glorified and sanctified be God's great name." These words were adopted from the Book of Ezekiel (38:23), in which God says, *Ve-hit-gadalti ve-hit-kadashti,* meaning "I will manifest my greatness and My holiness [and make myself known to many nations...]."

In response to the first word of the Kaddish, the congregation says, *Y'hay shmay rabba mevorach,* "May His great name be blessed." These words, taken almost verbatim from the Book of Daniel (2:20), came to be regarded by mystics as the essential element of the Great Doxology.

The Talmud[2] comments that when a congregation pronounces the words "May His great name be blessed," God is greatly pleased and says, "Happy is the King who is thus praised in this house."[3]

Today, the Rabbis' Kaddish is generally recited after the preliminary morning *(Shacharit)* service prior to the *Baruch She-amar* prayer. It is also recited following the Sabbath and holiday *Musaf* service prior to the *Alenu* prayer.

From the original Rabbis' Kaddish four additional forms emerged: the Complete (Full) Kaddish, the Half Kaddish, the Mourners' Kaddish, and the Burial Kaddish.

Why is the Rabbis' Kaddish recited primarily by mourners?

As discussed above, the Kaddish of the Rabbis was originally recited by all present at the conclusion of a Torah study session or a rabbinic discourse. When selections from the Talmud became part of the Preliminary Prayers *(Pesukay De-zimra)* of the morning service, it was considered appropriate to conclude this section with a recitation of the Kaddish of the Rabbis. But rather than have the entire congregation recite this Kaddish, the privilege was reserved for mourners, thus giving them an additional exclusive opportunity to recite the Kaddish.

On Sabbaths and holidays, after the *En Kelohenu* is sung, several selections from the Talmud are read, and once again the Rabbis' Kaddish is recited by mourners.

The complete text of the Rabbis' Kaddish can be found on pages 329 to 331.

Why was the Mourners' Kaddish introduced?

In the early Middle Ages, around the year 1000, the *Al Yisrael* paragraph was dropped from the Rabbis' Kaddish to create another Kaddish that would be recited by orphans at designated points in weekday, Sabbath, and holiday services. This version of the Kaddish was originally (and often still is) called *Kaddish Yatom,* the "Orphans' Kaddish." Today, however, this Kaddish is recited not only by orphans but by all mourners.

The earliest reference to the Kaddish as a mourner's prayer is found in *Or Zarua,* a book by Rabbi Isaac ben Moses of Vienna (1180-1260). The next reference to it appears in the *Machzor Vitry,* dated 1208, where we read: "The boy rises and recites the Kaddish." Undoubtedly, the Rabbis regarded the Kaddish as the perfect prayer for mourners, whose faith is being tested by the grievous loss suffered. They compared the mourner's anguish to that of Job, who, despite the death of all his children, was able to say: "Though He [God] slay me, yet will I trust in Him" (Job 13:15). For this reason the Kaddish is often described as "an echo of the Book of Job."

The idea of reciting Kaddish for the dead was encouraged by the thirteenth-century Kabbalists (mystics), who contended that this prayer has the power to redeem the souls of the deceased. This belief may have stemmed from a widespread legend that Rabbi Akiba had helped redeem the soul of a deceased man from the tortures of hell *(gehinnom)* by teaching the man's son to recite the

Kaddish at a synagogue service.

In most congregations, the Mourners' Kaddish is recited after Psalm 30 of the morning *(Shacharit)* service and after the *Alenu* at all prayer services.[4]

The complete text of the Mourners' Kaddish can be found on pages 332 to 334.

Why was the Full Kaddish incorporated into the synagogue service?

As mentioned earlier, the Rabbis' Kaddish initially was recited by all present after a study session or sermon, and later primarily by mourners at certain points in the prayer service. At an even later point, the sentiments expressed by the Kaddish so appealed to the public that the Rabbis of the post-talmudic period decided to introduce it in yet another form to be recited by the leader *(chazzan* or *baal tefila)* at the conclusion of various sections of the synagogue service.

This form of the Kaddish, which became known as the *Full Kaddish (Kaddish Shalem* in Hebrew), is marked by substituting a paragraph beginning with the word *titkabel* for the fourth paragraph of the Kaddish of the Rabbis (which begins with the words *Al Yisrael).* For this reason, the Full Kaddish is sometimes called *Kaddish Titkabel.*

The *titkabel* paragraph beseeches God to accept the prayers and supplications of the whole House of Israel *(titkabel* means "[May the prayers] be acceptable"), a distinctly appropriate conclusion for major sections of the synagogue service. Thus, the Full Kaddish is recited at the end of the morning *(Shacharit)* service on the Sabbath and holidays and at the conclusion of all other services after the recitation of the Silent Devotion *(Amida* or *Shmoneh Esray* in Hebrew).

Among Syrian Jews it is customary at a *brit* (circumcision) for everyone present who has ever lost a parent to join in reciting the Full Kaddish. This is explained as a way of demonstrating that on this day a new Jew has entered the Jewish fold to replace the loss of those being recalled through the recitations of the Kaddish.[5]

The complete text of the Full Kaddish can be found on pages 334 to 336.

Why do some authorities prohibit the recitation of the Full Kaddish in a house of mourning?

Since the *titkabel* paragraph of the Full Kaddish is a petition for the good and welfare of the whole House of Israel, many authorities consider it inappropriate for the mourner, when he leads the service in a house of mourning, to include this paragraph. Other authorities disagree and permit its inclusion.

Most authorities take the position that the *titkabel* is omitted when a mourner leads the service, but is included when a nonmourner serves as leader.[6]

Why was the Half Kaddish incorporated into the synagogue service?

After the Full Kaddish was introduced to mark the end of major portions of the prayer service, it was considered appropriate to do the same for the smaller prayer units. To distinguish between the two, the *Half Kaddish* (*Chatzi Kaddish* in Hebrew), consisting of only the first three paragraphs of the Full Kaddish, was introduced.

The primary points at which the leader of the service recites the Half Kaddish are:

- before the recitation of *Barchu* at morning services;
- before the *Amida* is recited at afternoon and evening services;
- before the congregant is called up for the *maftir aliya.*
- on those occasions when the *maftir* is read from a second scroll, the Half Kaddish is recited after the second scroll has been placed on the reading table,

and before it is opened for the reading. When selections are read from three Torot on a particular Sabbath, the Half Kaddish is recited after the reading has been completed from the second scroll. [7]

In some Sephardic congregations, when readings are conducted from two scrolls, it is customary for the honoree (oleh) to recite the Half Kaddish after the second Torah has been read.

Sephardim call Chatzi Kaddish by the name *Kaddish Le-ayla* because the last sentence of this short form of the Kaddish begins with the Aramaic word *le-ayla*.

The complete text of the Half Kaddish can be found on pages 336 to 338.

Why was a special Burial Kaddish introduced?

The first time a mourner recites the Kaddish is when the coffin is brought to the cemetery for burial. This Kaddish, known by its Aramaic name, *Kaddish De-itchadeta,* meaning "Kaddish of the Resurrection," was introduced by the Rabbis in order to console mourners by assuring them that death is only a passing stage; that life has meaning and purpose; that we may look forward to the days of the Messiah, when the dead will be revived. [8]

The Burial Kaddish, which in most communities is recited after the coffin is lowered into the grave, differs from the regular Mourners' Kaddish in that it makes direct reference to the world-to-come and to the resurrection of the dead, themes not mentioned in any of the other Kaddish forms.

It should be noted that many non-Orthodox rabbis, who do not subscribe to the concept of resurrection in a literal sense, choose to recite the Mourners' Kaddish at the cemetery funeral service.

The complete text of the Burial Kaddish can be found on pages 338 to 341.

Why is the language of the Kaddish Aramaic rather than Hebrew?

Aside from the final verse, "May the Creator of heavenly peace bestow peace upon us and all Israel, and let us say, Amen," the language of the Kaddish, in all its five forms, is Aramaic. For nearly a thousand years, from the time of Ezra in the fifth century B.C.E. until well after the end of the talmudic period, Aramaic was the vernacular of the Jewish masses in Babylonia and Palestine. Quite appropriately, the Kaddish was composed in the everyday, spoken language of the masses.

Why is a the Hebrew word *le-ayla* sometimes repeated in the Kaddish?

During the Ten Days of Awe, from the beginning of Rosh Hashana through Yom Kippur—a time of intense religious fervor—an extra word, *le-ayla,* is added to the third paragraph of all Kaddish forms. *Le-ayla,* translated as "beyond" or "above," emphasizes that God is to be exalted and glorified to the ultimate extent.

In some traditions, the conjunction "and" (*vav* in Hebrew) appears as a prefix to the second *le-ayla.* When this occurs, the contraction *mikol* is substituted for the two words *min kol* ("from all").

In the Italian liturgy, the second *le-ayla* is part of the Kaddish throughout the year. [9]

Why may Kaddish be recited only in the presence of a *minyan*?

In Jewish law, some prayers rank higher than others. The most important ones require the congregation to respond to words pronounced by the leader of the service. These include the *Barchu, Kedusha,* the Kaddish prayers—all of which may be recited only when a quorum of ten people, a *minyan,* is present.

The Kaddish requires a *minyan* because its opening words, *Yit-gadal ve-yit-kadash,* "Glorified and sanctified be God's great name," call for a response from the congregation, which is *Y'hay shmay rabba mevorach,* "May His great name be blessed." [10]

Why is one obligated to say Kaddish only for certain relatives?

The obligation to say Kaddish belongs primarily to sons. The Talmud[11] notes that "a son confers merit on his father." Traditionally, even in the absence of sons, daughters are not required to recite Kaddish.

Jewish tradition also requires that Kaddish be recited by other family members for each other. Basically, one is obligated to recite Kaddish for those relatives for whom one is obliged to sit Shiva, which includes mother, father, sister, brother, daughter, son, and spouse. The obligation to sit Shiva for the first six relatives is considered to be based on biblical law: these are the same blood relatives for whom, the Bible says, a Kohen may defile himself by becoming involved in their burial (Leviticus 21:2).

The Rabbis of the Talmud later enlarged the list of those for whom we are obligated to say Kaddish to include the wife (and subsequently the husband) and, still later, half-sisters and half-brothers.[12]

Why did the Rabbis not obligate women to say Kaddish?

Because of their obligation to care for family and home, the Talmud says that women are exempt from fulfilling many of the 613 commandments *(mitzvot)* that are time-specific, such as reciting the *Shema* and putting on *tefilin.*[13]

Since the Kaddish must be recited at a prescribed time of day, and since fulfilling the requirement might impose undue hardship upon women with family responsibilities, the Rabbis exempted females from the requirement of reciting this prayer. However, while women are not obligated to recite the Kaddish, they may do so.

In the Orthodox tradition a daughter who wishes to honor her departed father or mother generally satisfies that need by listening attentively as others recite the Kaddish and by responding "Amen" at the proper time. The daughter's attentiveness is regarded as the equivalent of her having personally recited the Kaddish.

There are authorities who see no legal objection to the recitation of Kaddish by daughters, but nevertheless do not recommend it. The Pitchay Teshuva commentary on the *Code of Jewish Law*[14] notes that if a man has no sons and wishes his daughter to say Kaddish for him, he has a legal right to make such a request. Nevertheless, he is urged not do so because such a practice weakens the established Jewish custom which assigns to sons the primary obligation of reciting Kaddish for parents.

The learned Henrietta Szold (1860-1945), organizer of Hadassah in 1918, had no brothers, and she recited Kaddish for her parents, insisting that Jewish law in no way prohibits a daughter from doing so. A famous chasidic woman *rebbe,* the Maid of Ladamir (1815-92), an only child, also recited Kaddish for her father, Monesh Werbermacher.

In Reform, Conservative, and Reconstructionist congregations today, female and male mourners alike recite Kaddish for family members.[15]

Why may one ignore a parent's wish that Kaddish not be recited?

The *Israeli Responsa Yearbook*[16] notes that a father will sometimes threaten a wayward son, warning that if the child does not improve his ways, he will not be permitted to say Kaddish for his father. But such a threat is meaningless because it is not the father's prerogative to order who shall and who shall not recite Kaddish. Although respect for parents is important in Jewish law, the need for praising God and accepting his decision is of paramount importance at this point in life.

Why are minors obligated to recite Kaddish for parents?

According to Jewish law, as an expression of love, minors of all ages are obligated to recite Kaddish for parents. In the Orthodox tradition, this applies only to boys below Bar Mitzva age. In the non-Orthodox tradition, the obligation also falls on girls below Bat Mitzva age.

Regardless of age, once a child is mature enough to distinguish right from wrong, he or she is expected to display respect towards parents. Accordingly, the law obligates a boy of any age to recite Kaddish for parents if he is capable of doing so. If he is not capable of reciting Kaddish by himself, he is to be assisted by an adult.

Girls are not obligated to say Kaddish, but may do so if they wish.[17]

Why is a boy often referred to as a *Kaddish* or *Kaddishl*?

Since in Jewish law it is the religious obligation of a son (not a daughter) to recite Kaddish for a parent, a young boy who is the only son in a family is sometimes referred to as a *Kaddish* or a *Kaddishl* (diminutive form), even during the lifetime of the parent.

Why is it not always proper for a man who has remarried to say Kaddish for his first wife?

If a man has remarried after the death of his first wife, it is not proper for him to recite *Kaddish* in the synagogue for her lest his new wife be offended. If children of the first marriage are still living with the father, they may observe these rites in the presence of their stepmother, since the Ten Commandments obligate children to respect their mother and their father. However, if the first marriage was childless or if there are no children alive from the first marriage, it becomes the obligation of the remarried husband to recite *Kaddish* for his first wife.

Rabbi Moses Sofer (1762-1832), the Hungarian authority on Jewish law, was of the opinion that when a man remarries after the death of his first wife, his primary obligation is to his second wife, and that his relationship to his first wife has totally ended. Most scholars do not agree.

Conservative, Reconstructionist, and Reform congregations that grant women equal status with men would also apply the above obligations to a woman who has remarried after the death of her husband.

Why do most authorities encourage adopted children to say Kaddish for their adoptive parents?

An adopted child is not a blood relative of the adoptive parents and hence, technically, is not required to say Kaddish for them. However, the Talmud[18] states that a man who raises an orphan is considered to be on par with the natural father, and many authorities are of the opinion that because of the close emotional ties that develop over the years, it is proper for an adopted child to say Kaddish for the adoptive parent.

The great thirteenth-century German talmudist Meir of Rothenburg said, "A man who calls his child 'son,' that child [even if adopted] is legally his son." Three centuries later, Moses Isserles included this view in his notes to the *Code of Jewish Law*.[19]

Why may Kaddish be recited for foster parents?

If foster parents raised and guided a child for an extended period of time, and a good relationship existed between them, the foster parents are considered to be in the category of adoptive parents, and it is proper that Kaddish be recited for them.

Why may a Jew recite Kaddish for a parent who has abandoned the Jewish faith?

There is a difference of opinion among authorities as to whether a child may recite Kaddish for an apostate parent—that is, one who has forsaken his faith and severed all ties with the Jewish community. Rabbi Moses Isserles (1525-72) wrote that a son may recite Kaddish for an apostate father who was murdered by idolators, because it is presumed that through his death the father has made atonement for his sin, and that in all probability the man repented just before life left his body.[20]

Other authorities follow the lead of the famous Rabbi Akiba Eger (1761-1837), of Posen, Poland, who ruled that a son is permitted to mourn and say Kaddish for an apostate parent even if the death was natural. This is in keeping with the talmudic view that the biblical commandment (Exodus 20:12) to honor one's father and mother is to be obeyed under all circumstances. It is also in keeping with the talmudic view that a Jew who has abandoned the faith is still considered to be a Jew.[21]

Why do most authorities consider it proper for converts to recite Kaddish for their non-Jewish parents?

As stated above, the Rabbis considered the fifth of the Ten Commandments, "Honor thy father and mother," to be a basic Torah precept that applies to Jews and non-Jews alike. Although converts to Judaism are not obligated to recite Kaddish for their non-Jewish parents, the Rabbis were in general agreement that converts are not prohibited from doing so.

The view that Kaddish *must* be recited by a convert

for his non-Jewish parents was first assumed in the twelfth century by Moses Maimonides, who wrote that a convert to Judaism must not cease respecting his Gentile parents. Although a convert is regarded in Jewish law as a newborn child, ties with the natural parents are not considered dissolved as a result of the conversion. This view was reiterated in Joseph Caro's *Code of Jewish Law*.[22]

In a 1933 responsum, Orthodox authority Rabbi Aaron Walkin ruled that a convert is *obligated* to recite Kaddish for his Christian father.[23]

Rabbi Chaim Denburg of Montreal, translator of the Yoreh Deah section of the *Code of Jewish Law,* which details the laws of mourning, dissents. In 1990, Denburg ruled that a convert must *not* say Kaddish for a non-Jewish parent.

Why is Kaddish not recited for infants who have lived less than thirty days?

An infant who has not survived at least thirty days is considered to be in the category of a nonviable fetus. Consequently, the various rites of mourning are not applicable. Keria (see Chapter Three) and Shiva (see Chapter Seven) are not observed for the infant, nor is Kaddish recited.[24]

Why is Kaddish recited for some children but not for others?

How old a deceased must be before family members are required to recite Kaddish has not been fixed by Jewish law. Some authorities say that Kaddish should be recited for any child who has lived thirty days or longer. Others believe the child must have achieved a certain degree of maturity and understanding of Jewish precepts. Basically, the decision to recite Kaddish for a minor is made on an individual basis.[25]

Why is Kaddish recited for some missing persons but not for others?

If there is adequate reason to believe that a missing person is deceased, Kaddish may be recited for that individual by family members. The only exception is the case of a missing married man, for whom Kaddish may not be recited unless there is absolute proof of death. This is so because if Kaddish were to be recited, it might convey to the public the impression that the man's wife is free to marry, when in fact she is classified as an *aguna,* a deserted woman, whose status is still that of a married woman.[26]

Why do nonblood relatives sometimes say Kaddish for the deceased?

While the opinion of authorities is divided, in cases where there is no surviving son, a son-in-law or any other family member may assume the obligation of saying Kaddish for the deceased as a token of love and respect.

Some authorities, fearing the evil eye, caution that if a person's parents are alive, that person should not say Kaddish for anyone, unless his or her parents grant permission.

Why is it generally inappropriate for a mourner to delegate the recitation of Kaddish to a nonfamily member?

Technically, Jewish law permits and even encourages a stranger to be designated and paid to recite Kaddish in place of a son or other relative who for any reason is unable to fulfill the obligation.[27] Nonetheless, most authorities discourage this dispensation since it reflects poorly upon the mourner, who should make every effort to display love for the deceased. In cases where there are no children or relatives capable of saying Kaddish, there is no question but that the synagogue sexton (or any stranger) may be engaged to do so and may be rewarded for his services.

The propriety of a stranger being designated to recite Kaddish was addressed by the eminent Joseph Hayyim, Sephardic rabbi of Baghdad (1835-1909), who ruled in the case of a spinster who had died and whose father had to be away on a business trip that strangers be hired for the purpose of saying Kaddish, for this benefits the soul of the departed.[28]

It is, however, considered inappropriate to engage a person to recite Kaddish who is already doing so for another person.[29]

Why was the time span for the recitation of Kaddish for parents reduced from twelve to eleven months?

"The dead are not forgotten until after twelve months [from the time of death], " says Rav in the Talmud,[30] and therefore the Kaddish for a deceased parent was originally recited for a twelve-month period. In talmudic times there was also a belief that the wicked are consigned to hell (gehinnom or gehenna) and are subject to punishment for a maximum of twelve months. To avoid the possibility of people erroneously concluding that the parent for whom Kaddish is being recited (for a twelve-month period) was wicked, scholars of the caliber of Rabbi Moses ben Israel Isserles (c.1525-1572) of Cracow reduced the requirement for the recitation of Kaddish for parents to eleven months. By ruling that Kaddish for a parent should not be recited for more than eleven months, Rabbi Isserles was eliminating the possibility of ascribing wickedness to the parent.

The eleven-month Kaddish period is counted from the date of burial. Even when the Jewish year has thirteen months, as in leap years, Kaddish, according to Isserles, should be recited only for eleven months.[31]

Most Jews follow the ruling of Isserles, although some, particularly Sephardim, do not. Spanish-Portuguese and Moroccan Jews, for example, generally conclude Kaddish for a parent after eleven months and one day.[32]

It should be noted that when reference is made to the Kaddish as being recited for parents for "one year," this is not always intended to mean a full twelve-month period.

Why do some mourners recite Kaddish for parents for twelve months less one week?

The famous sixteenth-century mystic, the Ari of Safed, ruled that since the soul of the departed is assisted in its heavenly ascent for twelve months by the prayers of the Kaddish, children should recite the mourner's prayer for parents for that full period. However, since the public may misunderstand this deviation from the popular practice of reciting the Kaddish for only eleven months, the followers of the Ari established the custom of ending the Kaddish recitation one week before the end of the full twelve months.[33]

Why, if a parent so instructs, may Kaddish be recited for a full twelve months?

If a parent has left instructions that Kaddish is to be recited for the full twelve months, or in a leap year for thirteen months, this request should be heeded even if a parent was known to be a righteous person. (See page 135 for the reason why Kaddish is not generally recited for twelve months.) By fulfilling the parent's wishes, the mourner is showing respect.[34]

Why is Kaddish for relatives other than parents recited for only thirty days?

In Jewish tradition, the death of a sibling, a child, or a spouse is considered to be a grievous loss, but not equal to the loss of a parent. Therefore, the number of days that

Kaddish must be recited for a brother, sister, son, daughter, or spouse was set at the lesser period of thirty days, the period referred to as *Sheloshim.* (See Chapter Nine for a detailed discussion of this thirty-day mourning period.)

Among Sephardim in the Spanish-Portuguese and the Judeo-Spanish communities, Kaddish for relatives other than parents is often recited for eleven months rather than thirty days.[35]

Why do the children of some suicides recite Kaddish for a full twelve months?

A suicide who was in full possession of his mental faculties is considered to be a wicked person. Because of the traditional belief that the wicked must spend the first twelve months after death in *gehinnom,* their children are required to recite Kaddish for the full twelve months rather than the more customary eleven months.

Why is the Burial Kaddish not recited for suicides?

Kaddish for suicides is to be recited by relatives for thirty days or for the full term, depending upon the relationship of the mourner to the deceased. However, to draw a distinction between a normal death and that of a suicide, the Rabbis suggested that the Burial Kaddish for the latter not be recited at the cemetery. This Kaddish, which in Aramaic is called *Kaddish De-itchadeta,* meaning "Kaddish of the Resurrection," would not be suited for someone who had shown disdain for life.[36] (See pages 96 and 153 for more on suicides.)

Why is the Kaddish generally recited in unison?

The practice of having mourners recite the Kaddish in unison developed in Sephardic congregations, where prayers generally are recited in unison. This custom was

adopted by the Ashkenazic community when it was recommended by Rabbi Jacob Israel Emden (1697-1776),
the foremost Ashkenazic authority of his time, as a more
orderly way of reciting the Kaddish.

In Orthodox synagogues in Israel, as well as in many
Orthodox synagogues in the Diaspora, the Kaddish is
not recited in unison. Each mourner recites the prayer
aloud at his own pace.

Why do mourners stand when reciting the Kaddish?

Like all prayers that may be recited only in the presence of a *minyan*—including the *Barchu, Hallel,* and
Kedusha—Kaddish must be recited in a standing position. Nonmourners are not obligated to say the Kaddish
and therefore do not stand as others are pronouncing
this declaration of faith.

However, chasidim—mourners and nonmourners—
always stand for Kaddish, whether it be the Mourners'
Kaddish or another form recited during the course of a
religious service. In recent years, so as to memorialize the
six million victims of the Holocaust, some national
youth organizations have instructed their members to
rise whenever any form of Kaddish is recited.

Why does one who is reciting Kaddish take three steps backwards when reciting the last sentence?

The last verse of the Kaddish is a quotation from the
Book of Job which beseeches God, "who makes peace in
the heavens," to bring peace to all mankind. With the recitation of this verse, the mourner concludes an audience
with God, who in Jewish tradition is portrayed as the
King of Kings. Just as one who has had an audience with
a king takes short steps backwards to mark the conclusion of the audience, rather than simply turning his back,
so does the mourner, after concluding prayers of suppli-

cation, retreat respectfully. After the retreat, the mourner promptly resumes his original position.

Why do we no longer bend the knee and bow when reciting the Kaddish?

Prior to the eighteenth century, Jews would bend the knee and bow when beginning the Kaddish and at several other points during its recitation. The Vilna Gaon of Lithuania (1720-97) condemned the practice, claiming that bowing and genuflecting were an integral part of the ceremonies of the Temple in Jerusalem and should not be performed after the Temple was destroyed.

This is the general practice today, although in some congregations members continue to bow when reciting the first and last word of the Kaddish, and also when pronouncing the phrases *Y'hay shmay rabba* ("May His great name be blessed"), *Yit-barach ve-yishtabach* ("Blessed and praised"), and *Brich Hu* ("Blessed is He").[37]

CHAPTER 7

The Shiva Period

Introduction

When the burial service has concluded and earth has been heaped upon the grave of the deceased, the first stage of mourning is over. Until this point the mourner has been referred to as an *onen* (feminine, *onenet*), meaning "one in distress." Hereafter, the designation *avel* (feminine, *avela*), "one who is sad, grieving," is used.

During the initial *onen* phase of mourning, bereaved family members are exempt from praying and carrying out other religious commandments *(mitzvot)* incumbent upon an adult Jew. However, once mourners return from the cemetery to begin the formal seven-day mourning period known as *Shiva*, they are obligated to observe all the laws and traditions of Judaism except for those specifically denied an *avel*.

Like the chapel and cemetery funeral services, the Shiva period is marked by simplicity. During this time of intense grieving, pleasurable activities are avoided.

In Chapter 24 of Ezekiel, some of the customs that a mourner is obligated to follow are mentioned for the first time. These include having friends prepare the post-funeral meal and refraining from wearing shoes. Most mourning customs, however, were initiated many centuries later by the Rabbis of the Talmud.

The Rabbis considered the first three days of Shiva to be the most acute,[1] and they expected that during this time mourners would adhere faithfully to all established rules. After three days, concessions are made for those whose livelihood is in jeopardy or who have other urgent responsibilities. But the Rabbis generally agreed that spending a full week in mourning is crucial for the psychological well-being of the individual, so crucial in fact that the mourner is mandated by Jewish law to mourn. The spirit of this attitude was captured by the nineteenth-century English poet Sir Henry Taylor: "He that lacks time to mourn, lacks time to mend."

Summary of Traditional Shiva Observances

Who observes Shiva

- Those who have lost a parent, sibling (including a half-brother and half-sister), child, or spouse are required to observe Shiva.
- Only adults (those past Bar or Bat Mitzva age) are obligated to sit Shiva.
- A child who becomes a Bar or Bat Mitzva during the Shiva week is not bound by the Shiva restrictions like other adults. Not all authorities agree. Some say that the child should observe Shiva fully.
- Adopted children, although not obligated to do so, may sit Shiva if they feel so inclined.
- Shiva is observed for most suicides.
- Most authorities deny all mourning rites for apostates. However, some allow Shiva to be observed under the overall talmudic dictum, "Once a Jew, always a Jew."
- Converts to Judaism may observe Jewish mourning rites for non-Jewish parents if they so wish.
- A bride or groom does not sit Shiva during the first week of their marriage.

- Shiva is not observed for persons who have been cremated.
- Shiva is not observed for a child who has lived less than thirty full days.

Instructions not to observe Shiva
- If a person leaves instructions that his family should not sit Shiva, his wishes are ignored.

Beginning and ending of Shiva
- Shiva begins immediately after interment. The day of interment is counted as day one of the Shiva period so long as there is sufficient time before nightfall for the mourners to settle in the Shiva house, remove their shoes, and sit on a low stool.
- Shiva ends on the seventh day, immediately after the morning service.

Reinterment
- When a body is removed from one grave and reburied in another, the immediate family sits Shiva for a second time on the day of reinterment, from the moment after burial until nightfall. All regular mourning rites, including Keria, must be carried out.

Shiva location
- Unless there are extenuating circumstances, Shiva is observed in the home where the deceased lived. If sleeping accommodations are not adequate, mourners may sleep elsewhere and return the next morning.

Meals
- The first meal eaten by mourners in a Shiva house must be prepared and served by neighbors or friends.

The memorial light
- As soon as the family returns home after the burial,

a candle or lamp supplied by the chapel is lit and kept burning throughout the seven-day Shiva period.

- Only one lamp is required to be lit for an entire family sitting Shiva in one house.

Covering mirrors and pictures

- All mirrors in the Shiva house are either covered, turned around to face the wall, or clouded over. Some Jews follow the practice of turning toward the wall photographs or works of art containing faces of people; others remove them completely.

Low Stools

- Mourners are obligated to sit on benches or stools no more than twelve inches high. Those with health problems are excused from this requirement.

Entertainment

- All forms of entertainment and social activity are forbidden during the Shiva week. These include attending a *Kiddush* (reception) after synagogue services.

Family cycle celebrations

- A Bar or Bat Mitzva may be held during the week of Shiva. The celebrant is exempted from Shiva and Sheloshim observances. However, the year-long restrictions remain in effect.
- During Shiva, a mourner may attend the wedding of a son or daughter and the *Brit* or *Pidyon Ha-ben* of a son.

Greeting and being greeted

- During the first two days of the Shiva week one may not greet mourners in the normal manner, and if greeted, mourners are not to return the greeting. On the third day of mourning, the mourners may return a greeting. This does not apply to the Sabbath, when greetings may be exchanged.

Delaying Shiva

- If a mourner lives far from where the death occurred and is unable to attend the funeral, he or she begins to observe Shiva at the moment of notification.

- If a mourner residing far from the site of the funeral has begun to sit Shiva in his or her own home, he or she may travel to sit with the other family members on the second day of Shiva.

- If due to illness or any other reason a mourner is unable to start sitting Shiva with the other family members, he or she begins whenever able to do so during the Shiva week. However, the mourner completes Shiva at the same time as the other mourners, even though he or she has sat for less than seven days.

- If a mourner failed to sit Shiva—intentionally or unintentionally—during the week following interment, the mourner must make up for it by sitting Shiva at any time before thirty days have passed.

- If because of illness or for any other reason mourners are unable to sit Shiva during the week after burial, they are not required to sit Shiva once thirty days have passed from the date of burial.

- If burial takes place on a festival or during the Intermediate Days (Chol Ha-moed) of a festival, mourners wait until the entire festival is over and then commence sitting Shiva.

- If a person was missing for a period of time and was declared dead by the courts, Shiva is to be observed when the ruling is made.

- If one learns of the death of a relative within thirty days of his or her passing, Shiva is to be observed. If notification is received on the Sabbath, the Sabbath is considered the first day of Shiva, although Shiva actually starts on the next day, since mourning is not permitted on the Sabbath. If the delayed news reaches the mourner on a festival, the full week of mourning rites commences after the festival is over.

- If one learns of the death of a relative after thirty days from the date of burial, he observes a token Shiva for a short while on the day the news is received.
- A planned wedding is postponed if the bride or the groom loses a loved one and must sit Shiva.
- Members of the family who escort the corpse for burial in a distant location begin Shiva after the interment, while members of the family who remain behind begin Shiva as soon as the body leaves their presence.

Cancellation of Shiva

- If the three Pilgrim Festivals (Passover, Shavuot, and Sukkot) or the High Holidays (Rosh Hashana and Yom Kippur) fall while Shiva is being observed, the entire week of Shiva is cancelled. Purim and Chanuka do not cancel Shiva, although at times Shiva rites are suspended or modified for the day.
- If thirty days have passed and a mourner has not observed Shiva, he or she is no longer required to do so. This applies to all relatives, including parents.

Leaving the Shiva house

- Under normal circumstances, except on the Sabbath, a mourner may not leave the Shiva house unless it is to attend a synagogue service in order to say Kaddish.
- It is permissible to sit on the porch or in the yard of the Shiva house. These are considered extensions of the home.
- If the mourner's livelihood is at stake, he or she may leave the house to attend to business after the morning (Shacharit) service of the third day of Shiva.
- A doctor may attend to patients who are in need of immediate care.

- A *mohel* in mourning may leave the house to per- form a circumcision. A *sandek* (person requested to hold the baby) may likewise leave the house to partic- ipate in the *Brit* ceremony.
- After the first three Shiva days (part of the third day is equal to a full day), a mourner may attend a funer- al of a relative and even a neighbor. If the relative is one for whom the person sitting Shiva is *obligated* to mourn, he or she may attend the funeral even on the first day of Shiva.
- A person who has difficulty sleeping in a strange bed or house may leave at night to sleep in his or her own home.
- If a mourner must leave the house of mourning, if at all possible he should do so after dark.

Personal grooming
- Luxurious bathing or showering is forbidden to mourners. For hygienic reasons the use of hot water is permitted.
- One may not shave, cut the hair, trim fingernails, use cosmetics, or wear jewelry. A woman may wear her wedding ring.
- The use of oils and lotions is forbidden, unless their use is required for health reasons.

Clothing restrictions
- Except for health reasons, during Shiva a mourner may not wear leather footgear. The mourner may wear cloth, felt, or rubber slippers. Those most me- ticulous in their observance often go about in stock- inged feet.
- Mourners who must leave the house of mourning to attend a weekday synagogue service—or for any other valid reason—may wear leather shoes. Some au- thorities suggest that the mourners first sprinkle

some earth in their shoes as a reminder of their status as mourners.

- The mourner may not change clothing, except for those garments that make contact with the skin.
- The washing of garments by mourners is prohibited because it involves work, which is forbidden during Shiva.

Sexual activity
- Kissing and embracing is forbidden during Shiva, as is all sexual activity.

Shiva on Sabbath and festivals
- Shiva is not fully observed on the Sabbath or festivals.
- Mourners end the Shiva observance on Friday afternoon sufficiently early to prepare for the Sabbath. On the eve of a holiday, the same rule applies. Conspicuous activities, such as the wearing of torn garment, are not observed on the Sabbath or festivals. Inconspicuous activities forbidden during the Shiva period continue to be forbidden on the Sabbath and festivals. These include sexual activity, luxurious bathing, and Torah study.
- The mourner may not lead a synagogue service on the Sabbath or festivals, unless no one else present is able to officiate.
- According to some authorities, spices are not used when reciting *Havdala* in a house of mourning.
- On the Sabbath and festivals mourners may greet people and may return greetings.

Torah honors
- A mourner may not serve as the Torah reader during the week of Shiva.
- A mourner should not be offered an *aliya* (Torah

honor) during Shiva, but if offered one in error, he must accept the honor.

- The mourner may be awarded the *hagbaha* (raising the scroll) or *gelila* (rolling the scroll) honors.

Shiva on Purim

- On Purim, a mourner may leave the Shiva house to hear the Megilla reading in the synagogue.
- The mourner may not be the Megilla reader for the congregation.
- Within the privacy of the home the mourner must carry out regular mourning rites, such as sitting on a low stool.
- Mourners may send Purim gifts *(Mishloach Manot)* to their friends and to the needy.

Shiva on Chanuka

- A mourner is obligated to kindle the Chanuka lights and to recite the appropriate blessings.

Shiva on Tisha B'Av

- On Tisha B'Av it is customary for mourners to go to the synagogue in the evening and the following morning to hear the Book of Lamentations *(Aycha)* read.

Prayers in the Shiva house

- Whenever possible, a *minyan* (religious quorum) is assembled and services are held morning and evening so that mourners will not have to leave the house to recite Kaddish in a synagogue.
- A mourner may lead the prayer service in the Shiva house.
- A Torah scroll is brought into the home and left there for the week if it will be read at least three times.
- On the first day of Shiva, some authorities maintain,

a mourner should not put on *tefilin*. However, the accepted practice is to do so.

Why is the period of mourning that follows burial set for seven days?

Shiva, the seven-day period of mourning (*shiva* is Hebrew for "seven"), although not directly mandated in the Bible, is nevertheless believed by the Rabbis to have the full force of biblical law.[2] This conclusion is based on an interpretation of the verse in Amos (8:10) in which the prophet speaks of feasts (festivals) and mourning in the same sentence:

> And I will turn your feasts [which usually lasted seven days] into mourning, and all your songs into lamentations; and I will bring sackcloth upon all loins; and baldness upon every head; and I will make it as the mourning for an only son; and the end thereof is a bitter day.

Since the festivals Passover and Sukkot are mandated in the Bible to be seven days long, the Rabbis declared that the initial period of mourning for the loss of a loved one should also be seven days.[3] Additional proof that the period of mourning should last seven days is adduced from the Book of Genesis (50:10), where it is written that Joseph mourned his father, Jacob, for seven days.

The Jerusalem Talmud[4] offers additional biblical evidence: "Moses instituted the seven days of feasting [for a bride, as indicated in Genesis 29:27] and the seven days of mourning [as indicated in Genesis 50:10]."

Modern scholars associate the designation of seven days as the initial mourning period with the belief that evil spirits have the power to harm family members for seven days after a death, but day by day they lose their power. The fact that condolence calls are paid during Shiva is also a factor in keeping the spirits at bay, since spirits are more prone to strike people who are alone.

Why must one sit Shiva only for certain relatives?

Shiva must be observed for the six relatives with whom one has blood ties. These, mentioned in the Book of Leviticus (21:1-3), are family members for whom a Priest (Kohen) must defile himself by becoming involved in their burial: father, mother, son, daughter, brother (by the same father), and unmarried virgin sister (by the same father).

To these six the Rabbis later added wife and husband, the Midrash explaining that no loss affects a person as deeply as the loss of a spouse. In addition, the Rabbis included half-sisters and half-brothers (but not stepsisters or stepbrothers), maternal or paternal.[6]

Why is a boy or girl under Bar or Bat Mitzva age not obligated to sit Shiva?

Boys under the age of thirteen and one day and girls under the age of twelve and one day are not yet adults under Jewish law, and they are therefore not obligated to sit Shiva or comply with other Shiva observances. However, if a minor loses a parent, and while the family is sitting Shiva the minor reaches Bar or Bat Mitzva age, authorities disagree as to how the minor, now turned adult, is to comport him- or herself. Some rule that he or she continues to be exempt from all laws of mourning.[7] Others maintain that the young adult is obligated to observe all mourning rites beginning with the thirty-first day after the burial and continuing until the end of the year. Still others rule that the young adult must observe all mourning rites from the moment during Shiva that he or she ceases to be a minor.[8]

Why is it proper to observe Shiva for a step-parent?

Although it is not mandatory that one observe Shiva for a stepmother or stepfather, it is proper that some, if not all, of the Shiva rites be observed.

The eminent Rabbi Judah the Prince (135-220 C.E.), nearing death, cautioned his children: "Take care that you show due respect to your mother." His colleagues wondered why he had left such instructions when the Bible itself (Exodus 20:12) commands that one honor his mother as well as his father. And the Talmud points out that the woman referred to was the children's stepmother, not their birth mother.[9]

Why do a bride and groom sometimes postpone Shiva to celebrate their honeymoon?

Although a newlywed who learns of the loss of a close relative is grief-stricken, he or she is not permitted to assume the role of mourner if news of the death reaches the couple immediately after the ceremony has been held and the marriage consummated. The couple first celebrates their honeymoon in a normal fashion, and when the honeymoon period is over, the mourner rends a garment and sits Shiva.

If the couple is apprised of the death before the marriage has been consummated, they must live apart for a full week, while the person who suffered the loss sits Shiva.[10]

Why is Shiva not observed for one who has left instructions that he be cremated?

Aside from the fact that cremation is a violation of the biblical law requiring that the deceased be returned to the earth from which man was originally formed (Genesis 3:19), Judaism considers cremation to be a pagan custom, and as such it is prohibited. The Rabbis insisted that the deceased be buried in the earth, not disposed of in any other way.[11]

Jewish law considers anyone who leaves instructions to have his body cremated as unworthy of having the rite of Shiva observed in his honor. However, many families today do observe Shiva in such an instance.

Why is Shiva not observed for missing persons?

In Jewish law, if the death of an individual cannot be definitely established, mourning rites are not observed. This applies to a person who has left home and never returned, to one who is missing-in-action in times of war, as well as to people who are assumed to have drowned.

The problem becomes complicated if the person leaves a wife behind. If the woman decides to sit Shiva, everyone will think that her husband is definitely dead and that the woman is free to marry. But in Jewish law such a woman is not a widow, but an *aguna,* "a deserted woman." Her marital status is moot and she may not remarry until her widowhood has been firmly established.

It is interesting to note that in the case of drownings, a distinction is made between a disappearance that occurs in a small body of water *(ma'yim she-yesh lahem sof)* and one that occurs in a large body of water *(ma'yim she-ayn lahem sof)*. If one disappears in a small body of water, where the entire shoreline is visible from any point, Shiva begins after all hope of recovering the corpse has been given up *(she-nit-ya-ashu le-vakesh)*. It is reasoned that if the person survived, he would have made his way to the shore and would have been seen leaving the water. Additionally, he would have made it known that he is alive. However, if a person disappears in a large body of water, where the entire shoreline is not visible, Shiva is not required because there is the possibility that the person may have emerged unnoticed.

Why are most suicides accorded full mourning rites?

Suicide in Jewish law is a serious offense. The Talmud says:

> For one who takes his own life fully aware of his action [the Hebrew word is *b'daat*], no rites are to be observed.... There is to be no rending of clothes and no eulogy. But people should line up for him [at the end of the burial ceremony], and the mourner's blessing should be recited [as the family passes through] out of respect for the living. The general rule is: Whatever rites are [normally] performed for the benefit of the survivors should be observed; whatever is [normally] done out of respect for the dead should not be observed.[12]

Jewish law does not, however, place all suicides in the same category. One category of suicide, as stated above, includes those who are in full possession of their physical and mental faculties (*b'daat*) when they take their lives. A second category includes those who act on impulse or who are under severe mental strain or physical pain when committing suicide. Jewish law speaks of an individual in this second category as being an *anuss,* meaning a "person under compulsion," and hence not responsible for his actions. All burial and mourning rites are observed for him.

The first *anuss* in Jewish history was King Saul, who, after being defeated by the Philistines on Mount Gilboa, realized what would have happened to him were he taken alive. He therefore impaled himself on his sword (I Samuel 31:4). This action gave rise to the expression *anuss k'Shaul,* meaning "as distressed as Saul."

Consequently, Joseph Caro, in his sixteenth-century *Code of Jewish Law,*[13] and most later authorities have ruled that the majority of suicides are to be considered as distressed as Saul and as having acted under compulsion when taking their own lives. As such, they are not responsible for their actions and are to be accorded the same courtesies and privileges granted Jews who have met a natural death.[14]

Reform Judaism does not consider the motivation of suicides. Those who take their own lives are accorded all funeral and mourning rites.[15]

Why are there differing opinions as to whether one who has abandoned the Jewish faith should be mourned at the time of his death?

The Talmud[16] says that mourning is not to be observed for any Jew who has become an apostate. In the Talmud a Jewish defector is placed in the same category as an intentional suicide and an executed criminal.

Scholars have pointed out that when Maimonides, in his *Mishneh Torah,* lists those for whom Jews do not mourn "because they have separated themselves from the community," he includes "apostates to idolatry."[17] Since today (and for the past eight or more centuries) a Christian is no longer considered to be an idolater in the eyes of Jewish law, the question of whether a family is to sit Shiva upon the death of one of its members who had earlier joined the Church is moot.

To be considered, however, is whether the apostate abandoned Judaism as an act of rebellion toward his family or teachers or whether he truly loved his newly adopted faith. When the motivation of the apostate is spite, some authorities argue, there is always a degree of hope that he may reconsider at a future date and return to the fold. Such an apostate is to be considered a full Jew, and when he dies, Shiva may be observed for him under the talmudic principle of "*Af al pi sche-chata, Yisrael hu* [A Jew continues to be a Jew even if he has sinned]."[18] However, when the motivation of the apostate is genuine love for another faith, the individual is not to be mourned.[19]

Some authorities are of the opinion that one who denounces Judaism publicly should not be mourned. His action, they believe, will encourage others to defect, and it is therefore inexcusable.[20]

Why does a Jew sometimes have to sit Shiva for a non-Jewish half-brother?

Rabbi Simon ben Zemach Duran (1361-1444), who served as rabbi of the Jewish community of Algiers, North Africa, was one of the outstanding fifteenth-century authorities on Jewish law. He is famous for his collection of responsa, entitled *Tashbetz,* and he himself became known by that name, which is an acronym for Teshuvot ben Zemach, "the responsa of the son of Zemach."

In one responsum,[21] Duran addressed a question concerning a Jew who had a son by a Jewish woman. The man later converted to Christianity and married a non-Jew. From this marriage he had a son, whom he brought up as a Gentile. If the non-Jewish son were to die, Duran was asked, would the Jewish half-brother be obligated to mourn for him as he would be required to do if the boy were his half-brother from a Jewish mother?

Duran replied: If the half-brother, brought up as a Gentile, dies while still a child, he is to be mourned, since it was not his fault that he was not taught about Judaism. But if this Gentile half-brother were to die when he was older and had an opportunity to learn about the religion of his father and still did not accept the Jewish way of life, then there is to be no mourning for him.

Duran, however, notes that Maimonides had a different view. He ruled that even if the half-brother died as a grown man, he is to be mourned because it is not his fault that he was brought up as a Gentile.

Why did the practice of sitting Shiva for a family member who converts to another faith gain wide acceptance?

The custom of sitting Shiva for a family member who has abandoned Judaism is based on a misunderstanding that dates back to the publication of the twelfth-century work *Or Zarua,* by Rabbi Isaac of Vienna. In this book, Rabbi Isaac reported that the great eleventh-century scholar Rabbenu Gershom ben Yehuda, known as the Luminary of the Diaspora *(Me'or Ha-gola),* sat Shiva for his son who had converted to Christianity. Upon publication of the book, it became widespread practice to sit Shiva for a child who converts, despite the fact that outstanding scholars, including Joseph Caro, author of the *Code of Jewish Law,* insisted that doing so is not demanded by the law and is not appropriate conduct.[22]

Why, then, did Rabbenu Gershom sit Shiva for his son? Further delving by scholars revealed that Rabbenu Gershom did not sit Shiva for his son at the time of the young man's conversion. He sat Shiva for him at a later date, at the time of the son's death. And the misunderstanding grew out of the misreading of one word in Isaac of Vienna's work. Isaac wrote that Rabbenu Gershom sat Shiva for his son—and he used the Hebrew word *shenishtamed,* meaning "who had converted." Some of the texts erroneously added one letter to the word and spelled it *ke-shenishtamed,* meaning "when he converted." Because of the error, it was believed that Rabbenu Gershom sat Shiva at the time of his son's conversion, when in fact he sat Shiva after his son died.

Sitting Shiva for a child who joins another faith has never been a legal requirement for Jews, and authorities do not favor the practice.[23] Mourning a member of the family who has abandoned Judaism runs counter to the basic talmudic principle that one never loses his Jewish identity; he may return to the fold unceremoniously whenever he so decides. To sit Shiva for a family member who converts is, in a sense, consigning that person to death, thus precluding the possibility of his ever returning to the faith of his ancestors.

Why must we ignore the instructions of a deceased that Shiva not be observed?

If a Jew leaves instructions that upon his death Shiva need not be observed, the request is to be ignored. Shiva, along with other mourning rites, are Jewish legal requirements, and no individual has the right to countermand them. Shiva, in fact, was instituted to give solace to the living as much as to honor the dead, so it is not within the province of the dead to nullify this rite.[24]

Why is it sometimes permissible to start the Shiva period even if the deceased has not actually been buried?

From time to time inclement weather or a strike by cemetery personnel delay the burial of the deceased. In such cases, the funeral service is held, the coffin sealed, and the body placed in storage for later burial. There are also occasions when a deceased is to be buried in a distant city. After the funeral, the coffin is sealed and sent off for burial.

In these instances, mourners not accompanying the body to the burial site do not have to wait until the body has been laid in the earth for the official seven-day mourning period to begin. For them, Shiva commences immediately after the coffin has been closed. This ruling is based on the view of Rashi that once the coffin has been covered, the body is considered to have been buried.[25] Those accompanying the coffin to the burial site begin Shiva immediately following interment.

Why, in Jewish tradition, are the first three days of Shiva considered to be the most critical?

In talmudic times, the first three days of Shiva were considered to be a period of heightened danger for the mourner. During this period, it was believed, the soul of the departed hovers over the grave seeking entry, and the mourner imagines that his life is being threatened.[26] By the end of the third day, noticing the change in the appearance of the deceased (as it begins to decompose), the soul departs, leaving the body to rest and thus freeing the mourner from danger.[27] Therefore, today, in cases where the full seven days of Shiva cannot be observed, at least the first three days are observed.

Why, in some cases, is one not obligated to observe the full Shiva period for a relative?

If, while one is in the midst of observing Shiva for a relative, a second relative dies, the mourner begins counting seven days of mourning for the second relative as soon as the second relative is buried. These days of mourning also count as part of the seven days of mourning for the first relative.[28] Thus, part of the Shiva period is being observed for both relatives at the same time.

The Rabbis of the Talmud[29] ruled that if a person is away from home and hence unaware that a death has occurred in the family, upon returning home the individual must join the other mourners in sitting Shiva until its conclusion. If the individual joins the family on the last day of Shiva, his Shiva observance lasts for that day only.

Why are those mourning the same person sometimes not required to sit Shiva for equal periods?

The Talmud[30] makes a distinction between mourners who have learned of a death in the family *before* thirty days have elapsed since the date of death and those who were apprised of the fact *after* thirty days have elapsed. News that reaches the mourner within thirty days is called *shmua kerova,* meaning "early tidings" or "early notification"; and news that reaches the mourner after the thirtieth day is called *shmua rechoka,* meaning "belated tidings" or "belated notification."

If news of a death reaches a family member before thirty days have elapsed, the mourner must carry out all the laws of mourning from the moment of notification. This is because notification has come sufficiently close to the day of burial and the mourner is in need of the opportunity to express his grief fully and formally. If the early tidings reach the mourner on a Sabbath, that day is counted as the first day of mourning, but the rending of the garment (Keria) is performed on the second day.

If news of a death is received after the thirtieth day, the mourner need observe only one day of mourning, for the structured seven-day period of mourning is no longer deemed necessary. The mourner in this instance is required to remove his shoes or sit on a low stool for a few minutes, thus symbolically satisfying the Shiva requirement. Only in the case of the death of a parent must the mourner also rend the garment.[31]

If belated tidings (after the thirtieth day following the burial) reach a mourner on a Sabbath or holiday, the Sabbath or holiday is counted as the only Shiva day the mourner is obligated to observe, even though public mourning rites are not observed on these days. In the evening, after dark, the mourner sits Shiva for one hour to fulfill the Shiva requirement.[32]

Why does a mourner never actually sit Shiva for seven full days?

Although the term Shiva, which literally means "seven," refers to the first seven days of mourning following burial, a mourner never actually sits Shiva for seven full days. This is so because in Jewish law part of a day is counted as a full day.[33] Thus, if a mourner manages to sit Shiva (by simply removing his shoes) even for a short time while it is still light on the day of the burial, it is considered as if he had sat for the full day. And that day is reckoned as the first day of the seven-day Shiva period.

On the seventh day of Shiva, the same rule applies. After morning services of the seventh day, a mourner is obligated to sit Shiva for only a short while (usually an hour or so), in order to give friends an opportunity to pay a last condolence call, and the person is then free to attend to normal business affairs.[34]

It should also be pointed out that although mourners do not sit Shiva on the Sabbath, it is counted as one of the seven days of the mourning period. (See below.)

Why do mourners suspend Shiva early on the eve of a Sabbath or holiday?

Jewish law requires that mourners sit Shiva until approximately one hour before sundown on a Friday or on the eve of a holiday. Precisely when Shiva is suspended varies with the amount of time required by the individual mourner to prepare food and dress for the Sabbath or holiday. That Shiva may be suspended at noon is a widespread misconception.

Why is the Sabbath counted as one of the seven days of mourning?

The Sabbath is counted as one of the seven days of mourning because although mourners do not have to abide by all mourning strictures on that day, they are still obligated to observe many of them.

Taking a clue from the prophet Isaiah (58:13), who referred to the Sabbath as a day of delight, the Rabbis limited the kind of mourning that may be observed on that day. They ruled that conspicuous mourning practices should not be observed, but inconspicuous ones are to be observed. Thus, the mourner is permitted to wear leather shoes, sit on a regular chair, dress in fine clothing, and attend synagogue services.[35] However, private mourning restrictions, such as sexual abstinence, remain in effect.

The importance of not observing mourning in public on the Sabbath has been drawn from an incident in the Talmud[36] in which the fourth-century Babylonian scholar Abaye is said to have observed Rabbi Joseph, who was in mourning, entering and leaving his house on the Sabbath with head covered.[37] Abaye asked Rabbi Joseph why he was observing a mourning practice—namely, keeping his head covered (see page 171)—on the Sabbath. Rabbi Joseph, quoting Rabbi Yochanan, replied: "Mourning in private may be carried out on the Sabbath."

All mourning practices are to be resumed on Saturday night after the *Havdala* prayer service.

Why is Shiva at times completely or partially cancelled?

When a holiday mandated in the Torah (the first five books of the Bible) falls in the midst of the Shiva period, Shiva is abruptly ended and is not resumed after the festival has concluded.[38] The same is true if mourning is started just moments before the onset of a festival: the entire mourning period is cancelled and need not be resumed after the festival.[39]

The Rabbis based these rules of cancellation on the biblical mandate that holidays be days of delight in which one must rejoice. Deuteronomy 16:14 demands: "You shall rejoice in your festivals." Clearly, a person who is observing mourning rites is not able to rejoice. Further, the Rabbis obviously felt that it would be incompatible for a mourner to resume formal grieving after celebrating the holiday.

Thus, if a burial takes place immediately before the major holidays of Rosh Hashana, Yom Kippur, Passover, Shavuot, and Sukkot, the entire Shiva period is cancelled. If there was sufficient time to begin Shiva before the onset of the holiday, wherever two days of a holiday are observed (as in the Diaspora) Shiva begins at night after the second day, and that second day of the holiday is counted as the first day of Shiva.[40]

On Purim, a minor biblical holiday, mourning is not fully observed, but the day is counted as one of the seven days of mourning. Chanuka is not a biblical festival, and mourning is therefore observed as it would be on a non-festival.

If a burial takes place during the Intermediate Days (Chol Ha-moed) of Passover or Sukkot, or on Rosh Hashana or Shavuot, the family begins sitting Shiva in the evening immediately after the holiday is over. Oddly enough, although in these instances Shiva starts after sundown, the entire day is counted as the first day of Shiva (and also as the first day of the thirty-day mourning period), leaving only six more days to complete Shiva.[41]

Why is the home of the deceased the proper place for mourners to sit Shiva and for services to be held?

The Talmud specifies that the proper place for services to be held during the week of mourning is the same house where the deceased lived. The scholar Rav maintains that[42] "even if there are no mourners to be comforted when a person has died, ten people should visit his home [and engage in prayer and study throughout the Shiva period]." Rashi (1040-1105) and other authorities likewise maintain that the proper place to sit Shiva is the house where the deceased lived.[43]

Abraham Danzig (1774-1820) of Vilna quotes Nachmanides,[44] who offers a mystical reason for observing Shiva in the home of the deceased. For seven days after a death, he says, the soul hovers about the house of the deceased, grieving and mourning for the body it once inhabited, expressing the hope that it will be reunited with it. The prayers that emanate from the house of mourning three times each day during the period of Shiva are a source of consolation to the unhappy spirit. For this reason, the sixteenth-century commentator Moses Isserles[45] says that services should be held in the home of the deceased even if there are no surviving family members sitting Shiva in that home.

Nowadays, when families are spread out geographically, and sometimes for other compelling reasons, it is often necessary for Shiva to be observed in more than one home. However, if at all possible, as a sign of respect, most rabbis encourage Shiva to be observed and services to be held in the house of the deceased.

Why are mourners sometimes permitted to leave the house of mourning overnight?

While authorities are in general agreement that mourners should sleep in the Shiva house as long as they can be comfortably accommodated, in special cases allowances may be made. These include a situation where a mourner finds it difficult to sleep in a strange bed,[46] or where interpersonal conflicts might arise.

Rabbi Moshe Feinstein[47] cautions that when a mourner leaves the house of Shiva to sleep elsewhere, it should be done late at night, when the streets are less traveled, so that there will be less likelihood of the mourner's actions being misconstrued. The principle involved here is that of marit a'yin (literally, "what the eye perceives"), which refers specifically to the fact that the wrong impression might be conveyed to an observer, who might conclude that the mourner is not sitting Shiva at all.[48]

Why is one sometimes cautioned not to borrow anything from a house of mourning?

Since in years past Shiva was virtually always observed in the house where the deceased lived and died, it was believed that a spirit of uncleanness and impurity (known in Hebrew as tuma) permeates the house of mourning. And because it was thought that all objects in that house also become impure, the practice evolved of not removing any object from the Shiva house, thus avoiding the spread of ritual impurity.

Today, this custom is still observed, notably by Moroccan Jews.[49] Generally, however, the practice is considered baseless.[50]

Why are mourners encouraged to stay indoors throughout the Shiva week?

Except for the Sabbath and holidays, which are days of joy in Jewish tradition, mourners are required to remain in the house of mourning for the duration of the Shiva period, unless there is compelling reason for them to leave.[51]

The Rabbis felt that during these initial seven days of grieving mourners are not in a sufficiently stable mental condition to become involved with society at large. Additionally, it was feared that should a mourner go out among people, he might forget that he is in mourning and become involved in inappropriate activities.

Why are mourners forbidden to work during the seven-day Shiva period?

From the words of the prophet Amos (8:10), "I will turn your holidays into days of mourning," the Rabbis infer that just as work is prohibited on holidays, some of which (Passover and Sukkot) extend for seven days, so it is forbidden throughout the seven-day Shiva period.[52]

The Rabbis reasoned that this is to the mourner's advantage to express grief fully, a process that takes at least an entire week. If the mourner were to interrupt the process by going to work, the expression of grief would be diminished, thus impeding the healing process.

Why is it permissible for some mourners to return to work before Shiva is over?

The Rabbis ruled that mourners whose livelihood is at stake—particularly the poor—may return to work after the morning prayers on the third day of Shiva. However, the mourner should make every effort to avoid performing work in public, lest his actions be misinterpreted.[53] The third-century talmudic scholar Bar Kappara, a disciple of Judah the Prince, theorized that the first three days of Shiva are all-important because after burial of a deceased the soul keeps returning to the grave in the hope of reentering the body. However, when it sees that the facial features have changed, the soul departs and it abandons the effort.[58]

The sixteenth-century scholar Solomon Luria was asked by a *melamed* (teacher) if he is permitted to teach his pupils during this Shiva period, since otherwise parents might take them to another teacher and the *melamed* would lose his livelihood. Rabbi Luria granted permission so long as it was well known that the *melamed* made a very meager living and that he was rushing back to work not out of pleasure, but out of need.[55]

Why is a physician permitted to attend to patients during Shiva?

Even if other physicians are available, in emergency situations a doctor in mourning is permitted to leave the Shiva house to care for his patients, because it is thought that patients heal faster when the doctor in whom they have placed their confidence cares for them. The preservation of life is a primary commandment of Judaism.[56]

Why may a *mohel* leave his house during Shiva to perform a circumcision?

The requirement that a boy be circumcised on the eighth day of life is of the highest priority in Jewish law. Therefore, a *mohel,* one who performs ritual circumcision, may carry out his professional duties even while observing Shiva for a loved one. During the first three days of the *mohel's* Shiva, the infant must be brought to the Shiva house, where the circumcision is performed. After the third day, the *mohel* may leave the Shiva house to perform the rite elsewhere.[57]

Rabbi Moses Isserles, in his notes to the *Code of Jewish Law,* says that if it is not feasible to bring the infant to the house of mourning, and if no other *mohel* is available, the mourner may leave his home to perform a circumcision even during the first three days of Shiva. (In the days of Isserles [sixteenth century], most circumcisions took place in the synagogue. Circumcisions are rarely held in the synagogue today.)

Why may a parent leave the Shiva house to attend the wedding of a child?

Authorities such as the noted Orthodox scholar Rabbi Moshe Feinstein[58] permit a parent who is sitting Shiva to leave the house of mourning to attend and participate in the wedding of a son or daughter. They caution, however, that the parent may neither partake of the food nor recite the Seven Benedictions *(Sheva Berachot)* in honor of the bride and groom, for these are pleasurable activities not in keeping with the spirit of mourning. (These benedictions, which are recited following the Grace After Meals at the wedding feast and at each of the festive meals during the week thereafter, are the same as those recited by the rabbi or cantor at the end of the wedding ceremony.)[59]

Why may a mourner not be married during Shiva?

The Talmud[60] discusses the question of a death in the family that occurs immediately before a scheduled wedding:

> If the bread had been baked [for the wedding], the meat slaughtered, and the wine mixed [diluted with water to make it less strong and ready for consumption], and the father of the groom or the mother of the bride dies [the two parties who usually make the wedding preparations], they move the body into

another room and lead the bride and groom under the canopy and the marriage is consummated. The couple then does not live together as man and wife but does observe the seven days of feasting with the recital of the *Sheva Berachot* each day. After that they observe the seven days of mourning.

Later authorities, however, ruled that it would be inappropriate for mourners to be married during the first thirty days of mourning (Sheloshim), and especially during the Shiva period—even if the wedding is held without music and an elaborate reception.[61]

Why do some mourners place a bit of sand or earth in their shoes if they must leave the house during Shiva?

Although no longer widely practiced, it was once popular for a mourner who had to leave the Shiva house for urgent business to place a bit of sand or earth in his shoes.

The discomfort of the sand or earth underfoot served to remind the mourner of his status as a bereaved person—and of the importance of returning to the Shiva house as soon as possible. The category of urgent business includes matters that must be attended to in order to prevent irreversible financial loss, such as distributing perishable goods that would be unusable if not sold that week.

Why is a memorial light kept burning in a house of mourning?

In Jewish tradition, a flame symbolizes the soul of man reaching ever upward. This is suggested by the verse in Proverbs (20:27), "The soul of man is the lamp of the Lord." By lighting a candle and keeping it burning throughout the Shiva period, it is believed that the soul of the departed is aided in its journey heavenward.

When the patriarch Rabbi Judah the Prince (135-220 C.E.), editor of the Mishna, was on his deathbed, he called for his sons and instructed them that "the light [which he used during his lifetime] shall continue to burn in its usual place."[62] This, say some commentaries, is the basis for the custom that a light be kindled in the house of mourning. Scholars, however, find no reference to such a practice being employed by Jews before the thirteenth century.

Today, a memorial candle or lamp is kept burning for the duration of Shiva. Some Sephardim, however, continue to keep one burning throughout the entire first year of mourning.

The memorial light for Shiva is often supplied by the funeral parlor. Although wax candles are traditionally used, electric bulbs are permissible.

Why were a towel and a glass of water once placed near the memorial candle in a house of mourning?

Sometime after the thirteenth century it became customary to place a towel and a glass of water near the memorial candle. According to popular belief, this would appease the Angel of Death, who might want to wash his sword in the water and dry it with a towel. There also existed the belief that man's soul returned to cleanse itself in the water. Nineteenth-century Jewish scholars condemned this practice and forbade it.

Why are the mirrors covered in a house of mourning?

Covering mirrors or turning them to face the wall in a house of mourning is a rather late innovation among Jews, one not mentioned in medieval sources.

Many reasons have been advanced for the practice, the most popular being that mirrors are associated with personal vanity and that during a period of mourning it is not appropriate to be concerned with one's physical appearance.

The covering of mirrors has also been explained as

an expression of the mourner's belief that despite the great loss just suffered, God should not be blamed. To see oneself in a sorry state, as a grieving mourner, is an affront to God, inasmuch as man was created in God's image.

Another reason proposed for covering mirrors is that prayer services are held in the house of mourning, and it is forbidden to pray in front of a mirror. (Note that there are no mirrors on synagogue walls.)

Finally, the practice of covering mirrors or of turning them to face the wall, which was common among early non-Jewish cultures, has been explained as an expression of man's primitive belief that man's soul was his image or shadow. The soul was reflected in a mirror (and in water). Since it was feared that when the soul of man is projected in a mirror the ghost of the deceased might snatch it away, pains were taken not to allow the man's image or shadow to make an appearance.[63]

Today, rather than cover mirrors or turn them around, some Jews apply sudsy water to them, which clouds the surface. Some authorities have ruled that mirrors in rooms not frequented by mourners need not be covered.[64]

In some households, because they might give pleasure to the mourner, pictures of loved ones are also covered.

Reform Jews, by and large, do not observe these customs.

Why do mourners sit on low stools during Shiva?

This ancient custom, according to some scholars, is based on the Bible's description of Job, who, having suffered misfortune, was comforted by friends who sat with him on "the earth." Today, mourners do not sit directly on the earth; rather, they sit as close to the earth as possible, usually on wooden stools. Jewish law merely demands that mourners not sit on chairs of normal height. This is a way of demonstrating that the mourners have reached a low point in life because of the loss of a loved one. Some explain the custom as a way of expressing the desire to stay close to the earth in which a loved one is now buried.

Sephardic communities do not use stools to the same extent as Ashkenazim. Jews who follow the Moroccan and Judeo-Spanish (Turkish, Greek, etc.) tradition sit directly on the floor, while Syrians sit on the floor but use thin pillows to lessen the discomfort.[65]

Why was the mourning practice of turning over one's bed discontinued?

In talmudic times, it was customary during the Shiva period for a mourner to turn over his bed or couch (called *kefiyat ha-mita* in Hebrew) and to eat and sleep on the overturned bed. Bar Kappara, the third-century Palestinian scholar, said that the bed symbolizes the place on which life is conceived, and now that death has taken its toll, the mourner is to be reminded of that fact by inverting the bed.[66]

By the Middle Ages this widespread custom had been abandoned because it was feared that the non-Jewish world would regard it as a form of sorcery, just as they considered throwing a clod of grass behind them after visiting a grave to be an act of magic intended to harm Christians.[67] But even much earlier, the Palestinian Talmud notes,[68] the practice had lost some of its popularity because of the ridicule heaped upon it by the Gentile world. The Rabbis were always careful to tone down a Jewish practice that might lead to a false accusation.

Why is black a traditional mourning color?

A talmudic legend tells of how immediately following Yom Kippur, the High Priest Simon the Just (died about 310 B.C.E.) announced that he would die within the year. When asked how he knew, the High Priest responded that every year, when he entered the Holy of Holies on the Day of Atonement to perform the special Yom Kippur service, he would see an old man dressed in white, and the old man would accompany him out of the holy chamber. This year, he said, the man was dressed in black and did not accompany the High Priest. Just as predicted, Simon died a short time later, after the Festival of Sukkot.[69]

This legend contributed to the association of the color black with sadness and hence with death, while white became a symbol of joy.

Although the Bible makes no reference to the wearing of black mourning garments, the Talmud[70] quotes Rabbi Yannai as having instructed, "Do not bury me in black garments [lest I appear to be without merit]," hence the association of black with death and mourning.

The *Code of Jewish Law*[71] declares that one should not mourn a relative who has not observed Jewish law, has not celebrated the holidays, and has not frequented a house of prayer or a house of study. Not only should one not grieve over such an individual's death, but he should dress in white and eat, drink, and be merry.

In his Siftay Kohen commentary on the *Shulchan Aruch*,[72] the Lithuanian scholar Shabbetai ben Meir Ha-Kohen (1621-62), better known as the Shach (an acronym formed from the name of his Siftay Kohen commentary), comments on this law: "From this ruling we may conclude that [under normal circumstances] one should wear black when mourning a relative. However, members of a community should follow their local custom."[73]

Today, the color of the clothing worn by mourners during the Shiva period is optional, although the majority tend to wear black or other subdued colors.[74]

Why is it traditional for mourners to keep their heads covered?

Covering the head by drawing a cloth over the face and lips is a mourning ritual that is as old as the Bible. It was a popular custom among Ishmaelites, and when adopted by Israelites, it became known as *atifat Yish-maelim,* "the wrapping of Ishmaelites."

In the Bible (II Samuel 9:5), when King David learned that his son Absalom had been killed in battle, he covered his face and grieved aloud: "O my son, Absalom! Absalom, my son, my son!" In the Book of Ezekiel (24:17), the prophet was commanded by God: "Cover not thy upper lip." The Rabbis of the Talmud[75] and later commentators such as Maimonides[76] concluded that the admonition regarding the covering of the head refers specifically to Ezekiel, and they deduced that all other mourners must therefore keep their heads covered.

In regard to covering the face, the Talmud[77] elaborates: "Any *atifa* [wrapping of the head] that is not like the *atifa* of the Ishmaelites is not a proper *atifa.*" We are told that when Rabbi Nachman (c. 235-324 C.E.) was in mourning, "he covered his face to the lip."

In time, a great many authorities began to disparage this practice of covering the head and face to the lips because it led to ridicule by non-Jews, particularly non-Jewish servants and maids. Gradually, it was abandoned in its original form and it became customary for mourners to keep their heads, but not their faces, covered.[78]

Many later legal authorities commented on the practice of mourners covering the head: the eleventh-century French authority Rashi was asked whether *avelim* (mourners) must keep their heads covered throughout the Shiva period. He replied: "Although non-Jews make fun of this custom, Jews should nevertheless follow the practice."

The thirteenth-century Spanish scholar Moses ben Nachman (Nachmanides) took the position that "the head is uncovered out of respect for the public." Thus, when a mourner is alone, he is to keep his head covered; and when visitors come to offer comfort, the mourner is to uncover his head as a sign of respect.[80]

Rabbi Jacob ben Moses Ha-levi Mollin (1360-1427), popularly known as the Maharil, indicates in his famous book on customs and ceremonies, *Sefer Ha-minhagim,* that it is proper for mourners to keep their heads covered at all times during Shiva. This is the practice generally followed today by traditional Jews. And, out of respect for the mourner, visitors to a house of mourning usually wear a headcovering as well.[81]

Why are mourners not permitted to wear leather shoes during the Shiva period?

"How lovely are your feet in sandals, O daughter of nobles!" proclaims the Song of Songs (7:2). In ancient times, footwear was a symbol of sensuousness and pleasure, and therefore, denying oneself this luxury became a way of expressing grief in Jewish tradition. In the Bible, Isaiah (20:2) was commanded to take the sandals off his feet as a sign of mourning. Originally, mourners went about barefooted during the Shiva period, even if it became necessary to leave the house for an urgent reason. The Rabbis later changed the law when the Gentile population began to ridicule the practice.[82] However, the wearing of leather shoes during Shiva remained banned because of the association of leather with luxury.[83]

In the Shiva house, mourners generally go about in stockinged feet or soft cloth slippers. Persons required to wear shoes for medical reasons may do so.[84]

On the Sabbath during the Shiva week, mourners may wear their usual shoes, leather or otherwise.

Why are some forms of bathing not permitted during the week of Shiva?

A distinction is made between bathing for cleanliness and bathing for comfort. Bathing for mere pleasure, namely bathing in hot water for an extended period, is definitely considered improper in Jewish law. However, showering and bathing for basic cleanliness is considered proper.[85]

Why is sexual activity prohibited during the week of Shiva?

Since in Jewish law sexual activity is engaged in not only for the purpose of propagation, as indicated in Genesis 1:28 ("Be fruitful and multiply and fill the earth"), but also as a source of pleasure, it is banned during the first seven days of mourning along with all other pleasurable activities.[86]

The Rabbis of the Talmud[87] base the law on II Samuel 12:24, which states, "And David comforted his wife Bathsheba [*after* the loss of their child] and cohabited with her." Since the verse mentions the act of cohabitation after mentioning the act of comforting, the Rabbis concluded that sexual activity did not take place until the week of Shiva had concluded.

Why are some women permitted to use cosmetics during the Shiva period?

Women generally are not permitted to use eye shadow, powder, lipstick, and other cosmetics during Shiva. However, some Orthodox authorities permit an unmarried woman who may be paid a condolence call by a potential suitor to use cosmetics and even jewelry during Shiva.[88]

Why is excessive grooming prohibited during the Shiva period?

Paying undue attention to one's physical appearance during the seven-day mourning period is considered a pleasurable activity and hence prohibited in Jewish law. The mourner is expected to refrain from shaving and cutting the hair during this time, although the simple act of combing the hair generally is considered acceptable.[89] It is interesting to note that in biblical times cutting one's hair and shaving one's face was considered a sign of mourning: Jeremiah 7:29 says, "Shear your locks and cast them away. Take up a lament on the heights." Jeremiah 41:5 describes the people of Shechem as having come "with shaven cheeks and rent clothing."[90]

Today, most mourners resume shaving after the Shiva week, but among Orthodox Jews, particularly in Israel, the practice is to not shave for thirty days after the death of a parent.

Why is the wearing of new or laundered clothing prohibited during Shiva?

During the Shiva period the mourner may not wear new or freshly laundered clothing. Doing so, said the Rabbis, would constitute a pleasurable activity. However, for hygienic reasons the mourner is permitted to change into freshly laundered garments that come into direct contact with the skin.

Why is the mourner not allowed to wash or iron clothing during Shiva?

The mourner is traditionally forbidden to wash or iron clothing during Shiva, even if the clothing is to be worn after Shiva or by a nonmourner. Washing or ironing would fall into the category of "work," which may not be performed by mourners during Shiva.

Why are all forms of merriment and entertainment prohibited during Shiva?

The Talmud[91] and the *Code of Jewish Law*[92] prohibit the mourner from attending weddings, dances, and parties during the seven-day mourning period because grief is most intense during this time and all forms of entertainment and gaiety are considered incompatible with the prevailing mood.

Why do some Jews abstain from consuming wine and meat during Shiva?

Some Jews, notably those in the Moroccan community, refrain from drinking wine and eating meat during Shiva because these foods are associated with joyous occasions. Others, such as the Judeo-Spanish Sephardim, do eat meat.[93] Ashkenazim consider the denial of these foods needless deprivation and follow their regular eating regimen.

Why were the Rabbis of the Talmud insistent that mourning be observed in moderation?

At one point in history, Jews took the words in the Book of Proverbs (31:6) literally. The author of the book, ascribed to King Solomon, suggested that strong wine should be offered to those who are "bitter of soul." This was taken to mean mourners. But with the destruction of the Second Temple many Jews became ascetics to demonstrate their grief over the loss of Israel's most holy place. They purposely refrained from drinking wine and eating meat, which had become symbols both of luxury and joyful living.

The Rabbis of the Talmud were annoyed at such behavior because they felt that it fostered a practice that would be damaging if it became widespread. "We should not mourn excessively," they said, "because we must not impose upon the community a hardship that would be difficult to bear."[94]

In arguing the point with the community of ascetics, Rabbi Joshua said, "My sons, why do you not eat meat or drink wine?"

They replied, "Shall we feast on flesh which used to be brought as an offering on the altar, now that the altar is destroyed? Shall we drink wine which used to be poured as a libation on the altar, when it no longer exists?"

"If that is so," Joshua responded, "we should not eat bread either, because the meal offerings have ceased."

"That is so. We can manage with fruit," replied the ascetics.

"We should not eat fruit either," said Joshua, "because there is no longer an offering of first-fruits."

"Then we can manage with other fruits," they said.

"But," Joshua replied, "we should not drink water either, because there is no longer any ceremony of the pouring of water [on the festival of Sukkot]."

To this they could find no answer, so Joshua said to them: "My sons, come and listen to me. Not to mourn at all is impossible, because the blow has fallen. To mourn overmuch is also impossible because we do not impose on the community a hardship which the majority cannot endure."

Mourning in moderation has become traditional Jewish practice.

Why are religious services held in a house of mourning?

Since a mourner is obligated to pray once his relative has been buried (he is not obligated to do so between the time of death and the time of burial), and since he generally is not permitted to appear in public during the week of Shiva, it is customary to assemble a quorum *(minyan)* in the house of mourning and to hold prayer services there.[95]

Why do some authorities maintain that a mourner should not be counted to a *minyan* on the first days of Shiva?

Rashi, the prominent eleventh-century scholar, was of the opinion that in the earliest stages of bereavement a mourner should not be counted to a *minyan*. He believed that this stressful period extends from the moment one learns of a death in the family until the end of the first day of Shiva, during which time the mourner is highly distraught and not totally in command of his faculties. Other authorities ruled that the period of not being counted to a religious quorum should extend even to the third day of mourning.

The more liberal view, which is accepted today, was expressed by Moses Isserles in his notes to the *Code of Jewish Law.*[96] Isserles contends that a mourner is to be counted to the *minyan* as soon as burial has been completed, when the stress begins to diminish. (See also Chapter One, page 23, for a discussion of the *aninut* period.)

Why do some mourners refrain from donning *tefilin* on the first days of Shiva?

When a death occurs, members of the immediate family are not obligated to pray or carry out other ordinary religious duties. This includes the donning of *tefilin* (phylacteries), which is considered to be a joyful religious experience and hence inappropriate during the first days of Shiva.

The Rabbis of the Talmud expressed varying opinions as to when the wearing of *tefilin* by mourners should be resumed. Rabbi Eliezer said that on the first day of Shiva one should not don *tefilin* at all, but on the second day he may put them on but not wear them all day long. (In talmudic times *tefilin* were worn throughout the day.) Rabbi Joshua said that the mourner may not don *tefilin* on the first or second day of Shiva, and on the third day he may put them on and wear them while reciting the morning prayers.[97]

Today, mourners generally resume doning *tefilin* at the first morning *(Shacharit)* service following burial.[98]

Why is a Torah scroll often brought into the Shiva house?

Whenever a *minyan* (quorum) is assembled for a Monday or Thursday morning service, it is customary to read a selection from the Torah scroll. To make it possible for mourners to fulfill this obligation, a Torah may be brought into the house of mourning so that the bereaved will not have to leave the Shiva home to attend synagogue services.[99]

The general rule established by the Rabbis is that a Torah may be brought into a Shiva house if it will be read on three consecutive reading days: Monday, Thursday, and the Sabbath. In such cases the Torah is kept there throughout the Shiva period rather than having it carried back and forth to the synagogue between readings. If this requirement cannot be fulfilled, a Torah may not be brought into a house of mourning because, say the Rabbis, it would be disrespectful to move the scroll from a synagogue to private quarters and not read from it on three consecutive days.

Some Jews, such as the Syrians, do not bring the Torah into a house of mourning under any circumstances.[101]

Why do Sephardim permit mourners to leave the Shiva house to attend synagogue services whenever the Torah is read?

In his *Code of Jewish Law,* sixteenth-century Sephardic authority Joseph Caro says: "The [general] rule is that a mourner should not leave his home [the Shiva home] on weekdays to attend synagogue services, but on the Sabbath he may do so. But our [Sephardic] custom is that he may leave his house [during Shiva] and visit the synagogue whenever the Torah is read."[102] Caro bases his ruling on the views of the Rabbis of the Talmud, who nowhere prohibit a mourner from attending synagogue services (even on weekdays) to hear the Torah being read.[103]

The Ashkenazic authority Moses Isserles, in his notes to Caro's code, permits the mourner to leave the Shiva house only on the Sabbath.[104]

Why is the *Tachanun* prayer omitted during the prayer service in a house of mourning?

The *Tachanun* prayer, is recited toward the conclusion of each weekday morning and afternoon synagogue service. On Mondays and Thursdays—days on which the Torah is taken from the ark for a public reading at the morning service—a lengthier form of *Tachanun* is recited.

Tachanun, which means "supplication, entreaty," is a plea to God that He be merciful and come to the aid of those in distress. The short form is essentially Psalm 6 with a brief introduction from II Samuel 24:14. In Sephardic liturgy, Psalm 25 is recited instead of Psalm 6. The long form is a combination of verses from various parts of Scripture.

Since *Tachanun* is a prayer for relief from the sorrows and tragedies of life, it is not recited in a house of mourning so as to spare the mourners additional reminders of their distress.[105]

Why is *Hallel* not recited in a Shiva home?

On Rosh Chodesh, which celebrates the coming of the new month, and on Chanuka, *Hallel* ("Psalms of Praise") is part of the normal liturgy. However, when these days fall during Shiva, this prayer is generally not recited at services held in a house of mourning, for mourners cannot sincerely recite such a prayer of unbounded joy and thankfulness. Some authorities maintain that because mourners are permitted to kindle the Chanuka lights and pronounce the joyful blessings, they should also be permitted to recite *Hallel.*

Mystics oppose the recitation of *Hallel* in the Shiva house. This is based on the belief that the spirit of the deceased hovers about a house of mourning, and to recite the verse *Lo ha-metim ye-halelu Ya,* "The dead cannot praise the Lord" (Psalms 115:17), would appear to be mocking the deceased.

In some communities, mourners leave the room while the rest of those assembled recite *Hallel.*[106]

Why is Psalm 49 recited at the end of most services held in a house of mourning?

Psalm 49, which begins with the Hebrew words *La-menatze'ach: li-venay Korach mizmor,* "To the leader: this is a Psalm for the family of Korach," exhorts us to face the fundamental issues of life honestly. It reminds us that death is a great leveler, a condition that befalls rich and poor alike. Because of this meaningful and comforting message, reciting Psalm 49 is deemed to be an appropriate way of concluding religious services during the Shiva period.[107]

Why may mourners sometimes leave the Shiva house to attend synagogue services?

While it is customary to make every effort to assemble a *minyan* and to hold religious services in the house of mourning during Shiva, when this is not possible, mourners may leave the Shiva house to attend synagogue services so that they will be able to recite the Mourners' Kaddish.[108]

Why may a mourner attend and participate in synagogue services on Tisha B'Av?

Tisha B'Av—the ninth day of the month of Av—commemorates the razing of the First and Second Temples in Jerusalem, in 586 B.C.E. and 70 C.E. respectively. Since all Jews observe Tisha B'Av as a day of mourning, the Rabbis felt that it is proper for mourners to join their fellow Jews at synagogue services on this day.[109]

The third of the three honorees called to the Torah at the Tisha B'Av morning service may be a mourner, because the Torah passage (Deuteronomy 4:25-40) read for this *aliya* expresses a mournful theme. The third honoree also recites the *haftara* selection from the Book of Jeremiah (8:13-9:23), the content of which is also sorrowful.

Why may a mourner leave the house of Shiva on Purim to hear the reading of the Scroll of Esther (Megilla) in the synagogue?

On Purim, a holiday that marks the miraculous rescue of Jews from a plot to exterminate them, everyone is ordered to be joyous. Therefore, conspicuous Shiva practices are not observed. These include sitting on a low stool and not wearing leather shoes. However, private mourning restrictions, such as sexual abstinence, remain in effect.[110]

On the eve and morning of the Purim holiday, mourners are encouraged to attend the synagogue reading of the Megilla, which recounts the miraculous turn of events that transformed catastrophe into victory. Mourners may join their families in the joyous Purim meal (se'uda), and they may also send out and receive holiday gifts. Some authorities, however, prohibit friends from giving gifts to those mourning the loss of parents, not only during Shiva but for the entire first year after the loss.[111]

When the first day of Shiva and Purim coincide, it is proper according to some authorities for those preparing the Meal of Condolence to omit serving eggs, a symbol of mourning, and instead to serve wine and meat, symbols of joy.

On Shushan Purim, the day following the holiday, the same rules that apply to Purim are in effect.

Why do mourners not join the other worshippers at the beginning of the Friday night synagogue service?

It has become traditional for mourners who come to the synagogue to attend the Friday night service during their Shiva week not to join the other worshippers at the beginning of the service. They wait outside the doors of the sanctuary and enter as the last stanza of the *Lecha*

Dodi prayer is being chanted. This stanza is a song of welcome to the Sabbath Bride, and reciting it is considered an appropriate way of welcoming the bereaved to the community at large for the duration of the Sabbath.

After the *Lecha Dodi* is concluded, as the mourners take their seats in the synagogue, the congregation greets them with the traditional mourner's greeting: *Ha-Makom ye-nachem etchem be-toch she'ar avaylay Tziyon vi-Yerushala'yim,* "May the Lord comfort you along with all the mourners of Zion and Jerusalem."

Sephardim use the expression, *Min ha-Shama'yim te-nuchamu,* "May Heaven comfort you."

Why do mourners traditionally not occupy their usual synagogue seats during Shiva?

To emphasize that a great upheaval has taken place in their lives, it has become customary for mourners to change their usual synagogue seats for the duration of the mourning period. (This may extend for up to one year for those mourning the loss of a parent.) Moses Isserles, the sixteenth-century Ashkenazic authority, considers this practice an appropriate way of calling attention to the fact that all is not normal in the life of these congregants.[112]

The Sephardic contemporary of Isserles, Joseph Caro, did not consider it important for mourners to change their seats.[113] Nonetheless, most Sephardic Jews today do follow the practice.[114]

It is interesting to note that in some congregations, such as the synagogue in Barcelona, Spain, a special "mourners' bench" is set aside in the rear of the sanctuary to be occupied by mourners only. In the Doheny Synagogue, in Budapest, Hungary, it is customary for ushers *(gaba'im)* to escort mourners and present them to the rabbi, who awaits them near the pulpit. The rabbi offers them words of consolation, and the mourners are then escorted to seats on the side, toward the front of the synagogue.

Why should a mourner not be offered an *aliya* during the week of Shiva, even on a Sabbath or holiday?

Mourners who visit the synagogue during their week of Shiva should not be called to the Torah, even on the Sabbath or holidays when mourning is suspended, because the Torah blessings that have to be recited include expressions of joy that are not in consonance with the inner feelings of grief and sadness being experienced by the mourner.

The *Code of Jewish Law*[115] points out that a Priest (Kohen) may be not be awarded an *aliya* while observing Shiva even if there is no other Kohen present in the congregation. In this case, the first *aliya* is given to a Yisrael (Israelite).

Not all authorities agree, however, some contending that it is proper to award an *aliya* to a Kohen during Shiva since the first Torah honor must always be assigned to a Priest if present.[116]

Why must a mourner accept an *aliya* if called to the Torah on a Sabbath or holiday?

As stated above, a mourner attending a synagogue service on a Sabbath or holiday should not be offered an *aliya.* However, if called to the Torah, the mourner must accept the honor because to do otherwise would be an affront to the Torah. Members of the congregation, unaware that the individual is in mourning, might think that the Torah is being blatantly rejected.[117]

Why is it proper to offer a mourner some Torah honors?

While a mourner may not be offered an *aliya* on the Sabbath during Shiva, he may be honored with other Torah assignments, such as the raising and dressing of the Torah (*hagbaha* and *gelila*) and the removing and returning of the Torah to the ark. These various honors do not involve the recitation of the Torah blessings, which express joyous sentiments.

Why is a mourner sometimes prohibited from leading a prayer service?

Generally, during the Shiva period a mourner may not lead the Sabbath synagogue service, an activity that must be performed in a spirit of joy. However, an exception is made when there is no one else present who is capable of leading the congregation in prayer.

At weekday services held in the house of mourning, it is customary for one of the mourners to lead the prayer service. Many consider this to be helpful to the soul of the departed.[118]

Why is a mourner prohibited from serving as a Torah reader?

The Book of Psalms (19:9) says: "The precepts of the Lord are just, making the heart rejoice." From this verse the Rabbis concluded that it is inappropriate for a mourner, who is in a saddened state, to serve as a Torah reader (baal koray). Reading "the precepts of the Lord" to the public is a joyful activity and thus not permissible during Shiva. However, if no other person capable of reading the Torah is present, some authorities permit the mourner to do so.

The Code of Jewish Law[119] points out that if the Torah reader is a professional who is engaged by a congregation on a permanent basis, he should not go to his synagogue on the Sabbath of Shiva, but should attend another house of worship. If no other synagogue exists, he should frequent his own but should not read from the Torah even if called upon. Some contemporary authorities are more lenient in this matter.[120]

Why must a Priest (Kohen) refrain from pronouncing the Priestly Benediction during the Shiva period?

Because a Kohen during the Shiva period is in a downcast state, he is not permitted to participate in pronouncing the Priestly Benediction *(Birkat Kohanim)* at public services. He may not do so even if no other Kohen is present to bless the congregation, but must instead leave the synagogue before that point in the service (that is, as the *R'tzay* prayer is being recited). If, however, the Priest has not left the synagogue and is asked to go up to the ark area to offer the Priestly Benediction *(duchen* in Yiddish), he must do so, for to decline would be an affront to the congregation.[121]

Why is a mourner generally forbidden to "study Torah"?

During Shiva, studying the Bible, the Talmud, or other religious works is prohibited. In Jewish tradition such activity is considered joyous and therefore not to be engaged in by the bereaved. However, the Rabbis of the Talmud permitted the study of solemn subjects, including sections of the Book of Jeremiah, the Book of Lamentations, the Book of Job, as well as books pertaining to the laws of mourning.[122]

Some authorities permit the reading of chapters from the Book of Psalms because they offer comfort to the mourner, while others prohibit it because it constitutes study and hence is a pleasurable activity. Most contemporary authorities, however, permit the study of new and unfamiliar parts of the Bible and Talmud because these would contain a degree of difficulty, thus mitigating the slight pleasure that might be derived from their study.

Why does the Shiva period end early on the morning of the seventh day?

In Jewish tradition, part of a day is considered equal to a whole day.[123] Thus, if a mourner sits *Shiva* for as little as one hour on the day of the funeral, that is considered as one full day of *Shiva*. The same holds true if a mourner sits *Shiva* for only a short time on the seventh day: that is considered a full day.

Generally, on the seventh day mourners sit on their stools after the morning service and receive words of consolation from those present. With this action, the Shiva period is considered ended.

Why do mourners sometimes walk around the block at the end of the Shiva period?

In some Jewish communities, it is customary, when Shiva is over, for all mourners to walk together for a short distance, usually around the block. This symbolizes their return to society and the real world from which they have withdrawn for a week. The origin of this custom is obscure, and its practice is not mandated by Jewish law.

CHAPTER 8

Comforting the Mourner

Introduction

In his essay "The Right to Kill," Hayim Greenberg (1900-1953), editor of *The Jewish Frontier*,[1] reminds us that logotherapy, healing through words, is as old as the human race. The ancient Persians called our attention to three kinds of doctors: the herb-doctor, the knife-doctor, and the word-doctor. Jews were considered to be especially proficient at word-doctoring.

The healing power of the spoken word is highlighted in a story that once made the rounds in chasidic circles concerning the Magid ("Preacher") of Kosenitz, who was terminally ill. When the preacher's famous friend known by the nickname "the Yid [Jew]" learned of the illness, he sent two of his students to the preacher's bedside to read Psalms and sing Sabbath melodies to him and thereby cheer him up. The students arrived on a Friday afternoon and began their mission. With each word offered, the preacher grew stronger and stronger, and eventually he recovered and praised "the Yid" for allowing him more time to complete his unfinished tasks on earth. The soft, moving words of the students had served as balm to the ailing preacher.

In a similar vein, Jewish law and tradition suggests that we use carefully selected words to comfort the bereaved in their time of need. We are obliged to monitor our words and follow prescribed psychological guidelines. One of the admonitions of the Sages was "Do not try to comfort a mourner while his loved one is still un-buried."[2] Accordingly, when the funeral is over and we visit the mourner in the hope of offering comfort, we keep silent until the mourner shows an interest in speaking. And when we are engaged in conversation, we do not shy away from speaking about the deceased, fearing that it will sadden the mourner. On the contrary, the mourner appreciates hearing words of praise about the deceased, said scholar and physician Moses Maimonides. "Those who grieve," he wrote in his twelfth-century Guide of the Perplexed, "find comfort in weeping and having their sorrow aroused."

Jewish tradition also reminds us that after the first week, month, and year of mourning have run their course, the time for grieving is over and the time for consoling has come to an end.

Summary of Traditional Observances Relating to Comforting Mourners

Consoling mourners
- Visiting mourners during the week of Shiva is a primary obligation of Jews.
- The first meal eaten by mourners after the funeral, which is called the Meal of Condolence, must be prepared by neighbors or friends rather than by the mourners themselves. Subsequent meals may be prepared by the mourners. Rolls, bagels, and hard-boiled eggs are the primary fare of the Meal of Condolence.

Posture
- Mourners sit on low stools when receiving visitors. They need not stand, even for important visitors.
- When eating meals, mourners sit on regular chairs around a table. On all days except the Sabbath, when conspicuous mourning is prohibited, if guests are present they slice the bread for the mourners.

Bringing gifts
- It is permissible for persons paying condolence calls to bring gifts of wine, liquor, or food.

Mourners as hosts
- Mourners are not expected to act as hosts. However, sometimes an urn of coffee and light refreshments are set out for visitors to help themselves.

Greetings
- Traditionally, visitors do not greet mourners in the normal fashion. If mourners are greeted, they should not be expected to respond.

When to visit
- Except for close relatives and friends, it is customary

not to pay condolence calls until the third day of Shiva. If this is not feasible, visits may be made even during the first three days.

- Visits may be made on weekdays during the day or evening. Under normal circumstances, condolence calls are not made on the Sabbath or holidays.

Conversation
- Jewish law demands that one wait for the mourner to initiate conversation. Long visits and lengthy conversations are discouraged unless one senses that such is the desire of the mourner.

Upon leaving
- Upon taking leave of the mourner, it is traditional among Ashkenazim to say, *Ha-Makom ye-nachem etchem be-toch she'ar avelay Tziyon vi-Yerushala'yim,* "May the Lord comfort you together with all mourners of Zion and Jerusalem." Sephardim say, *Min ha-Shama'yim te-nuchamu,* "May Heaven comfort you."

Why is the practice of comforting mourners so strong in Jewish tradition?

The Rabbis of the Talmud consider the act of condoling, of offering sympathy to mourners, to be a great *mitzva,* a godly act, the kind of activity in which God himself is involved.[4] The first such instance is found in the Bible, where after the death of Abraham, God revealed Himself, paid Isaac (Abraham's son) a condolence call, and blessed him.[5]

The Hebrew expression for comforting mourners is *nichum avelim*. When one comforts a mourner, he is said to be *menachem avel*.

Why has the expression beginning with the words *Ha-Makom ye-nachem etchem* become the traditional condolence salutation?

According to tradition, upon the conclusion of the funeral rites at the cemetery, visitors form two rows so that mourners may pass through and receive words of condolence from those assembled. Among Ashkenazim the expression used is:

הַמָּקוֹם יְנַחֵם אֶתְכֶם בְּתוֹךְ שְׁאָר אֲבֵלֵי צִיוֹן וִירוּשָׁלָיִם.

> *Ha-Makom ye-nachem etchem betoch she'ar avaylay Tziyon vi-Yerushala'yim.*

> May the Lord comfort you together with all the mourners of Zion and Jerusalem.

The loss of the Second Temple in 70 C.E. was a serious blow to Jews everywhere, a catastrophe for which Jews were to be in perpetual mourning. Reference to it is made whenever we take leave of mourners at the cemetery or when paying a visit to a Shiva house. By associating the mourner's personal loss with the national catastrophe that befell all Jews when the Temple was destroyed, we are expressing how deeply we empathize with the bereaved. (For further discussion of the evolution of the mourner's greeting, see pages 113-14.)

The traditional expression of condolence among Sephardim is:

מִן הַשָּׁמַיִם תְּנוּחָמוּ.

> *Min ha-Shama'yim te-nuchamu.*

> May Heaven comfort you.

Why are mourners sometimes offered a cup of wine upon returning from the cemetery?

The Talmud speaks of a "cup of mourners,"[6] which apparently alludes to the wine that was customarily offered to mourners upon their return from the cemetery.

The origin of the custom has been attributed to Rabbi Chanan, who interpreted the verse in Proverbs (31:6), "Give strong drink to him that is ready to perish, and wine unto the bitter of soul," to mean that wine was created specifically for the purpose of comforting mourners.

The practice of offering wine to mourners is not commonly followed today.[7]

Why is the post-funeral meal prepared by neighbors or friends of the mourners?

The first meal eaten by mourners following a funeral, known as the "Meal of Condolence," must not be prepared by the mourners themselves. Jewish law imposes that obligation upon neighbors and friends.[8] The Rabbis of the Talmud reprimanded those who did not fulfill their neighborly responsibility, commenting that such behavior reflects a lack of sensitivity to the grief of others.

Rabbi Yerucham offered a very pragmatic reason for the introduction of this law. He says that after the funeral the mourner is in such distress that if left to his own devices, he might not eat at all.

Allusion to a Meal of Condolence is first made in the Book of Ezekiel (24:17-18). In anticipation of the imminent fall of Jerusalem, the prophet Ezekiel is told by God that in mourning the loss of his wife he is not to follow the customary mourning ritual of eating food belonging to others, but that he should prepare his own food. The Meal of Condolence should, God said, be reserved for the greater public tragedy that was foreseen. In later times the Rabbis ruled that the first full meal eaten by the mourners after returning from a burial should be prepared by neighbors and friends.[10]

Why is the Meal of Condolence referred to as Se'udat Havra'a?

When David mourned the death of his close friend Abner, commander of Saul's army, the people came out to comfort David and "to cause David to eat bread" (II Samuel 3:35). The Hebrew word used here for "to cause to eat" is *le-havrot,* from which is derived the Hebrew name for the Meal of Condolence, *Havra'a* or *Se'udat Havra'a.*

Se'udat Havra'a is also referred to in English as the Meal of Healing, for it is thought to be of great help in assuaging the grief of mourners. Knowing that one's neighbors and friends are supportive contributes to the process of healing.

Among Sephardim in the Syrian and Moroccan communities, it is the Chevra Kadisha that prepares the Meal of Condolence. Among Syrians, the meal is served after the Keria ritual has been performed. The rending of the garment takes place in the Shiva home, not earlier as in most other communities. See Chapter Three, Rending the Garment, for a full discussion of the Keria ritual.[11]

Why does the Meal of Condolence generally include rolls, bagels, and hard-boiled eggs?

The menu for the first meal in the house of mourning is designed to include foods that symbolize eternal life: round rolls and bagels, oval eggs and lentils—all of which are symbolic of the cyclical, eternal, continuous nature of life. After serving these ceremonial foods, a regular meal is usually eaten.[12]

A second traditional explanation is that round and oval foods, particularly eggs, are served at the Meal of Condolence because these items have no mouth, that is, they have no opening. They represent the mourner, still in shock, who has no words for anyone.[13]

The Talmud[14] offers a third explanation for the serving of round and oval foods to mourners who have just returned home from burying their dead. The Rabbis say that the soup of lentils that Jacob made for his father, Isaac, was cooked on the same day on which his grandfather, Abraham, died, and that it was specifically prepared as a Meal of Condolence for Isaac.

Among Judeo-Spanish Jews—those living in the general area of Turkey and Greece—families sit on the floor when eating the Meal of Condolence, which consists of olives, eggs, and bread.[15]

The practice among Ethiopian Jews has been for the attendants at the burial, who lay the corpse in the grave and fill it with earth, to return to the house of mourning, where they eat peas and drink coffee.[16]

Why do some authorities consider it improper to bring gifts of food to a Shiva house?

Although in talmudic times it was customary for visitors to bring gifts of food to a house of mourning during the Shiva week,[17] some authorities prohibited the custom because it imitates a non-Jewish practice (chukat ha-goy), and because it is a way of offering a greeting to the mourner, which the Rabbis forbade. Distinguished authorities such as Rabbi Moshe Feinstein[18] reject the above reasoning and permit the bringing of food and drink to a Shiva house. They view this as a way of empathizing with those in mourning.

Why are light refreshments sometimes served to visitors in a house of mourning?

While it is contrary to Jewish tradition for mourners to act as hosts to visitors who come to offer condolences, it is not improper for an urn of coffee and light refreshments to be set out on a table for visitors to help themselves. Since visitors often travel long distances to pay their respects, making refreshments available is considered a courtesy.

Why were colored glasses once used when serving visitors in a house of mourning?

The Talmud[19] indicates that at one time, when drinks were served in a house of mourning, the rich were served in white glass vessels and the poor in colored ones. When it became apparent that the poor were being slighted or embarrassed because they could not afford the more expensive white glasses, the Rabbis ruled that everyone should be served in colored glasses.[20]

Why are Jews obligated to pay a condolence call during the first week of mourning?

'Comfort ye, comfort ye, My people,'
saith the Lord...

From this opening verse of Chapter 40 of the Book of Isaiah, the intention of which is to allay the fears of the threatened people of Jerusalem, the message was drawn that in times of tragedy every individual needs comforting.

The condolence visit Jews are obligated to pay during the Shiva period helps sustain the mourner during the initial period of distress, depression, and loneliness that follows a death.

Why is it recommended that one wait until the third day of Shiva before paying a condolence call?

The proper time for casual acquaintances to visit the mourner is after the first two days of Shiva. The Rabbis of the Talmud advised, "Do not comfort a mourner while his deceased relative is still before him [in the mind's eye]." Because memories are vivid and grief is most intense during the first two days of Shiva, visitors should wait until the third day before paying a condolence call. An exception is made for the very closest of friends and for those who would have no other opportunity to pay their respects to the bereaved.[21]

Why is it considered improper to offer condolences over the telephone rather than in person?

Offering condolences to a mourner is best done in person. To resort to the telephone to offer sympathies can be considered only second best and is acceptable only when traveling to the Shiva home would be exceedingly difficult or prohibitively costly.[22] Otherwise, authorities feel, there should be no excuse for anyone's neglecting the duty to personally comfort a mourner.[23]

Why does Jewish law demand that one refrain from engaging in undue conversation when visiting a mourner during Shiva?

The mere presence of a visitor in a Shiva house is what offers the most comfort to the mourner. Words are unnecessary. The Bible, in describing the classic mourner, Job, says that when Job was mourning the loss of his family, he was visited by three friends, who sat with him for seven days without uttering a word, "for they saw how very great was his suffering" (2:13). And the Bible (Job 3:1) later says: "After this, Job opened his mouth and said...." Only when Job was finished talking did his friend Eliphaz the Temanite begin to speak (4:1).

In talmudic times it was customary in Babylonia for mourners, when being visited, to cover their heads and faces with a hood, a practice common among the general population. The Rabbis of the Talmud encouraged this behavior and urged mourners to be sure to cover their mouths, leaving only the nose and eyes exposed. This reminded the mourners to be silent.[24] For a mourner to be engaged in much conversation might leave the impression that he has forgotten his sorrow.

Rabbi Yochanan points out[25] that "as soon as the mourner nods his head [indicating that he would like the visitors to take leave of him], the comforters are no longer allowed to remain seated by him."

In the Midrash,[26] the Rabbis suggest that a visitor can bestow no greater favor upon a mourner than to be silent in his presence, unless invited to speak. This message was driven home by an incident that occurred when the wife of Rabbi Mana of Sepphoris (fourth century C.E.) died. His colleague Rabbi Abun came to pay a condolence call. Rabbi Mana said: "Are there any words of Torah you would like to offer us in our time of grief?" Rabbi Anun replied: "At times such as this, the Torah takes refuge in silence."

This does not mean that one need remain absolutely silent when in the company of a mourner, but idle chatter should be avoided. The visitor is best advised to be prepared to respond to the mourner rather than to initiate conversation.

Why is it considered improper to exchange casual words of greeting when paying a condolence call?

To pretend to be casual about the mourner's situation is considered an affront. Accordingly, authorities such as Rashi, citing God's words to Ezekiel (24:17), "Sigh in silence," state that those visiting the mourner during Shiva should refrain from extending customary greetings such as "hello," "good morning," "how are you?" and *"shalom."* The mourner is obviously experiencing a great sorrow at this time, and an honest, positive response to these greetings can surely not be expected.

Some authorities are more lenient in this matter, maintaining that expressions such as "good morning" or "how are you?" are not intended to be taken as questions that call for a response.

Why does Jewish tradition advise us not to expect a normal response from a mourner whom we greet?

When a mourner does not respond to words of greeting, it should be recognized that the individual has been traumatized by recent events and cannot be expected to respond normally. A visitor should not be insulted if a mourner does not respond to a greeting.

The Talmud [27] advises that a mourner react in the following manner to those who greet him: "On the first and second day of mourning he should say to them, 'I am a mourner.' On the third day, he may return their greeting in hushed tones, but in no case should he greet anyone first." [28]

Why is it permissible for a mourner to be greeted and to respond to a greeting on the Sabbath?

As far back as biblical times, the prophet Isaiah (58:13) characterized the Sabbath as "a day of delight." Therefore, although the Sabbath is counted as one of the seven Shiva days, public mourning observances are discontinued on that day. On Sabbaths (and on holidays, which are also days of delight) a mourner dresses up, attends synagogue, and carries on somewhat normally by greeting people and returning their greetings. At nightfall, full mourning is resumed. [29]

What are phrases such as *alav ha-shalom* and *zichrono li-veracha* often used when mentioning the name of the deceased?

When mentioning the name of the dead, as a sign of respect many people add the words *alav ha-shalom* ("May he rest in peace") or *aleha ha-shalom* ("May she rest in peace"). For a learned person or a righteous person, the phrase *zichrono li-veracha* ("May his memory be a blessing") is appended for a male, and *zichrona li-veracha* ("May her memory be a blessing") for a female.

For persons who have led saintly lives, the expression *zecher tzadik li-veracha* ("May the memory of the righteous one be a blessing") is popularly used when the name of the deceased is mentioned.

Why are the words "until one-hundred-twenty" often spoken in a house of mourning?

The Bible (Deuteronomy 34:7) says that when Moses died, "his eyes had not dimmed and his vigor had not diminished." And he had reached the ripe old age of 120! This had led to the popular Yiddish expression *Biz hundert und tsvansig,* "May you live to 120," which is often uttered in a house of mourning when visitors speak of the living. The phrase is also used among nonmourners to wish someone long life.

Among the great leaders of Israel who lived to age one-hundred-twenty, mentioned most often are Hillel, Rabbi Yochanan ben Zakai, Rabbi Akiva, and Yehuda Hanasi.

Why do many people refrain from asking a mourner to be seated?

There is an old superstition, still observed by many, that when being paid a condolence call, the mourner rises to greet the visitor and the visitor must never say to the mourner, "Sit down." To do so, goes the superstition, would be "opening one's mouth to Satan," for it might be construed as saying to the mourner, "Sit down and may your misery continue." To give Satan the opportunity to open his mouth would be inviting him to cast an evil spell.[30]

Why is the Mishna sometimes studied by visitors to a house of mourning?

During the Shiva period, with the exception of certain subjects, mourners are prohibited from participating in the pleasurable activity of studying Torah. But according to tradition it is helpful to the soul of the departed if Mishna, the first part of the Talmud, is studied in a house of mourning by those who come to pay their respects. Mishna study is usually conducted in the late afternoon, between the afternoon service (Mincha) and the evening service (Maariv). Studying is done aloud so that the mourners can hear the words, although they do not actively participate in any of the discussion.

This custom is said to have originated in sixteenth-century Safed, when the prominent scholar Rabbi Isaac Luria, better known as the Ari, called attention to the fact that the words Mishna and neshama (meaning "soul") consist of the same Hebrew letters. He concluded that studying Mishna in a house of mourning is helpful to the soul in reaching its heavenly destination.

While any of the Six Orders of the Mishna may be studied, two chapters from the order Tohorot are generally selected—specifically Chapter 24 of the tractate Kelim and Chapter 7 of Mikvaot.

CHAPTER 9

The Post-Shiva Period

Introduction

The Rabbis of the Talmud prescribed that following the week of Shiva three more weeks be set aside as a time during which the mourner can learn to adjust to the loss experienced. They saw this period as crucial to the mourners' making a successful reentry into daily life. The one-week period of Shiva plus the three-week mourning period that follows it is known as *Sheloshim,* meaning "thirty." The full thirty-day period of mourning commences on the day the deceased is buried and concludes following the morning prayer service on the thirtieth day after burial. For individuals mourning relatives other than parents, the period of formal mourning concludes at this point.

Those mourning the death of a parent are obliged to observe many of the mourning rites for *yud bet chodesh,* "twelve full Jewish calendar months," although the recitation of the Kaddish prayer ends after eleven months. The twelve-month mourning period begins on the first day of Shiva and ends twelve months later on the anniversary of the date of death.

As will become evident in this chapter, many authorities are relatively lenient in their interpretation of Jewish law with regard to post-Shiva mourning rites. This is in keeping with the well-established principle that in matters of mourning one should be less demanding whenever possible. Thus, for example, the Rabbis ruled that a man mourning a parent does not have to allow his hair or beard to grow for a full twelve months, nor must he refrain from wearing laundered or new clothes for that length of time.

Taking societal attitudes into consideration and being concerned that the mourner would appear unkempt, the Rabbis ruled that once thirty days have passed, a mourner for a parent may wear laundered clothes or even new clothes if someone else dons them for just a short while, thus technically rendering them used.[1] Some authorities have also expressed leniency with regard to listening to music or watching television programs during the post-Shiva mourning period. In formulating the laws of the post-Shiva period, rabbinic intent has always been to provide adequate time for the expression of grief without overburdening the bereaved.

Summary of Traditional Post-Shiva Observances

THE SHELOSHIM PERIOD

Thirty Days vs. Twelve Months
- Mourning for all relatives except parents continues for three weeks after Shiva, until thirty days have passed from the day of burial. This thirty-day mourning period is called *Sheloshim,* meaning "thirty." Mourning for parents extends for twelve months. This period of time is called *Yud Bet Chodesh,* meaning "twelve months."

Kaddish during Sheloshim
- Kaddish recitation for all relatives except parents concludes at the end of Sheloshim. Kaddish for parents is recited for eleven months.

Minors who come of age

- A minor who becomes Bar or Bat Mitzva during Sheloshim, even though considered an adult, is not bound by the Sheloshim restrictions that apply to other adults. Not all authorities agree, however. Some say that the child should observe Sheloshim along with the other mourners.

- A parent in mourning may prepare the festivities of a Bar or Bat Mitzva once Shiva is over.

Religious celebrations

- During the three weeks of Sheloshim that follow Shiva, all mourners may attend religious celebrations, such as a *Brit, Pidyon Ha-ben,* a Bar or Bat Mitzva, and a wedding.

Leading a religious service

- A mourner during Sheloshim should be given the opportunity to lead the synagogue service. Those in mourning for parents are given preference over those mourning other relatives.

Attending social functions

- During Sheloshim, mourners should not attend purely joyous social functions.

Clothing

- One should not buy or wear expensive clothing during Sheloshim.

- Garments rent for relatives other than parents may be basted after Shiva and fully mended after Sheloshim. Garments rent for parents may never be fully mended. However, after Sheloshim the garments may be basted and worn again.

When Sheloshim is cancelled

- A festival (Passover, Shavuot, Rosh Hashana, Yom Kippur, and Sukkot) cancel Sheloshim observance if

Shiva had already ended before the onset of the holiday.

- If Yom Kippur occurs in the midst of the Shiva period, Yom Kippur cancels Shiva and Sukkot cancels Sheloshim.

Weddings during Sheloshim

- If a wedding had been scheduled and a death occurs that obligates the bride or groom to sit Shiva, the wedding is postponed until after Sheloshim. An exception is made if a great financial loss will be incurred by cancelling the wedding, in which case the wedding may be held after the Shiva period.
- A mourner for a relative other than a parent may escort the bride and groom down the aisle at a marriage ceremony during the three weeks of Sheloshim. One in mourning for a parent may do so only after Sheloshim.

Second marriages

- A widow must wait three months before remarrying. A widower must wait until the three Pilgrim Festivals have passed.
- If a widower has not yet fathered children, or if he has small children from his previous marriage who require care, he may marry immediately after Shiva.

Synagogue seating

- When attending synagogue during the remaining weeks of Sheloshim following Shiva, most authorities suggest that the mourner not occupy his usual seat. Some say that the new seat should be six feet distant from the old one; others suggest that the mourner need only move to the seat next to his usual one. Those mourning parents change seats for a full year. The rabbi of a synagogue is not required to change his seat. Every community has its own customs.

Entertainment
- Traditionally, mourners may not attend or listen to entertainment programs on stage, screen, radio, or television during Sheloshim. Some authorities are more lenient in this matter.

Personal grooming
- Luxurious bathing is prohibited during Sheloshim.
- Cutting nails with clippers or scissors is forbidden during Sheloshim.
- Traditionally, those mourning a relative other than a parent may trim their hair and shave only after Sheloshim has ended. Those in mourning for a parent may not cut their hair or shave after Sheloshim until such time as they are criticized for being unkempt. Current popular practice is for everyone to shave after Shiva.
- Unmarried women may not use eye-shadow, face-powder, and other makeup during Sheloshim, but married women may use cosmetics of all kinds after Shiva.

THE TWELVE-MONTH (YUD BET CHODESH) PERIOD

To whom it applies
- Whereas mourning for relatives other than parents ends after thirty days, mourning for parents extends for a full twelve months, although Kaddish is recited for only eleven months.
- A child who has lost a parent and becomes a Bar or Bat Mitzva during the twelve-month mourning period following burial is bound by all the year-long restrictions.

Kaddish

- For parents, one recites Kaddish for eleven months, beginning with the day of burial. This rule applies to leap years as well as ordinary years. Some authorities say that Kaddish should be recited for eleven months less one day.
- Traditionally, the primary obligation to say Kaddish rests upon sons, but women may do so if they wish.

Personal attire

- Traditionally, those in mourning for a parent do not change into new or laundered clothing until the advent of a major holiday or until reprimanded by friends for being unkempt.

Social gatherings

- A mourner for a parent may not arrange dinner parties or social gatherings during the year-long mourning period. However, the mourner may accept invitations to the homes of friends on holidays.
- The mourner may join in group activity if the primary purpose is business rather than pleasure.

Entertainment

- While mourners for parents are traditionally forbidden to attend a musical performance or play a musical instrument for twelve months, a more lenient ruling permits listening to appropriate mood music. Listening to and viewing informational programs on radio and television have also been ruled permissible.

End of Yud Bet Chodesh

- The twelve-month mourning period for parents is counted from the date of death and concludes at the end of twelve full Hebrew months. If a death occurred on the first day of Adar, the mourning period ends at the end of the first day of Adar one year later. The principle of part of a day counts for a full day does not apply here.

- In a leap year, when there is a thirteenth Hebrew month in the Jewish calendar, mourning ends after twelve full months.

Why were a thirty-day and a twelve-month mourning period introduced?

Although the first seven days of mourning—the Shiva period—are considered the most agonizing and traumatic for the mourner, the grieving process does not end abruptly after seven days. For this reason, and also so that mourning should not be carried on indefinitely, the Rabbis imposed two formal mourning periods in addition to Shiva.

The first, known as *Sheloshim* (Hebrew for "thirty"), is based on a statement in the Bible (Deuteronomy 34:8): "And the Israelites mourned Moses in the steppes of Moab for thirty days." This Sheloshim period begins immediately after burial, which is the first day of Shiva, and concludes after the morning prayers thirty days later. Once Shiva ends, many of the mourning restrictions that apply to the first seven days are lifted. For the remainder of the first month, the mourner may resume a more or less normal lifestyle. After the Sheloshim period, those mourning the loss of a relative other than a parent may carry on in their customary fashion.

Those mourning the death of a parent continue to be bound by restrictions for twelve Jewish calendar months *(yud bet chodesh)*. Given the trauma experienced when a child loses a parent, the Rabbis felt that this amount of time is necessary for recuperation.

Unlike the Shiva and Sheloshim periods, which commence on the day of burial, the twelve-month period is counted from the date of death and extends through the first anniversary of that date. Thus, for one who died on the first day of Nissan, the twelve-month period ends at the end of the first of Nissan one year later.

When a death occurs in a Hebrew leap year, a year with thirteen months, containing an Adar II in addition to Adar I, the twelve-month mourning period is considered complete at the end of Adar I, after twelve months have elapsed from the date of death.

Why does the Sheloshim period end early in the morning on the thirtieth day after burial?

Just as the Shiva mourning period ends after mourning *Shacharit* services on the seventh day after the burial, so does the Sheloshim period end after morning services on the thirtieth day after burial. In Jewish law, part of a day is the equivalent of a full day.[2]

Why is Sheloshim observed for less than thirty days if Passover falls during the Shiva period?

As stated in Chapter Seven, page 161, if Passover falls at any point during the seven-day Shiva period, Shiva is abruptly cancelled and need not be resumed after the holiday. It is as if the mourners had sat Shiva for a full seven days. For the duration of the Passover holiday, which is a seven-day biblical holiday but which most Jews outside of Israel celebrate for eight days, mourning is not observed. The days of Passover, however, are counted as part of the thirty-day mourning period—seven in Israel and eight in the Diaspora. After the completion of Passover, the balance of Sheloshim is observed: sixteen more days in Israel,[3] and fifteen more days in the Diaspora. The intent is for the Sheloshim period to end thirty days after burial.

Reform Jews follow the Israeli practice of observing

Passover for seven days. See page 212 for further information.

Why, in connection with the observance of the thirty-day mourning period, is Shavuot considered to be a seven- or eight-day holiday?

In the Bible, Shavuot (Pentecost), which commemorates the giving of the Torah on Mount Sinai, is a one-day holiday, and it is celebrated as such in Israel today. In the Diaspora, except for Reform Jews who follow the biblical mandate, Shavuot is a two-day holiday.

As with Passover (see the previous answer), if Shavuot falls during the Shiva period, mourning restrictions are cancelled, although it is considered as if the mourners had sat Shiva for a full seven days.

With regard to calculating the number of days remaining in the thirty-day Sheloshim period, the Rabbis considered the Shavuot holiday to be comparable in length to Passover and Sukkot. Thus, in Israel, for the purposes of Sheloshim, Shavuot is considered to be a seven-day holiday.[4] The seven days of Shiva plus the days of Shavuot (a total of fourteen) are deducted from the thirty-day count, leaving sixteen more days to complete the Sheloshim period.

In the Diaspora, for the purposes of calculating Sheloshim, the two-day Shavuot holiday is reckoned as an eight-day festival. Thus, when the seven Shiva days are added to the eight days of holiday observance (a total of fifteen), there remain fifteen days to complete the thirty-day mourning period.

The reason offered for counting the Shavuot holiday as a seven- or eight-day festival is that, in Temple times, if one failed for some reason to offer the festival sacrifice on Shavuot, he could still bring a sacrifice within the next six days. Thus, the Rabbis thought of the holiday as being of seven-day duration. See page 212 for further information.

Why is the thirty-day Sheloshim period reduced to eight days when Sukkot falls during the Shiva period?

In the Bible, the festival of Sukkot, which commemorates the forty-year trek of the Israelites through the desert on the way to the Promised Land, is observed for seven days. (In Israel today, only the first day of the festival is observed as a full holiday, while in the Diaspora the first two days are observed as full holidays. The one-day holiday of Shemini Atzeret ("the eighth day of assembly") immediately follows Sukkot.

As with Passover and Shavuot, the other two Pilgrim Festivals, if Sukkot falls during the Shiva period, mourning restrictions are cancelled, but it is considered as if the mourners had sat Shiva for a full seven days. During the Sukkot holiday and the Shemini Atzeret holiday that follows it, mourning rites are not observed.

In calculating the number of days remaining in the Sheloshim period, the Shiva period is counted as seven days, Sukkot is counted as seven more, and Shemini Atzeret is counted as an additional seven. This makes for a total of twenty-one days that are deducted from the thirty-day Sheloshim period, leaving nine more days to complete Sheloshim. In the Diaspora, where Simchat Torah is observed immediately after Shemini Atzeret as a separate holiday (in Israel, Simchat Torah is celebrated as part of Shemini Atzeret), the above count is increased from twenty-one to twenty-two, leaving only eight days to complete the Sheloshim period.

The reason for counting Shemini Atzeret as a seven-day festival is that in the Talmud both Shemini Atzeret and Shavuot are referred to by the name *Atzeret,* meaning "assembly." And, since for the purpose of calculating days of mourning the Rabbis considered Shavuot to be a seven-day holiday (see the previous answer), so too is Shemini Atzeret considered to be a seven-day holiday for mourning purposes.

See page 212 for further information.

Why is the thirty-day mourning period abbreviated if Rosh Hashana or Yom Kippur falls during Shiva?

As with all major Jewish holidays, if Rosh Hashana falls at any point during the Shiva period, the balance of Shiva is cancelled. After Rosh Hashana is over, Shiva is resumed, but those mourning laws that apply to Sheloshim are observed. When the Day of Atonement arrives, all remaining Sheloshim observances are cancelled. The catharsis experienced by the mourner during the Yom Kippur fast day is considered to have contributed sufficiently to the healing process to allow the mourner to curtail the Sheloshim period.

If Yom Kippur falls during the Shiva period, the laws of Shiva are immediately cancelled. The restrictions that apply to the thirty-day Sheloshim period are observed from the end of Yom Kippur until the beginning of Sukkot five days later. At that point all Sheloshim restrictions are cancelled.[5]

See below for further information.

Why is the Sheloshim period sometimes cancelled after Shiva has been observed?

If Shiva has been completed and one of the biblical holidays of Passover, Shavuot, Rosh Hashana, Yom Kippur, and Sukkot fall at any point during the remaining days of Sheloshim, the Sheloshim period is completely cancelled by the holiday. The same reasoning that was applied by the Rabbis for cancelling the Shiva period when a holiday intrudes applies here. See page 161 for further information.

Why do many authorities today allow those mourning the death of a parent to cut their hair after Sheloshim?

The talmudic tractate Moed Katan[6] states that those mourning a relative other than a parent may trim their hair after thirty days from the date of burial.[7]

Although the eighth-century talmudic tractate Semachot (9:10) states that those in mourning for a parent wait for the approach of the next holiday (Passover, Shavuot, Rosh Hashana, or Sukkot) before cutting their hair, the sixteenth-century *Code of Jewish Law*[8] subscribes to an earlier view set forth in the Talmud.[9] The ruling there is that the mourner should wait until friends reprimand him for his unkempt appearance.

Today, most authorities consider it permissible for those mourning a parent to cut their hair after Sheloshim as soon as they begin to sense that their appearance is even the least bit disturbing to others.

With regard to facial hair, it was traditional for those mourning a parent to wait to be rebuked by friends for being unkempt. Today, however, many authorities are of the view[10] that shaving may be resumed immediately after the Shiva period. This is the accepted practice.

Why are those mourning the loss of a parent prohibited from changing clothing for an extended period of time?

The Rabbis recognized that those mourning the loss of a parent generally have a need to express grief for a longer time than those mourning other close relatives. They therefore ruled that such mourners may not change into new or laundered clothes until the advent of a major festival or until friends reprimand them for being unkempt.[11] In some cases, this period could extend for as long as six months, such as when a death occurs immediately after Sukkot, with the next holiday being Passover.

Later Rabbis were more lenient with regard to the changing of clothes, allowing the mourner to wear new clothing if it is first worn by someone else for even a few minutes, thus technically making it a used garment.

The above restrictions apply particularly to outer garments, those visible to the public. Garments that make direct contact with the skin may be changed at any time.

Why are those mourning relatives other than parents permitted to wear new or laundered clothing after Shiva?

While those mourning a parent may not wear new or laundered clothing until after Sheloshim, those mourning relatives other than parents may do so after Shiva—during the last three weeks of Sheloshim.[12] The Rabbis required less grieving time for siblings and other close family members, an attitude that is also reflected in the fact that the recitation of Kaddish for relatives other than parents is required for thirty days only.

Why do some mourners attend social events during Sheloshim?

The Talmud[13] says: "For all dead [other than a parent] one enters a house of rejoicing after thirty days, but for a father and mother [because the grieving is more intense] one may not enter such an establishment until after one year has passed."

This rule applies to purely social events where there is music and dancing, but does not apply to religious celebrations such as a circumcision or wedding ceremony. In fact, even those mourning parents may attend a religious celebration, such as a Bar Mitzva party, during the remainder of the Sheloshim period after Shiva has ended—so long as they do not participate in the merrymaking. Joining with those engaged in celebrating a religious ceremony is considered to be a religious duty *(mitzva)*.[14]

Those mourning relatives other than parents may participate in all social events after Sheloshim. However, those mourning parents must abstain from social activities, such as going to parties or restaurants, even where no music is played. Such mourners may, however, engage in social activities that are basically of a business nature or that are for the welfare of the community.[15]

Why do some authorities permit mourners to engage in pleasurable activities during the post-Shiva mourning periods?

The Rabbis of the Talmud[16] forbade all mourners from participating in activities during the Sheloshim period. Those mourning parents must refrain from doing so during the entire twelve-month mourning period. However, many modern Orthodox and Conservative rabbis have interpreted this ruling liberally based on their defintion of "pleasurable." For example, they distinguish between music listened to for sheer pleasure and more subdued mood music that induces contemplation and reflection. The former is considered unacceptable and the latter acceptable.

Rabbi Emanuel Rackman, an Orthodox authority, says: "There is no prohibition against the sound of music as such... [It is proper for mourners to listen to classical music] that induces a mood that the laws of mourning promote." The same principle, he says, applies to plays and movies: "The light, the gay, the humorous—these are to be avoided. However, a drama or film that would contribute to one's philosophical musing or meditation is precisely what the occasion demands."[17]

The stricter view prohibits the mourner from listening to all forms of instrumental music. However, playing a musical instrument is permitted if necessary for one's livelihood.[18]

Pleasurable activities engaged in for health enhancement, such as working out in a gym or participating in an outdoor sports activity, are generally permitted by more liberal authorities. Engaging in personal hobbies and cultural activities, such as visiting museums and libraries, are likewise considered within the bounds of propriety after Sheloshim for those mourning parents, and after Shiva for others. The prohibition against studying Torah and other pleasurable subject areas ends for all mourners once Shiva is over.

Why may a mourner sometimes get married immediately after Shiva?

Ordinarily, a mourner is not permitted to marry during the first thirty days of mourning,[19] but an exception is made if wedding preparations were made before the death occurred and a great financial loss might be suffered.[20]

Why must a widower wait for the passing of the three Pilgrim Festivals (Passover, Shavuot, and Sukkot) before remarrying?

The *Code of Jewish Law*[21] states that a man whose wife has died must wait for the three Pilgrim Festivals to pass before remarrying. The commentators on the *Code* point out that this period of waiting is necessary to allow time for the memory of the man's deceased wife to fade somewhat. Being required to celebrate three joyous festivals before remarrying helps soften the sorrow and improve the bereaved's state of mind.

This reasoning notwithstanding, the Rabbis ruled that a widower who has not yet fathered children, or who has young children in need of care, or who is himself in need of a homemaker may remarry immediately after Shiva,[22] without waiting for the passing of the three Pilgrim Festivals.

Why must a widow wait for three months after the death of her husband before remarrying?

A widow is permitted to remarry sooner than a widower (see the previous answer) because, in the opinion of the Rabbis, the unmarried lifestyle is much more difficult for a woman than for a man.

Generally speaking, a widow may remarry after three months because this is sufficient time to determine if she is pregnant. If the woman were to remarry earlier, the paternity of the child could be in doubt. However, under circumstances where it is definite that the woman is not pregnant, she may be granted permission to remarry immediately after the Shiva period.[23]

Why does a Priest (Kohen) in mourning for a parent refrain from pronouncing the Priestly Benediction?

A variety of customs govern the times when a Kohen is to appear to pronounce the Priestly Benediction (duchen), as recorded in the Book of Numbers (6:24-26). In some parts of Israel, mainly Bnei Brak and Jerusalem, the Priestly Benediction is pronounced every day; in other parts of Israel, only on the Sabbath and festivals. In some Ashkenazic communities of the Diaspora, the benediction is pronounced only on holidays; among some groups it is omitted if the holiday falls on a Sabbath. Sephardim *duchen* every Sabbath.

A Kohen in mourning for a parent may not recite the Priestly Benediction during the entire year of mourning. Rabbi Moses Isserles, the Ashkenazic commentator on Joseph Caro's sixteenth-century *Code of Jewish Law* explains that one must be in a joyous mood when bestowing a blessing, and a mourner for a parent is not in that frame of mind during the twelve-month mourning period.[24]

Why are some people under the impression that mourners should not visit a loved one's grave during the first year after burial?

Grave visits during the first year are considered psychologically undesirable. Mourners often experience unwarranted feelings of guilt after the death of a loved one, and to visit the grave too early might intensify those feelings.

However, Jewish law does not prohibit such visits. In fact, the sixteenth-century *Code of Jewish Law*[25] says that the grave of a scholar may be visited on the seventh and thirtieth day after burial. An authoritative book on mourning by the contemporary Rabbi Yekutiel Greenwald[26] emphasizes the point: "There is a widespread notion that we may not visit the grave of our departed until twelve months after a death, but that is not true." Dr. Michael Higger, a noted contemporary scholar,[27] reminds us that Jews living in Arabic lands used to follow the practice of visiting the cemetery each morning of the Shiva week.

Today, Sephardim often visit a grave immediately after Shiva or Sheloshim. Ashkenazim, however, generally wait until the thirty-day Sheloshim period is over, while others wait a full year.

As a general rule, most people wait until a tombstone has been erected before beginning regular grave visits.

CHAPTER 10

———✦———

Graves and Monuments

Introduction

Orthodox scientist and Judaic scholar Yeshayahu Leibowitz was once asked by an interviewer, "Where do you want to be buried?"

"While I'm living, no one buries me," he replied. "And when I die, I no longer exist. Therefore, when I die, it is not I being buried. My body is being buried, but that is not me. When I die, I am no longer I."

Leibowitz was then asked: "What about the fact that when we die we are placed in a grave? Doesn't that mean anything?"

"It means nothing," said the professor. "Even the grave of my deceased son, my dear, beloved son, is of no interest to me. I find no consolation for his loss, the pain never lessens. In the short time left me [Leibowitz was eighty-seven years old at the time of the interview], I shall continue to live with the tragedy. But his grave—that is not him. That is only the place harboring his body."[1]

Jewish law makes no requirement that the grave sites of loved ones be visited. However, most Jews visit graves regularly, hoping to rekindle loving moments that they shared with the deceased. While not all modern Jews accept the talmudic[2] sentiment that the purpose of visiting a grave is to invoke the spirit of the deceased so that it might intercede before God for the sake of the living, many do believe that by visiting the grave site they are able to sustain the feeling of closeness they once enjoyed with the departed.

This chapter is devoted to a discussion of those practices and customs that concern erecting a monument to the deceased, the proper inscriptions to be placed on the monument, the appropriate time to make grave visits, and the protocol to be followed when planning an unveiling.

Summary of Traditional Observances Relating to Graves and Monuments

Visiting graves
- Graves may be visited at any time. Some Sephardim visit graves even during the Shiva week.

Flowers on graves
- Some authorities prohibit decorating graves with flowers because it is an imitation of a Gentile practice, but this view is not shared by all authorities.

Erection of monuments
- It is not mandatory that a monument be erected, but it is traditional to do so.
- The monument should not be ostentatious.
- The monument may be erected at any time after the week of Shiva, although most people wait for a number of months to allow the earth to settle.

Unveiling
- It is not mandatory that an unveiling ceremony be held.
- The most popular practice is to hold an unveiling approximately one year after the date of interment.

Tombstone inscriptions
- The inscription on a tombstone should indicate the

Hebrew name of the deceased and the Hebrew date of death. Although some authorities object, the secular name and secular date of death may also be included.

- Ashkenazim inscribe the Hebrew name of the deceased and the Hebrew name of the deceased's father. Sephardim record the Hebrew name of the deceased's mother rather than that of the father.

Eulogies

- Since it is customary to deliver a eulogy at an unveiling, unveiling ceremonies should not be scheduled on days when eulogies are forbidden. These include Rosh Chodesh, the entire month of Nissan, Chanuka, the day after each of the Pilgrim Festivals *(Isru Chag),* the four days between Yom Kippur and Sukkot, Friday afternoon, and immediately before a festival.

Why is a tombstone erected over the grave of a deceased?

It is incumbent upon the heirs of the deceased to honor their loved one by erecting a monument in his or her memory.[3] According to scholars, the practice of erecting a monument over a grave dates back to biblical times. When Rachel died on the road to Bethlehem, Jacob "set up a pillar upon her grave" (Genesis 35:30).

Several other reasons are given for the custom of erecting a tombstone:

- The stone is considered a symbol of respect and affection for the deceased inasmuch as it helps keep the memory of the person alive.

One of the foremost authorities of the Middle Ages, Rabbi Solomon ben Adret of Barcelona, Spain (1235-

1310), was probably the most influential individual in establishing the custom of setting tombstones over graves as normative Jewish practice. He emphasized that doing so is a worthy way of honoring the dead.

- The tombstone marks the place of interment of a deceased so that visitors can locate the proper grave.

- The stone serves notice on Priests (Kohanim) that the site is a place of burial and that they must therefore not approach it. (Priests, according to biblical law, are rendered impure if they come in close proximity to the dead.)[4]

- The tombstone was once thought to help incarcerate the ghost of the deceased, which is anxious to leave the grave and seek out its enemies for revenge but is now unable to because of the weight of the stone.

While most Rabbis of the Talmud believed that it is proper and desirable to erect a monument over a grave,[5] there were those, such as the illustrious scholar Rabbi Simeon ben Gamaliel (second century C.E.), who felt that memorials of this type should not be erected for righteous and learned people.[6] "Righteous people are not in need of monuments," he said. "Their teachings are their monuments."

Why were footstones once considered inappropriate for use as monuments?

The question of whether it is proper to place a monument at the foot of a grave as well as at the head was first addressed early in the twentieth century by Rabbi Meir of Zhabaraz. He condemned the introduction of footstones because it represented a marked departure from what was customary until that time among traditional Jews and was therefore in violation of the rule that one should not change the customs of one's ancestors. Rabbi Meir also points out that because the head, which houses the brain, is the most important part of the anatomy, the tombstone should be placed near the head of the corpse rather than near its feet. That is why, when the body is prepared for burial (during the *tohora*), the head is the first part of the body to be washed.[7]

Why is it recommended that the tombstone selected be simple?

Elaborate headstones are considered to be ostentatious. Scholars urged that headstones be very simple as an expression of the equality of all people and to reinforce the words of the Book of Proverbs (22:2): "The rich and the poor meet together [in death]. The Lord is Maker of them all."

Why is a tombstone sometimes called a *tziyun*?

Ordinarily, a tombstone is called a *matzeva* in Hebrew, a term first used in the Book of Genesis (35:20). In later biblical times the word *tziyun,* meaning "sign," was used to designate a grave marker. In II Kings 23:17 King Josiah is said to have seen a *tziyun* over the grave of a prophet.[8] This term is rarely used today.

Why did the Rabbis of the Talmud call a monument by the name *nefesh*?

In rabbinic literature, in addition to the more common appellation *matzeva,* the tombstone placed on a grave is often called *nefesh*.[9] According to a widespread ancient Jewish belief, the soul (*nefesh* in Hebrew) hovers over the spot where a person is buried. This belief, promoted by the foremost Kabbalist of the sixteenth century, the Ari of Safed, suggests that the soul continually floats over the grave. To honor the soul and to give it a specific area within which to dwell, the grave is marked by erecting a tombstone over it.[10]

Why has there been objection to burying the dead in mausoleums?

Although the Rabbis of the Talmud were aware that Abraham was buried in Me'arat Ha-machpela (Genesis 23:9), a cave located in Hebron, they nonetheless ruled that it is a violation of Jewish law[11] for a corpse to be buried in hewn rock, which prevents it from making direct contact with the earth. It is known that the prominent rabbinic authority Isaac Elchanan Spektor (1817-96) permitted burial in a mausoleum, but only as temporary measure, until arrangements could be made for permanent burial in the ground.

The stone structures that are built over graves in Jewish cemeteries are not usually mausoleums in the accepted sense of the word. Most often these are erected after the deceased has already been buried in the earth. (See the next answer.) In Jewish law, burial in mausoleums is permitted only when a coffin placed in it is covered by earth.[12]

Why do we sometimes find a tentlike structure erected over the grave of an outstanding religious leader?

The burial place of a Jewish notable often became the locus of pilgrimages by his disciples. To mark the grave site as a place of special significance, a tentlike structure was usually erected over it.

The general term used to refer to the tentlike structure was *ohel,* meaning "tent." A more ornate, stone canopy was referred to as a *nefesh* (plural, *nefashot*), meaning "soul."[13]

The canopy is a symbol of royalty, and the practice of bestowing royal treatment upon leaders of great merit is quite old. The cemetery in Tiberias, Israel, has a very elaborate *ohel* for Moses Maimonides. It should be noted, however, that there was a desire on the part of some scholars to abolish the custom of erecting superstructures over graves because it smacked of ostentation and was an imitation of non-Jewish practice.

Why has there been strong objection to erecting an iron gate or railing around a grave?

The prominent nineteenth-century Hungarian authority Rabbi Jacob Tennenbaum (1832-97), when asked whether it is permissible to erect an iron gate around a grave, noted three objections to the practice. First, he said, it is an imitation of what non-Jews do. Second, it is disrespectful to the other dead in the cemetery whose graves are not so protected. Third, it is demeaning to poor families who are unable to afford such luxury. Tennenbaum concludes that in instances where there is no objection from the owners of nearby plots, a simple railing be erected.[14]

Another reason offered for the objection to iron railings or gates is that iron, as a symbol of war, has no place in a cemetery.

Why do most authorities suggest that the wording on a monument be concise?

Authorities are of the opinion that, in keeping with the principle that every aspect of burial ought to be simple, it is preferable that the words inscribed on a monument be minimal. It is essential only that the Hebrew name of the deceased (including the name of the deceased's father) and the Hebrew date of death appear on the face of the tombstone. Among Sephardim it is customary to inscribe the name of the deceased's mother on the tombstone as well.

Why do the tombstones of some famous pious Jews have no superlatives engraved upon them?

Over the centuries, some of the most illustrious scholars have left strict instructions that the inscriptions on their tombstones not contain any words of praise. Their works, they felt, should serve as their lasting memorial. Rabbi Akiva Eger (1761-1837), one of the foremost rabbinical authorities of his time, instructed that nothing but the words "Here lies buried Rabbi Akiba Eger" should appear on his tombstone.[15]

Yet, it was not unusual for elaborate inscriptions to appear on tombstones of important rabbis and scholars. The tombstone of an illustrious seventeenth-century Dutch rabbi, Manasseh ben Israel, for example, bears these words: "The rabbi did not die. His light is not yet extinguished. He lives in the heights. By his pen and the sweetness of his speech his remembrance will be eternal, like the days of the earth."[16]

Why do some Jews refrain from inscribing English dates on monuments?

Some authorities caution that it is improper to inscribe the Civil (secular) date of death on a monument and that only the Jewish (Hebrew) date may be used.[17] Use of the secular date, they maintain, is an acknowledgment of the birth of Jesus.

In 1992, the Supreme Court of Israel ruled that in addition to the Hebrew inscription a gravestone may be inscribed in any foreign language, with the dates of birth and death according to the secular calendar.

Why do two Hebrew letters usually appear on the top of tombstones?

Most tombstones with Hebrew inscriptions engraved upon them have the Hebrew letters *pay* and *nun* appearing at the very top. *Pay nun* are the first letters of the words *po nikbar* (the masculine form) or *po nikbera* (the feminine form), meaning "here is buried." These letters may also stand for *po nitman* or *po nitmena,* meaning "here is hidden."

Occasionally, the letters *pay tet* appear on tombstones. These two letters stand for *po tamun* (masculine) or *po temuna* (feminine), both of which also mean "here is hidden." *Po nitman (nitmena)* and *po tamun (temuna)* are considered a softer way of saying "here is buried."

Among Sephardim, it is common practice to place the letters *mem* and *kuf* on the gravestones of both males and females. The *mem* stands for *matzevet* and the *kuf* for *kevurat,* the phrase meaning "the tombstone of the burial place of [so and so]."[18]

Why do the Hebrew letters *tav, nun, tzadi, bet,* and *hay* often appear on monuments?

These five letters are the first letters of the Hebrew words *tehi nishmato (nishmata) tzerura bi-tzeror ha-cha'yim,* meaning "May his (her) soul be bound up in the bundle of life," signifying that not all life is over, that only life on earth has come to an end. The words imply a belief in the resurrection of the dead and a world-to-come, concepts held dearly by Jews throughout the ages and enunciated by Maimonides as the thirteenth of his Thirteen Articles of Faith.

The phrase has its origin in words first spoken by Abigail to David, who was in flight from King Saul. Abigail, who later marries David, assures him that his life is secure, that God will protect him. She says to David (I Samuel 25:29), "If anyone sets out to pursue you and seek your life, the life of my lord [David] will be bound up in the bundle of life in the care of the Lord."

Why do the letters SBAGDG appear on some tombstones?

Beginning in the seventeenth century, the epitaphs on the tombstones of many Spanish Jews included the abbreviation SBAGDG, which stands for *Sua bendita alma goze de gloria,* meaning "May his blessed soul enjoy glory." It was not until the nineteenth century that Ashkenazim permitted words in the vernacular to be inscribed on tombstones.[19]

Why does Jewish law prohibit engraving the human likeness on tombstones?

The adornment of tombstones with engravings of the human image is considered to be a violation of the Second Commandment (Exodus 20:4 and Deuteronomy 5:8): "You shall not make for yourself a sculptured image...." Although the practice is not common in Western countries, evidence of it can be seen in such places as Odessa, Ukraine, where the Jewish cemetery contains stone monuments with etchings of the human likeness. This practice is today being replicated in Brooklyn, New York, by recent immigrants, many of whom come from Ukraine.[20]

Although the placement of a photograph of the deceased on a tombstone is not prohibited per se in Jewish law, it is discouraged as being in poor taste and out of place in a cemetery.[21]

Why are some tombstones engraved with unusual designs and ornamentation?

From the seventeenth century onward, it became popular in many Jewish communities to engrave tombstones not only with floral decorations and baskets of fruit, but also with symbols representing the actual occupation of the deceased. A neckchain, for example, would be engraved on the tombstone of a jeweler, a parchment with a goosefeather on the tombstone of a scribe (sofer), a book or a row of books on the tombstone of a scholar or writer.

The tombstone of a Kohen (Priest) was usually engraved with two outstretched hands, representing the manner in which the Kohen holds his hands when pronouncing the Priestly Benediction during a religious service. And the monument of a Levite—one who served the Kohen during Temple times—would be decorated with a basin or ewer, vessels used in washing the Priest's hands before the Priestly Blessings were pronounced.

Occasionally, tombstones would have engravings symbolizing the name of the person. Thus, a lion might appear on the face of a monument of someone named Aryeh or Leib, a deer on that of someone named Tzvi or Hirsh, a fish on that of someone named Fischel, and a dove on the tombstone of someone named Yona (Jonah).

Why do some people refrain from reading inscriptions on tombstones?

Some Jews still abide by the widely held superstition with roots in talmudic literature that when visiting a cemetery, one should avoid reading inscriptions on tombstones. Reading tombstones, it is claimed, leads to memory loss.[22]

Why are tombstones usually erected about twelve months after death?

There is no prescribed time after burial when a monument must be erected, but most families wait for about one year before doing so. According to an old Jewish tradition, immediately after burial the soul of the deceased is confused and travels back and forth between the grave and the house where the deceased lived. As time passes, the soul's desire to be reunited with the body lessens, and after twelve months the hankering has diminished considerably, making it a good time to establish a permanent memorial on the grave site.

This belief notwithstanding, most authorities are of the opinion that a monument may be erected any time, even immediately after Shiva. The reason usually given for waiting for a whole year after death—especially for a parent, for whom Kaddish is said for a year (less one month)—is that there is no need before then to erect a tombstone to serve as as an additional reminder. In addition, arranging for the erection of a monument can be very painful, and the bereaved should be spared that discomfort for a considerable period of time.

A more practical reason for waiting a year before erecting a monument is to give the earth a chance to settle, so that the heavy tombstone will not sink into the ground.

Why is one to ignore the wishes of a deceased who requested that a tombstone not be erected over his grave?

There is a strong obligation upon family members to accord due respect to the deceased. Since one way of fulfilling this requirement is to erect a monument to the deceased, instructions requesting that a monument not be erected may be ignored. In cases where a deceased leaves instructions that a monument not be erected, families are advised to install a stone that is very simple and modest.[23]

Why is the dedication of a tombstone called an "unveiling"?

Prior to commencing the formal ceremony at which the tombstone is dedicated, a cloth is draped over the stone so as to conceal the words engraved on it. After the recitation of appropriate prayers and psalms by the rabbi or other leader of the service, a member of the family is given the honor of literally unveiling the monument, thus revealing it to the public for the first time.

Following the official unveiling of the stone, the rabbi or leader of the service reads aloud the inscription etched into it. The El Malay Rachamim prayer is then recited and a brief eulogy customarily given. If a minyan (religious quorum) is present, Kaddish is recited by the immediate family.

Why is a formal unveiling ceremony not a legal requirement?

Although monuments have been erected over graves for many centuries, the custom of conducting a special ceremony at which the tombstone is unveiled to friends and loved ones is relatively new. The practice was instituted toward the end of the nineteenth century both in England and the United States in order to formalize and dignify the erection of the monument. Whereas Americans refer to the ceremony as an "unveiling," the British call it a "tombstone consecration."

Although a formal ceremony does add dignity to the erection of a tombstone, there is no religious obligation under Jewish law to conduct one. Many families prefer to mark the occasion informally by reciting psalms and personalized prayers. It is unnecessary to have a rabbi officiate.

Why is an unveiling sometimes conducted more than once?

If a tombstone has been badly damaged and the family wishes to replace it, or if the family decides that it would like to erect a more presentable tombstone in place of an old one, it is considered proper to hold a second unveiling for the new stone.

Why are stones sometimes placed on monuments by those visiting graves?

The Talmud and later rabbinic writings are replete with references to the powers of the dead. The souls of the deceased were believed to be aware of everything that transpires here on earth, to be privy to all laudatory and derogatory remarks made about them, and to have the power to reward or punish, as they see fit. The only thing the souls of the dead lack is the power of speech.[24]

In order to bridge this absence of direct communication between the living and the dead, it became common practice, at the conclusion of a cemetery visit, to place one or more small stones on the cemetery marker as a way of reminding the dead that the living have not forgotten them. In some locales it became customary to leave grass instead of stones on the grave marker. In time, these gestures lost their original superstitious associations and simply became a way of showing respect to the dead. It also became a kind of "calling card" that serves as a reminder to the living that relatives or friends have come to visit.[25]

Reform Jews do not, as a rule, leave reminders on tombstones.[26]

Why are some communities more amenable than others to the practice of adorning graves with flowers?

During World War II, the chaplaincy committee of the National Jewish Welfare Board (representing Orthodox, Conservative, and Reform rabbis) ruled that on Memorial Day, as a way of honoring the dead, it is permissible to decorate military graves with flowers. The committee did, however, object to permanent plantings.

In Israel today, placing flowers on graves, particularly in military cemeteries, is more accepted than in the Diaspora. In fact, floral shops and stands are found near cemeteries in many parts of the country. Outside of Israel, traditional Jews generally do not encourage (and often do not permit) the adorning of graves with flowers, but they do permit the use of shrubbery. Liberal Jews in the Diaspora have no objection to the use of flowers on graves.

Sephardic practice varies from community to community.

Why do some Jews place the left hand on a loved one's tombstone during a cemetery visit?

When visiting the resting place of a loved one, some Jews today follow the old practice of laying the left hand on the tombstone—or on the grave itself—and uttering a fifteen-word Hebrew prophecy from the Book of Isaiah

(58:12), which translates as:

> Men from among you will rebuild ancient ruins,
>   You shall restore foundations laid long ago.
> And you shall be called "Repairer of Fallen
>   Walls, Restorer of Streets for Habitation."

The Rabbis associated Isaiah's prophecy and its promise of God's protective care with the later prophecy of Hosea in which Israel affirms its loyalty to God. Hosea, speaking in the name of God, says (2:21-22):

> I will betroth you to Me forever.
> I will betroth you to Me in righteousness, in
>   justice, in goodness and in mercy.
> And I will betroth you to Me in faithfulness.
> Then shall you know the Lord.

This prophecy of Hosea consists of exactly fifteen Hebrew words, just as the prophecy of Isaiah does. It is reasoned that since the words of Hosea are spoken whenever one wraps the *tefilin* straps around the left arm and hand (unless he is a lefthanded person), it is this hand that should touch the monument when reciting the words from Isaiah.

Why do Jews traditionally visit the cemetery before the High Holidays?

Visits to the cemetery during the month of Elul (the month preceding Tishri, the month of the High Holidays) are common. This tradition, which was introduced by Ashkenazim, was first noted in the writings of the Maharil, Rabbi Jacob ben Moses Ha-levi Mollin (1360-1427), the outstanding German authority on Jewish customs and ceremonies. The sixteenth-century Moses Isserles, in his notes to the *Code of Jewish Law*,[27] describes the practice of people coming to the cemeteries before the High Holidays to visit the grave sites of their loved ones.

This practice spread to all segments of the Jewish community and today it has become a traditional way for Jews to prepare spiritually for the Days of Awe.

Why do some people visit the graves of loved ones on fast days?

Visiting the cemetery on fast days in order to pray at the graves of loved ones and saintly persons is an old Jewish tradition.[28] It was believed that prayers recited at graveside would be more efficacious than prayers recited elsewhere, and that the dead would be more inclined to "intercede" for the living.

The concept of "merit of ancestors" (zechut avot) as a contributing factor to our salvation is underscored throughout Jewish literature. The Midrash[29] emphasizes this point in its comment on the verse in the Book of Psalms (80:9), "Thou didst pluck up a vine out of Egypt." The Rabbis comment:

> Just as a vine leans upon dead pieces of wood, so does living Israel lean upon the [dead] Patriarchs [Abraham, Isaac, and Jacob].

Why were frequent cemetery visits discouraged by the Rabbis?

The Rabbis of the Talmud[30] discouraged frequent visits to the graves of relatives because the living were in the habit of praying to their dead to intercede in their behalf. This was considered a sacrilegious act. In Judaism, unlike other religions, prayers are to be addressed to God alone, not to an intermediary.

To curb excessive cemetery visits, the Rabbis specified when it is proper to visit the grave of a deceased relative. The approved times include the month of Elul (which precedes the High Holidays), the days between Rosh Hashana and Yom Kippur, Tisha B'Av, and the anniversary of the loved one's date of death (Yahrzeit). Visits are also sanctioned at the conclusion of the Shiva and Sheloshim periods and at the end of the twelve-month mourning period.[31] Cemetery visits on the Sabbath and holidays (including the Intermediate Days of festivals, Rosh Chodesh, and Purim) are not permitted.

Despite the established tradition concerning frequent visits to graves of relatives, Rabbi Menachem Mendel Schneerson, the Lubavitcher *rebbe,* would spend at least two afternoons each week visiting the graves of his wife and his father-in-law, the previous Lubavitcher *rebbe,* at the Old Montefiore Cemetery, on Long Island, New York. After these visits, he would spend the balance of the day at work in a small enclosure adjacent to his predecessor's grave.[32]

Why is it prohibited to bring certain articles into a cemetery or to perform religious activities there?

Since the deceased can no longer carry out the religious commandments incumbent upon the living, Jewish law[33] insists that the living avoid carrying out their religious obligations in the presence of the deceased. Thus, because the dead can no longer pray or don *tefilin,* it is in violation of Jewish law to conduct a formal prayer service or wear phylacteries in a cemetery. Based on similar reasoning, because the dead can no longer enjoy physical pleasure, it is also generally prohibited to bring food into a cemetery.[34]

These prohibitions are based on the interpretation of a verse in Proverbs (17:5), "He who mocks the poor [*lo'eg le'rash* in Hebrew] blasphemes God." In Jewish literature a poor man is equated with a dead man. Hence, those lying in their graves are sometimes referred to as "the poor ones."

Why are there certain circumstances under which food and drink may be served in a cemetery?

When cemeteries were far from cities and a trip to the cemetery might occupy as much as one full day, it was considered proper to serve food to those who made the long trek. Serving food in the cemetery was done out of necessity rather than in a spirit of celebration.

Today, with travel time reduced considerably, many rabbinic authorities consider it inapproppriate for food or drink to be served at graveside after a funeral or unveiling. Some rabbis, however, still permit the practice—if the food is limited to wine, liquor, and cake. This, they argue, affords those present the opportunity to toast each other with the word *le-cha'yim,* "to life."

Why are some selections from the Book of Psalms particularly appropriate for recitation at the cemetery?

There is no formal prayer protocol when visiting the cemetery. However, an old tradition suggests that Psalms 16, 17, 33, 72, 91, 104, and 130 are most appropriate for mourners to recite when visiting the grave of a loved one, particularly at the end of Shiva, Sheloshim, and the twelve-month mourning period. These selections evoke healthy emotions that the mourner should be encouraged to experience. They express a renewal of faith in God as Master of the Universe, as One who champions the cause of the lonely and despondent, and as One who will assist and watch over all who have been crushed by personal tragedy.

Why is the Aleph Bet Psalm popularly recited by those making grave visitations?

After one or more of the psalms mentioned in the previous answer have been recited by the visitor to a grave, the visitor often then recites Psalm 119, the Aleph Bet Psalm. Psalm 119 is a paean expressing man's loyalty to the Torah and his acceptance of it as a source of salvation. It is the longest chapter in the Bible, consisting of twenty-two sections of eight verses each, a total of 176 verses. Each group of eight verses begins with a different letter of the Hebrew alphabet, starting with *aleph* and ending with *tav.*

Sephardim, in particular, make use of Psalm 119 to memorialize their dead. They select verses from this psalm so that, when put side by side, the first letter of each verse selected will spell out the name of their loved one.

Why do some people drop a clump of grass on a grave before leaving the cemetery?

Based upon the verse in the Book of Isaiah, "O let your dead revive! Let corpses arise! Awake and shout for joy, you who dwell in the earth!" (26:19), the custom developed of dropping a clod of grass on a grave when visiting a cemetery. The clump of earth with the grass attached is associated with the concepts of resurrection of the dead and renewal of life. See Chapter Five, page 114, for a more detailed discussion of the reasons behind this practice.

Why was it once customary for visitors to a cemetery to toss metal on the ground?

Eleazar ben Judah of Worms (1160-1238) was among the first to call attention to the custom of throwing pieces of metal, specifically iron, when visiting a cemetery. This was based on the superstition that metal objects keep evil spirits at bay. The superstition also manifested itself in the custom of placing a metal key to the synagogue under the pillow of a dying person. It is also the reason why pregnant women kept a knife with them when alone and why the knife of a *mohel* (one who performs ritual circumcision) was kept under the baby's pillow on the night before his circumcision.[35]

Why do people soliciting alms frequently appear at cemeteries?

The custom of giving charity when death strikes is of post-talmudic origin. Although neither the Bible nor the

Talmud refer to the practice specifically, the Talmud[36] interprets the verse in the Book of Proverbs (10:2 and 11:14), "Righteousness [tzedaka] delivers from death," to mean that giving "charity" eases the trauma of losing a loved one. Righteousness is equated with charity because the Hebrew word for righteousness, *tzedaka,* is also the Hebrew word for charity.

Thus, people at funerals and those visiting a cemetery at other times will often find the indigent soliciting alms and repeating the phrase *tzedaka tatzil mi-mavet,* "charity delivers from death."[37]

Why do some people wash their hands upon entering and leaving a cemetery?

Many Jews follow the tradition demanding that before entering a cemetery to recite prayers at the grave of a loved one, the hands should be washed so that the person will be in a state of purity. Based on the old folk-belief that evil spirits follow those who have visited a grave, and that water will wash away the demons, it is also common for people to wash the hands immediately upon leaving a cemetery.

Why do some Jews take a different route when returning home from a cemetery?

The tradition of visitors to the cemetery not returning home via the same route by which they came is based on an ancient superstition that demons and harmful spirits hover over the cemetery and also follow mourners when they leave the cemetery. By taking a different route, it was believed, the visitors can outwit the evil spirits.[38]

Why is indiscriminate disinterment contrary to Jewish law?

Jewish law, which views a disturbance of the deceased as *nivul ha-met,* "an offense to the dead," is strongly opposed to removing a body from its burial place.[39] Once buried, the body must be left undisturbed.

For this reason, authorities[40] caution that a body may not be disinterred simply to be reburied in a cemetery that is nearer to the homes of family members. It is evident that the motivation here is not to honor the dead *(kevod ha-met)* but to make grave visits easier for the living.

However, opposition to disinterment is not absolute. If it was understood at the outset that the burial was temporary, and that as soon as arrangements could be made the deceased would be transferred to a family plot or to Israel, such reinterment is permitted. (Burial in Israel's sacred soil has always been looked upon with favor by rabbinic authorities.) Similarly, if a Jew had been buried in a Christian cemetery, it is considered an honorable deed to remove the body of the deceased and to transfer it to a Jewish cemetery so that the body may rest in Jewish soil.

The custom among Spanish-Portuguese Jews is to announce at the time of burial that the interment taking place is conditional *(al tenai),* and should it be decided in the future to disinter the body, the action will not be in violation of Jewish law.

CHAPTER 11

Memorializing the Dead

Introduction

Ecclesiastes (1:4) put it succinctly: "One generation goes, and another comes, but the earth remains the same." The words of this biblical philosopher-preacher are only partially true. People go and people come and the world continues on its course, but the world does not remain the same for those who have seen loved ones pass on.

Two of the tools that Jewish tradition has proposed for dealing with the trauma of death are Yahrzeit and Yizkor. Yahrzeit, the anniversary of the date of death, and Yizkor, a synagogue memorial service held four times each year, are times for remembering. They tie the present to the past.

These rites, which are not mandated by law but have become a strong part of Jewish tradition, help us sustain the bond that we, the living, have shared with our parents and other loved ones. They afford us an opportunity to acknowledge the debt we owe our forebears for the values they have imparted to us and the legacy they have bequeathed us.

The concept of Yahrzeit was introduced in talmudic times, but its actual observance did not become common until the Middle Ages. Over the centuries, most Jews have come to think of Yahrzeit as a sad occasion, which historically it was, but some of the giants of Jewish history have viewed it otherwise—namely, as a day to applaud the past and express our fond remembrance of those who enriched our lives.

One outstanding figure who believed that the end of life should be celebrated rather than mourned was Rabbi Shimon bar Yochai, the charismatic second-century mystic and talmudic authority reputed to be the author of the *Zohar.* Rabbi Shimon left instructions that his death be memorialized joyfully. Consequently, his Yahrzeit date became known as *Yom hilula de-Rabbi Shimon bar Yochai,* "a day of celebrating the life of Rabbi Shimon bar Yochai." To this day, on Lag B'Omer, the day of his death, many of Rabbi Shimon's followers make a pilgrimage to his grave on the top of Mount Meron in the Galilee. There, they engage in study and joyfully celebrate his life.

Throughout Jewish history there have been many distinguished leaders who have expressed a similar view of the positive nature of Yahrzeit. A notable example is the writer Sholom Aleichem who, although not a mystic, requested in his will that on his Yahrzeit family members should assemble and read some of his more humorous stories.

The Yizkor memorial prayers were originally recited only on Yom Kippur, the Day of Atonement, when we pray for forgiveness for our sins. According to Rabbi Moses Isserles, the prime Ashkenazic commentator on the *Code of Jewish Law,* the reason why Yom Kippur was designated as the day on which Yizkor was to be recited is that the dead, like the living, are also in need of forgiveness.[1]

Isserles was reiterating an old rabbinic interpretation found much earlier in the Midrash. In commenting on the verse in the Book of Deuteronomy (21:8), "Forgive, O Lord, Thy people Israel whom Thou hast redeemed [from Egypt]," the Rabbis say that "Thy people" refers to the living, and "whom Thou hast redeemed" refers to the dead.[2]

But this approach was merely an attempt to give the

Yizkor service a biblical foundation. The facts of history point to a more mundane and practical origin. Scholars are pretty much in agreement that the recitation of Yizkor on Yom Kippur became a widespread practice after the First Crusade (1096 C.E.), when a zealous army of Christians marched uncontrolled through one European country after another, on their way to Palestine to free the Holy Sepulchre from the hands of unbelieving Arabs and Muslims. In their mad frenzy, the zealots rallied the faithful with the charge: "Why kill God's enemies in a distant land while Jews, equally opposed to Christianity, are close at hand!" And soon the chant reverberated everywhere: "Kill a Jew and save your soul!" As a result, thousands of Jews perished.

When the Crusades ended, European communities recorded the names of all the fallen Jews in a communal record book known as *Memorbuch*. In the years that followed, it became customary to read the names publicly during the synagogue service on Yom Kippur and the three Pilgrim Festivals.[3]

When we recite Yizkor today, we remember not only our own relatives and friends, but all Jews throughout the ages who lost their lives for no reason other than that they were Jews.

Summary of Observances Relating to Yahrzeit and Yizkor

YAHRZEIT

For whom Yahrzeit is observed
- The observance of Yahrzeit is particularly incumbent upon those who have lost parents. It is also customary to observe Yahrzeit for other relatives for whom one sits Shiva. Yahrzeit may be observed for grandparents

as well as for other relatives and friends.

- Observance of Yahrzeit for a minor or by a minor (under Bar/Bat Mitzva age) is optional.
- Yahrzeit may be observed for a deceased spouse if it will not offend the present spouse.
- Yahrzeit is observed for suicides.

When Yahrzeit is observed

- Yahrzeit is observed on the anniversary of the Hebrew date of death. If the interment took place more than three days after the date of death, the *first* Yahrzeit is observed on the date of burial. In subsequent years, Yahrzeit is observed on the date of death.

Duration of observance

- Yahrzeit is observed for a full twenty-four-hour period from twilight of the evening before until nightfall of the Yahrzeit date.

Neglecting to observe Yahrzeit

- If one forgot or was unable to observe Yahrzeit on the proper date, he or she may do so at a later date selected at random.

When date is unknown

- When the date of death or interment is unknown, mourners may select a date on which they will always observe Yahrzeit.

Leap years

- If a person died during the extra month, Adar II, that is added in leap years, in subsequent leap years the mourner observes Yahrzeit on the date of death in Adar II. In nonleap years, when there is no Adar II, the mourner observes Yahrzeit on that date in Adar I.

Yahrzeit light

- A candle or memorial lamp is kept burning for a full

day, from twilight the night before until nightfall of the actual Yahrzeit date. Electrified memorial lamps may be used.

- It is not proper for a remarried widower or widow to kindle a lamp in the presence of his or her new spouse.

Leading a prayer service

- A mourner observing Yahrzeit for a parent has preference in leading the synagogue service even over a mourner in the midst of the Sheloshim period.

Aliyot

- A person observing Yahrzeit for a parent is entitled to an *aliya* (Torah honor) on the day of Yahrzeit or on the day closest to it during the preceding week.

Yizkor

For whom Yizkor is recited

- Yizkor is recited for deceased parents and all other relatives for whom one sits Shiva. It may also be recited for other relatives and friends. Minors (under Bar/Bat Mitzva age) may recite Yizkor if they wish.
- Yizkor is recited for suicides.

Duration of observance

- The obligation to observe Yizkor continues throughout a person's life regardless of how long ago a relative has passed away.

Where Yizkor is observed

- One may recite Yizkor in the privacy of the home, since a religious quorum *(minyan)* need not be present when Yizkor is recited. However, in the synagogue a more formal service is held.
- Yizkor is conducted in Ashkenazic synagogues, but

rarely in Sephardic ones. In recent years some Sephardic congregations have introduced a modified form of Yizkor that is recited after the *Musaf* service.

When Yizkor is recited
- Yizkor is recited four times a year: on Yom Kippur, Shemini Atzeret (the holiday after Sukkot), the last day of Passover, and Shavuot. Some authorities are quite emphatic that Yizkor must be recited even before the year-long mourning period has ended, and even during the Shiva week. The common practice, however, is not to recite Yizkor during the first year after a death.

Leaving the synagogue
- Some synagogues encourage those who have not lost parents to leave the synagogue when Yizkor is being recited, but this is not a universal practice.

Memorial lights
- A memorial candle or lamp is lighted at home or in the synagogue on the eve of the day when Yizkor is recited and kept burning for twenty-four hours, until the end of the holiday.
- Electric memorial lamps may be used.

Why was the Yahrzeit observance introduced?

Although Yahrzeit is described in the Talmud[4] as a time for remembering parents, its observance did not become widespread until the eleventh and twelfth centuries, when the Crusaders rampaged through Germany and other countries of Europe to fulfill their mission of rescuing the Holy Sepulchre (burial vault) of Jesus from the hands of the Saracens (Arabs and Muslims). En route to the Promised Land, the Crusaders vented their anger on countless innocent Jews.

At first these Jewish martyrs were memorialized as a group by their respective communities, but later it was customary for family members to memorialize their loved ones individually on the anniversary of the date on which they were killed.

Today, Yahrzeit is set aside as a time for remembering each deceased individual, parents as well as other close relatives.

Why is the word *Yahrzeit* used to denote the anniversary of a death?

The Yiddish word *Yahrzeit*, derived from the German *Jahrzeit*, meaning "anniversary," was first used in the writings of the fourteenth-century German scholar Rabbi Jacob Mollin (Maharil) and his Austrian contemporary, Rabbi Isaac of Tyrnau, both of whom wrote books on Jewish customs and ceremonies.

Sephardim use the word *Nachala*, "inheritance," for Yahrzeit. The modern Hebrew term is *Yom Ha-shana*, "day of the year, anniversary."

Scholars point out that the German word *Jahrzeit* was similarly used in the Christian Church to denote an occasion of honoring the memory of the dead.[5]

Why is Yahrzeit generally observed on the anniversary of the date of death?

Unless there are extenuating circumstances (see the next question), Yahrzeit is observed on the anniversary of a person's death rather than on the anniversary of burial.

Aside from the fact that it is most fitting to observe Yahrzeit on the date on which the life of a loved one actually ended, it is also more practical to do so because often a burial is delayed due to a strike, inclement weather, and similar unforeseen happenings. In such a case, if the date of burial were to be designated as the Yahrzeit in the future there might be confusion as to the date on which Yahrzeit should be observed.

When we speak of the date of death as the date of Yahrzeit observance, it should be noted that in the Jewish calendar a day begins after dark on the evening before the actual date. Accordingly, Yahrzeit observance for a person who died on Monday during daylight hours begins with the Sunday evening *Maariv* service.

Why is Yahrzeit sometimes observed on the date of burial?

Although a majority of authorities say that Yahrzeit should be observed on the date of death,[6] there is a body of opinion which contends that in cases where a burial takes place three or more days after a death, the first Yahrzeit should be observed on the date of burial, and in subsequent years it should be observed on the date of death.[7] (See the previous answer for the probable reasoning behind this.)

Why is a Yahrzeit sometimes observed in a month other than the one in which the death occurred?

Normally, Yahrzeit is observed annually on the Hebrew date of death. An exception is when a death occurs on the thirtieth of Cheshvan or Kislev. These are the two months in the Jewish calendar when the number of days is not fixed. In some years they have twenty-nine days and, in others, thirty days.

The question arises as to when Yahrzeit should be observed if a death occurred on the thirtieth day of one of these months, when in the following year or years that month has only twenty-nine days. While there are differences of opinion, the prevailing view is that one should set as the permanent date of Yahrzeit the date on which

Yahrzeit is observed on the first anniversary of death.

Thus, if the first Yahrzeit fell in a year when Cheshvan or Kislev has only twenty-nine days, henceforth Yahrzeit should always be observed on the twenty-ninth of the month. If the first anniversary fell in a month that had thirty days and a subsequent year has only twenty-nine days, Yahrzeit should always be observed on Rosh Chodesh. (It should be noted that the thirtieth day of a month is always the first day of Rosh Chodesh of the month that follows.)[8]

If a person dies during the month of Adar, there are likewise instances when Yahrzeit might be observed in a month other than the one in which the death occurred. This relates to the fact that in the Jewish calendar ordinary years have twelve months and leap years thirteen. The twelfth month of the year is Adar, and the thirteenth month is called Adar II (Adar the Second in English, Adar Sheni in Hebrew). In leap years, Yahrzeit is always observed in Adar II regardless of whether the actual day of death was in Adar I or Adar II. If a death occurred in Adar II, and the year in which Yahrzeit is to be observed has only one Adar, Yahrzeit is observed in Adar I.

Why, if the date of death is unknown, should a later rather than an earlier Yahrzeit date be established?

If the family knows the precise month in which a loved one died but is not certain of the day of death, the last day of the Hebrew month in which the person died should be established as the day of Yahrzeit. Some have explained that by designating the last day of the month, it is as if the family is prolonging the lifespan of the deceased. However, to avoid the complications discussed in the previous answer, the thirtieth day of Cheshvan or Kislev should not be selected.

Why, when the precise dates of death of both parents are unknown, should one designate a different Yahrzeit date for each parent?

If one is not sure of the dates of death of one's parents, such as those who were Holocaust victims, a separate Yahrzeit date for each should be set so as to accord each proper respect. However, if one is absolutely sure that both parents died on the same day, Yahrzeit is observed for both simultaneously.

Why is it sometimes permissible to observe Yahrzeit after the actual Yahrzeit date has passed?

If one forgets to observe Yahrzeit on the official date, he may do so belatedly when reminded of the neglect. Since the observance of Yahrzeit is not a strict legal obligation that must be performed at a precise time, it is quite proper to do so even after the official date.

Persons who do not know the Hebrew date of death may observe Yahrzeit on the English date.

Why is it traditional for one observing Yahrzeit to lead the prayer service?

Mystics believe it is balm for the soul of the deceased when a relative acts as leader of a prayer service (shaliach tzibur) on the anniversary of a loved one's death. By acting as leader, the relative has an opportunity to recite not only the Mourners' Kaddish, but also the other forms of Kaddish that are part of the service. The soul of the deceased, the mystics say, delights in all this activity and soars blithely upward to find its place in the Garden of Eden.[9]

Why did it become customary for mourners to recite Kaddish when observing Yahrzeit?

In the Middle Ages, the custom arose in Germany and nearby countries to recite Kaddish for a parent on the day of Yahrzeit. Later, the practice was extended to include other relatives as well.

Hayyim Schauss, author of the classic *Lifetime of a Jew*,[10] points out that originally Spanish and Oriental Jews were opposed to the recitation of Kaddish on the Yahrzeit day because to them this implied that the deceased parent had remained in *gehinnom* (hell) for more than one year. (See page 135 for more on this theme.) Later, influenced by the great kabbalist Isaac Luria of Safed (the Ari), the opposition of Sephardim was overcome. They accepted the Ari's explanation that even the souls of the good and righteous, who are already in the Garden of Eden (paradise), are elevated to an even higher sphere when Kaddish is recited for them on the day of their Yahrzeit.

On the day of Yahrzeit, beginning with the evening *Maariv* prayers, Kaddish is recited by family members of the deceased at each of the three religious services of the day.[11]

Among Syrian Jews it is customary to observe Yahrzeit by reciting Kaddish for as many as seven days before the actual Yahrzeit date, always beginning on the preceding Friday night.[12]

Why, on the day of Yahrzeit, does the obligation to say Kaddish for a parent never terminate?

The eminent Sephardic rabbi Yosef Chayim of Baghdad (1835-1909) was asked whether a son must continue to say Kaddish for a parent even after twenty years have passed since the parent's death. True to his mystical approach, Rabbi Yosef Chayim responded that a son is obligated to say Kaddish regardless of how long ago the parent died. He explains that even after a soul enters paradise, it is not fully perfected, and the soul relishes all the spiritual help it can receive in order to be elevated to an even higher degree of perfection.[13]

The same ruling would apply to other relatives for whom one observes Yahrzeit.

Why do some people fast on the day of Yahrzeit?

The Talmud[14] makes reference to the practice of not eating meat or drinking wine on the day that a person's father or teacher died. Abstaining from these foods is tantamount to fasting because meat and wine were considered to be the basic elements of a good meal.

Based upon this talmudic reference, the Rabbis concluded that just as one fasts on the day of a father's or teacher's death, so should one fast on the *anniversary* of the death of a parent or any other close relative. This custom of abstaining from food and drink on the day one observes a Yahrzeit continued for many centuries, but never became law. It gained popularity only in the thirteenth century after it was recommended by Judah the Pious of Regensburg (died 1217).

By the sixteenth century, many authorities, particularly Rabbi Moses Isserles, whose notes to the *Code of Jewish Law* are an integral part of the text, were making a strong case for fasting on the day that one observes Yahrzeit, insisting that doing so encourages one to turn inward and to reflect upon the meaning and value of life. Such reflection, it was contended, will not only improve the quality of life of the mourner, but will redound to the merit of deceased relatives whose full acceptance in paradise will be speeded up.[15]

Fasting is forbidden on the Yahrzeit day if it falls on the Sabbath, on one of the major festivals, on the minor holidays of Chanuka and Purim, during the entire month of Nissan, on the days between Rosh Hashana and Yom Kippur, or on the day before Yom Kippur. As a general rule, on all days on which the *Tachanun* prayer (see page 180) is omitted from the morning *(Shacharit)* service, fasting is not permitted.[16]

Nowadays, fasting on the date of Yahrzeit is not widely practiced.

Why do people give charity on the anniversary of a death?

When observing Yahrzeit, it is recommended that one make a charitable contribution. This practice is an outgrowth of a medieval custom whereby those visiting a cemetery pledged charity (tzedaka) in memory of the deceased. The custom has its roots in the biblical verse "Righteousness [charitable acts] saves from death" (Proverbs 10:2 and 11:4).[17]

Why may an onen sometimes attend the synagogue to observe Yahrzeit?

On days—excluding the Sabbath—that fall between the time of death and the time of burial of a loved one, the onen, as the mourner is then called, is exempt from prayer and other religious obligations.

Authorities disagree as to the propriety of an onen's observing Yahrzeit on these days. However, if the Yahrzeit should fall on a Sabbath, when all forms of public mourning are suspended, all would agree that he may attend a public service to recite Kaddish.[18]

Why is it customary for an individual who is commemorating a Yahrzeit to be awarded an aliya?

Mystics consider receiving an aliya important on a Yahrzeit day because listening to the Torah reading is the equivalent of engaging in Torah study. And, they say, when a relative is studying Torah, the soul of the deceased, which is believed to float between the upper and lower regions, is elevated to its proper place in heaven. For this reason, many Jews read the Psalms and study Mishna on a Yahrzeit day.[19]

In traditional synagogues it is customary for one who

will be observing Yahrzeit during the coming week to be called to the Torah on the Sabbath (or Monday or Thursday) preceding the Yahrzeit day. In many synagogues, after the Torah reading has been completed, the *El Malay Rachamim* prayer is recited on behalf of those who are to observe the Yahrzeit on that day or during the week that follows. In some congregations the *El Malay* memorial prayer is recited during the Sabbath afternoon *(Mincha)* service in behalf of all who will be observing Yahrzeit during the ensuing week.

Why does the Yahrzeit observance for a male have higher priority than that for a female?

As discussed above, it is traditional for one observing Yahrzeit to be called to the Torah on the Sabbath preceding the Yahrzeit date, or on any other day of that week when the Torah is read. If there is no Bar or Bat Mitzvah that day, the person observing Yahrzeit is called for the special honor of *maftir.*

A question arises when two men have Yahrzeit on the same day, one for a father and the other for a mother. Who, then, is awarded *maftir?*

The consensus among authorities is that the person observing Yahrzeit for a father is to be awarded the *maftir,* while the other person is to be awarded one of the other *aliyot.* The Rabbis so ruled because men are obligated to fulfill more commandments *(mitzvot)* than women, and, therefore, a father is more deserving of the higher honor. (Women are not obligated to observe positive commandments that must be carried out at a specific time, such as donning *tefilin,* which is done during morning prayer.)

Why do Sephardim usually award the seventh or last Sabbath *aliya* to one observing a Yahrzeit?

It is customary in most Sephardic synagogues for the person observing Yahrzeit to be honored with the last mandated *aliya* of the day, which on a Sabbath is *shevi'i,* the seventh *aliya,* the *aliya* that precedes the *maftir.* If more than seven *aliyot* are awarded on a particular Sabbath, the person observing Yahrzeit is awarded the last *aliya* before the *maftir,* which Sephardim call *mashlim* (Ashkenazim call it *acharon*), meaning "completion [of the prescribed readings of the day]."

Before the *maftir* honoree is called to the Torah, the Half-Kaddish is recited. The honor of reciting the Half-Kaddish is bestowed upon the person who has been awarded *mashlim.*

If two Torah scrolls are read from on the same day, the person observing Yahrzeit is called for *maftir,* and the Half-Kaddish is recited after the reading from the second scroll.[20] In the Ashkenazic tradition, the Kaddish is recited after completing the reading from the first Torah scroll.

Why do some people observe Yahrzeit for grandparents?

In Jewish tradition grandparents are like parents, and they must be accorded the same degree of respect. Therefore, especially when the children of the deceased are both alive, grandchildren should assume the Yahrzeit responsibility.[21]

Why does a person who has remarried refrain from observing Yahrzeit for his or her deceased spouse?

Most authorities consider it improper for a man who remarried after the death of his first wife to observe Yahrzeit for her, to recite Kaddish for her, or to light a memorial candle for her in his home, lest his new wife be offended. Non-Orthodox Jews apply the same ruling to women who have remarried.

Some scholars permit the remarried spouse to observe the Yahrzeit ritual if it can be done inconspicuously.

Why do some authorities consider it proper to observe Yahrzeit for infants?

Jewish law does not consider a child less than one month of age to be a full-fledged person, and traditional Jews therefore do not observe Yahrzeit for an infant who lived less than thirty days. However, some authorities maintain that Yahrzeit should be observed. This is in keeping with the mystical belief that, like adults, children need the encouragement of the living as they journey after death toward their eternal resting place.[22]

Why do some people visit the graves of loved ones on the day of Yahrzeit?

The eleventh-century French scholar Rashi quotes earlier scholars to the effect that in talmudic times it was customary to observe the anniversary of death of illustrious persons.[23] Students and others would assemble at the grave of a respected scholar on the anniversary of his death to listen to a learned discourse.

In Jerusalem today, on Shavuot, which is thought to be the anniversary of the death of King David, some follow the old tradition of making a pilgrimage to the City of David, located at one of the entrances to the Old City.[24]

In time the custom of visiting the grave site on the anniversary of death was adopted by the public at large as a way of showing respect to their loved ones.

Why does a person observing Yahrzeit sometimes furnish refreshments following synagogue services?

Mystics believe that after death, year by year, the soul of the deceased is elevated to higher levels until it reaches its ultimate goal and stands in the presence of God.

Chasidim of the eighteenth century, particularly in Poland, built on this mystic belief and transformed the observance of Yahrzeit from an occasion of mourning to an opportunity to express joy and piety. They commemorated the anniversaries of death of their revered *rebbes* through song, dance, general rejoicing, and by serving cake and brandy. This chasidic tradition was adopted by Jews at large, and now it is commonplace for those observing Yahrzeit to sponsor a *Kiddush*—a light reception —following a synagogue service, at which time cakes, cookies, wine, and *shnapps* (liquor) are served.

Why do we light candles to memorialize the dead?

In Jewish tradition, the flickering flame of a candle, represents the spirit of God and the soul of man. King Solomon, in the Book of Proverbs (20:27), wrote,"The soul of man is the lamp of the Lord."

Despite the ancient roots of candlelighting, the use of a candle or memorial lamp in the observance of Yahrzeit (and Yizkor) did not take hold until late in the seventeenth century. Up until that time Jews were averse to lighting candles to memorialize the dead because this was a common Church practice.

Among some Sephardim, particularly Moroccans, it is customary to keep a memorial candle burning in one's home throughout the first year after the death of a loved one.

Why are Yahrzeit candles lighted on the night before the actual day of the anniversary of death?

The Yahrzeit candle must burn for a period of twenty-four hours. In the Jewish calendar, a day begins after dark on the day preceding it. The full twenty-four-hour Yahrzeit period therefore begins with nightfall on the day preceding the actual anniversary of death and concludes at twilight on the following day (the actual anniversary of death). Thus, a Yahrzeit to be commemorated on the fifteenth of Adar begins after sunset on the fourteenth of Adar, at which time the Yahrzeit candle is lighted.

Why do authorities recommend that individual Yahrzeit candles be lighted for two parents whose Yahrzeits fall on the same date?

Some authorities recommend that a Yahrzeit candle be lighted for each parent on the anniversary of his or her death, even if both parents died on the same day. Not to kindle a separate light for each parent, these scholars contend, would be disrespectful. Similarly, it is sometimes suggested that several siblings living together under one roof light individual candles for each parent.[25]

For relatives other than parents, authorities generally agree that it is not necessary for more than one memorial candle to be lighted in the same household.

Why do many authorities suggest that only wax candles or oil lamps be used as memorial lights?

Many authorities are of the opinion that memorial lights used for Yahrzeit must conform to the definition of the Hebrew word *ner*. *Ner*, which is translated as "candle" or "lamp," implies the presence of a flame produced by a wick and fuel (wax or oil). The flickering flame is a reminder of the lights that burned on the *menora* in the ancient Temples of Jerusalem. The light from an electric bulb would not fit the definition of *ner*.

Some authorities, however, do permit the use of electric memorial lamps. Rabbi Ovadya Yosef, former Sephardic Chief Rabbi of Israel, considers it quite proper to use an electric Yahrzeit lamp.[26]

For safety reasons, all authorities agree, it is permissible for the sick and elderly to memorialize their dead through the use of electric memorial lamps. Similarly, when necessary, electric candlesticks and candelabra may be used as a substitute for the customary Sabbath candles.[27]

Why was it once common for people to light Yahrzeit lamps in the synagogue rather than at home?

Up until the beginning of the twentieth century, it was quite common for Orthodox Jews to light Yahrzeit lamps in the synagogue. This was particularly helpful to persons for whom a Yahrzeit fell on one of the festivals, because those who were late in coming to the synagogue could still light their lamps by taking fire from a lamp that was already burning. (To strike a match on a holiday is forbidden, but to light a fire from an existing flame is permitted.)[28]

Those of a mystical bent believe that each year on the anniversary of death the soul is given permission to soar above the world, and when it approaches the synagogue where it had spent much time of its earthly existence, it is pleased to see a candle burning in its memory and thus to know that it has not been forgotten.

Today, most Jews light a Yahrzeit lamp at home, but many Sephardim still light one in the synagogue as well. On the eve of Yom Kippur, before Kol Nidre, members of traditional synagogues often light a Yahrzeit lamp in the synagogue rather than at home.

Nowadays, most synagogues set aside wall space on which small plaques memorializing their deceased members are affixed. Next to each plaque is an electric memorial bulb which is lighted whenever Yahrzeit or Yizkor is observed.

Why was Yizkor introduced into the synagogue service?

In one of the earliest commentaries on the Bible, the Midrash Tanchuma (composed in the fifth century, at about the time that the final editing of the Babylonian Talmud was begun), we find the first reference to the concept of Yizkor. The Midrash, in commenting on Deuteronomy 32:1, says: "It is the duty of the living to redeem the dead. Therefore, it is our custom to memorialize the dead on Yom Kippur."

The actual introduction of Yizkor as a formal part of the Yom Kippur service occurred in the eleventh or twelfth century when many thousands of Jews were murdered indiscriminately by the Crusaders as they made their way to the Holy Land in an attempt to wrest it from the Muslims. The Memorial Prayer (*Yizkor* in Hebrew) expressed the hope that the deceased would intervene before God and effect an amelioration of suffering.

The earliest reference to the formal Yizkor service is found in the eleventh-century *Machzor Vitry,* which was composed by Rabbi Simcha ben Samuel of Vitry, a pupil of Rashi.[29]

In Ashkenazic congregations today, the Yizkor service is held after the Torah reading, before the *Musaf* service begins. However, the Yizkor service never gained a foothold in the Sephardic service, probably because the countries in which most Sephardim lived were not affected by the Crusades.

Why is Yizkor recited on the Day of Atonement and on the three major festivals?

The early Rabbis believed that every individual, no matter how seemingly pious, sinned at some point during the course of his life. *"En mita b'li chet,"* they said. "There is no death without sin."

Because the Rabbis associated death with sin, and because Yom Kippur is the day of atonement for sins, it was considered an appropriate time to memorialize the dead. By reciting the Yizkor prayer for loved ones on this solemn day, it was believed that the souls of the dead would be aided in gaining entrance to paradise.[30]

In the course of time, the public felt that it would be appropriate to publicly remember their dead on more than just one occasion during the year, and Yizkor was therefore introduced as part of the service on the major holidays of Passover, Shavuot, and Shemini Atzeret.[31]

Why was there opposition to the introduction of Yizkor into the synagogue service?

The eminent Babylonian scholar Hai Gaon (939-1038) and his prominent disciple Nissim ben Jacob opposed the custom of praying for the dead on Yom Kippur and on festivals. They also opposed donating charity in memory of the dead, as the Yizkor prayer requires. These scholars believed that the only things important to God are the good deeds an individual actually performs during his lifetime. They felt that charitable acts by the descendants of the deceased cannot elevate the souls of the deceased.

The attitudes of Hai Gaon and his disciple did not find favor with the masses, who wanted to maintain strong links with their departed. The observance of Yizkor therefore grew in popularity.

Why is Yizkor recited on the last day, rather than the first day, of festivals?

Some scholars are of the opinion that memorial prayers are recited on the last day of the major festivals, so as not to detract from the joyous mood which these holidays were intended to engender.

A second reason for selecting the last day of festivals for the recitation of Yizkor is that they both mark endings: one, the end of a holiday; the other, the end of a life.

Why is Yizkor recited on Shemini Atzeret?

The Bible (Leviticus 23:36) calls the holiday that immediately follows the seven-day Sukkot holiday Shemini Atzeret, "the Eighth Day of Assembly." Because Shemini

Atzeret has been so named, it is often thought of as the eighth day of Sukkot, although in actuality it is an independent holiday. (The "eighth" simply refers to the eighth day after the beginning of the Sukkot holiday, and does not imply that it is the eighth day of Sukkot, since Sukkot is only a seven-day holiday.)[32]

Because the Rabbis of the Talmud thought of Shemini Atzeret as the conclusion of Sukkot, this day rather than the seventh and final day of Sukkot was selected for Yizkor recitation.

Why have Sephardic congregations introduced a Yizkor service in recent years?

Historically, Yizkor is alien to the Sephardic service. In recent years, some Sephardic congregations have introduced Yizkor in order to accommodate members who have Ashkenazic antecedents, but the Sephardic prayerbook does not include a Yizkor service. In Sephardic congregations that hold a memorial service, Yizkor is a supplementary service that follows *Musaf.*

Why may Yizkor be recited during the first year following the death of a person?

Although many Jews are under the impression that Yizkor may not be recited during the first year after a death, no such prohibition actually exists. Yizkor may be recited beginning with the first festival following the death of a loved one, even if that festival falls immediately after the Shiva period. Since Yizkor is a positive expression of faith in God and love for a departed relative, there is no valid reason for postponing its recitation for an entire year.

Why is it permissible to recite Yizkor at home?

Some prayers in the Jewish liturgy rank higher than others. In order for one to recite the words of the Kaddish, a *minyan* (quorum of ten) must be present because the prayer calls for an "Amen" response by a congregation. The Yizkor prayers do not call for such a response. They are very personal in nature and are recited silently. For this reason, if an individual cannot attend a synagogue service, he or she may recite Yizkor at home.

Why is one permitted to recite Yizkor in a language other than Hebrew?

In the past, many authorities insisted that Yizkor be recited only in Hebrew,[33] although they permitted women, whose knowledge of Hebrew was generally far less than that of men, to do so in the vernacular. Modern rabbis believe that prayers recited in the vernacular are also valid and that Yizkor may therefore be recited in any language.

Why do some people leave the synagogue when Yizkor is recited?

Although there is no requirement that one leave the synagogue during Yizkor, if worshippers are not memorializing a loved one, many authorities believe that they are tempting fate if they do not absent themselves when the memorial prayers are being recited. Consequently, in traditional synagogues, worshippers who still have their parents are urged to leave the synagogue during Yizkor.

Several reasons have been advanced for the institution of this practice. One is that the evil eye may bring harm to parents who are still living should their children stay in the synagogue while others are remembering their dead. A second reason is that if one has no need to recite Yizkor and remains silent while others nearby are reciting the memorial prayers, it might appear disrespectful. Third, those reciting Yizkor might feel envious of worshippers who have not lost a loved one and are therefore not reciting a Yizkor prayer.[34]

Why do some people believe that Yizkor need not be recited for children who have have not reached maturity?

In some communities it is customary not to recite Yizkor for boys who died before age thirteen or for girls who died before age twelve. This is based on the fact that a boy who has not yet become a Bar Mitzva or a girl who has not reached Bat Mitzva age is not obligated to assume religious obligations. Since one of the purposes of reciting Yizkor is to elevate the souls of the dead and negate their sinfulness on earth, it is argued that because a child who died before Bar or Bat Mitzva age was too young to be classified as a sinner, reciting Yizkor for him or her would be inappropriate.

The more common practice, however, is for parents to recite Yizkor for all deceased children who lived for at least thirty days, at which age an infant is considered viable in Jewish law. This stems from the belief that even the youngest of infants harbor remembrances gained in a previous life.[35]

Why is Yizkor recited for suicides?

Although a distinction is made between planned suicides and those done impulsively under great stress, the majority of rabbinical authorities today are of the opinion that it is an act of kindness to memorialize those who have taken their own lives.[36]

Why do authorities disagree as to whether it is proper to say Yizkor for a first spouse?

Some authorities have ruled that it is improper for a widow or widower who has remarried to recite Yizkor for a first spouse, lest the new spouse be offended. Most authorities, however, permit the recitation of Yizkor in such cases since the prayer is always recited silently, and it is unlikely that the current spouse would be aware of it and thus offended.[37]

Why may one recite Yizkor for loved ones other than relatives?

In Jewish tradition there is no objection to Yizkor being recited for persons other than family members. In fact, the Yizkor service includes prayers that may be recited for the dead of the whole household of Israel.

Why may Yizkor be recited by converts for their non-Jewish parents?

Basically, the Yizkor prayer is applicable to all parents who have gone to their eternal rest, whether Jewish or not. Since Jewish authorities are in agreement that converts to Judaism owe their non-Jewish parents the honor and respect called for in the Fifth Commandment (just as is expected of a Jew by birth), Yizkor and all other Jewish mourning and remembrance rites must be observed by converts for their natural parents.[38]

Why are candles kept burning during the days when Yizkor is observed?

The flame of a candle symbolizes the eternity of the soul. As is the practice in connection with the observance of Yahrzeit, it is customary to keep a candle or lamp burning for twenty-four hours on each of the four occasions when Yizkor is recited: Yom Kippur, Shemini Atzeret, Passover, and Shavuot.

Why do siblings living under the same roof sometimes light more than one memorial lamp for Yizkor?

Most authorities agree that when a number of siblings are members of one household, they need light only one Yizkor memorial lamp, while some believe that it would be more respectful and personally meaningful if each person were to light an individual memorial lamp.

Why is there no prescribed structure to the Yizkor service?

Since Yizkor became part of the prayer service much later than the rest of the synagogue liturgy, it does not have roots as deeply embedded in Jewish tradition. Therefore, the Yizkor service held in Ashkenazic congregations throughout the world on four occasions during the year does not follow a standard format. (As noted earlier, Sephardim traditionally do not observe Yizkor.)

Most Yizkor services open with a prayer that begins with the words *Adonai, ma adam va-tay-da'ayhu?* ("O Lord, what is man that Thou art mindful of him?"). This prayer, which consists of verses from the Book of Psalms and the Book of Ecclesiastes, is followed by a recitation of Psalm 91, which begins with the words *Yoshev be-se-ter Elyon* ("He who dwells in the shelter of the Most High"), a reference to loved ones being memorialized at the service.

Psalm 91 is followed by the silent recitation of personalized Yizkor prayers. Most prayerbooks contain prayers for a mother, father, husband, and wife, as well as a general memorial prayer for other female and male relatives and friends. In addition, to parents and spouses, relatives most often memorialized are sons, daughters, brothers, sisters, and grandparents.

The leader concludes the Yizkor service by chanting the *El Malay Rachamim* prayer for all the departed mentioned by those present at the memorial service. A second *El Malay Rachamim* prayer, added after World War II, is recited to memorialize the Six Million who were martyred during the Holocaust.

Orthodox congregations end the Yizkor service at this point. Conservative and Reform congregations often conclude the service with the recitation of Psalm 23 and the recitation of the Mourners' Kaddish in unison.

(See page 348 for Yizkor prayers that may be recited in the privacy of the home.)

Why, in some communities, is the matronymic rather than the patronymic form used when memorializing the dead?

When Ashkenazim recite the memorial prayer for a parent, the deceased is referred to as _____, the child of _____, first giving the deceased's name and then the deceased's father's name (for example, Yosef ben [son of] Yaakov or Dina bat [daughter of] Yaakov). Sephardim, however, use the matronymic rather than the patronymic form. Thus, for example, the deceased would be referred to as Yosef ben Rachel or Dina bat Leah, first giving the deceased's name and then giving the deceased's mother's name.

When a prayer for the recovery of an ill person is recited, both Ashkenazim and Sephardim employ the matronymic form only.

The source for the Sephardic practice is the *Zohar*,[39] where it is explained that the true identity of a person's mother is always certain, but the true identity of a person's father is not always known.

CHAPTER 12

The Afterlife

Introduction

Eschatology—the branch of theology that deals with death, resurrection, and immortality—has been of great interest to Jewish philosophers and scholars over the centuries. As we study the variety of views expressed about life in the hereafter, it becomes evident that it is impossible to integrate them into a whole and label them as *the* Jewish view. There are diverse, distinct beliefs about the nature of the soul, the meaning of resurrection, and the nature of existence after death.

In the Bible itself there are no clear-cut references to an afterlife. However, some students of the Bible chose to believe that She'ol, mentioned in Numbers 16:33 ("They [all Korach's people] went down alive into She'ol") is a reference to hell, or Hades, where the wicked received punishment for having rebelled against Moses. Other students of the Bible believe that the story describing Elijah's ascent to heaven in a chariot of fire (II Kings 2:11) constitutes proof of the existence of heaven as the place where the righteous are rewarded after death.

The most definitive allusion to an afterlife is found in the Book of Daniel, one of the later books of the Bible which was composed early in Second Temple times and which describes Jewish life, after the return to Palestine from the Babylonian Exile.

In Chapter 12 we read: "Many of those who sleep in the dust of the earth will awake, some to everlasting life, some to eternal life; others to reproaches, to everlasting abhorrence."

This is in sharp contrast to Job 14, where the author compares man to a flower that ceases to exist once its end has come:

> He [man] blossoms like a flower
>   and withers,
> He vanishes like a shadow,
>   and does not endure.

Toward the end of the Second Temple period, substantially different views of the existence and nature of an afterlife emerged.

The Sadducees, consisting of prominent aristocrats, priests, and other influential members of society, refused to accept interpretations linking biblical texts to the concept of an afterlife. They believed solely in the here and now. Reward and punishment, they believed, will be administered in this life, the only life we know.

By contrast, the Pharisees, the less affluent members of society, believed that the Bible is subject to interpretation. Even vague biblical allusions to a hereafter are to be taken seriously, and this fed their hope that a better life awaited them after earthly existence. The Pharisees embraced the concepts of resurrection of the dead, judgment day, and the coming of the Messiah, views expressed throughout the Talmud by the many Rabbis who were of the Pharisaic persuasion.

Later Rabbis expanded upon the Pharisaic belief in the afterlife, which they called the *olam ha-ba,* the "world-to-come." They explored the meaning of immortality, the nature of reward and punishment, and the advent of the Messiah and the Messianic Age.

No general consensus was reached, and the debate on the nature of an afterlife continues to this day. As Professor George Foot Moore of Harvard so aptly put it, "Any attempt to systematize the Jewish notions of the hereafter imposes upon them an order and consistency which does not exist in them."[1]

Why did the concept of an afterlife become an integral part of Jewish tradition?

The idea that man's earthly adventure does not terminate with his physical demise took on importance for Jews during the centuries following the Babylonian Exile (sixth century B.C.E.) and especially when the Second Temple was destroyed in 70 C.E. In order to endure under the degrading and oppressive conditions of the Babylonian captivity and to cope with prolonged suffering during the Roman occupation of Palestine, which led to the destruction of the Second Temple, the Jewish people were eager to accept the concept of an afterlife.

Why did some of the Rabbis of the Talmud characterize the present world as a vestibule leading to a future world?

In the talmudic tractate Ethics of the Fathers (4:16), Rabbi Jacob expressed an outlook on life that captured the imagination of many Jews: "This world is like a vestibule [prozdor] before the world-to-come [olam ha-ba]," he said. "Prepare yourself in the vestibule so that you may enter into the grand salon."

To encourage this hopeful outlook among Jews, the Rabbis of the Talmud set forth various scenarios about the beautiful, easy life that lay ahead for those who conduct themselves properly in this world. One vivid scenario describes the world-to-come as "not like this world. In this world, man [often] has trouble harvesting and crushing [grapes], but in the world-to-come a man will place one grape [which, as all other grapes, will, be huge] on a wagon or a ship, transfer it to a corner of his house, and use its contents to make enough wine to fill a large keg...."[2]

It is this type of world, which the Rabbis called *olam ha-emet* ("world of truth"), that was foreseen as awaiting man after life on earth.

Why did the concept of heaven and hell enter Jewish tradition?

The Bible and later Jewish literature concentrate on man's conduct on earth rather than on what awaits him in the world-to-come. The concept of heaven (also referred to as "paradise" or the "Garden of Eden") and hell (also referred to as hades; *gehinnom* in Hebrew; *gehenna* in Greek) as places where reward and punishment will be meted out is not directly mentioned in the Bible. Only after the destruction of the First Temple in 586 B.C.E. and the subsequent years of exile in Babylonia (later conquered by Persia), when Jews came under the strong influence of the Zoroastrian belief in an afterlife, did the idea of heaven and hell become the subject of serious discussion among Jews.

Although most prominent scholars throughout the ages have rejected the idea of a literal heaven and hell, others have expressed the belief that these are real places "created by God."[3] The illustrious Rabbi Yochanan ben Zakkai, the Talmud tells us,[4] wept before his death because he was not sure whether he was destined for paradise or for hell.[5]

While over the centuries there have been rabbis and scholars who have held fast to the concept of heaven and hell as an actual physical place, the vast majority take these terms figuratively.

Why did the term *Gan Eden* become synonymous with heaven?

The Garden of Eden (*Gan Eden* in Hebrew) mentioned in the second chapter of the Book of Genesis was a heavenly place on earth where Adam and Eve enjoyed luxurious living. It was quite natural, then, for the Rabbis to assign the name *Gan Eden* to the place where the righteous would go after death to enjoy their reward for having been virtuous while on earth.

In the Septuagint, the Greek translation of the Bible, the Hebrew term *Gan Eden* is translated as "paradise," a word derived from the Persian for "park" or "garden."

Why was it thought that *gehinnom* is the place to which sinners would be consigned?

Side by side with the view that the righteous would spend their afterlife in the Garden of Eden, it was commonly believed that those who did not live exemplary lives on earth would be consigned to hell, referred to in Hebrew as *gehinnom.*

The Books of Joshua (15:8), II Kings (23:10), and Jeremiah (7:31) refer to *gehinnom* as "the valley of the son of Hinnom," a place south of Jerusalem where children were sacrificed to the god Moloch. The accursed valley later became the burning place for all the city's refuse, which led to the word *gehinnom* becoming synonymous with all that is evil and sinful. Hel (Hell), the Old Norse goddess of the underworld, later became synonymous with *gehinnom.*[6]

Why did the leviathan become associated with paradise?

One of the most graphic descriptions of paradise is found in the Talmud. There, we find paradise pictured as a large banquet hall in which sumptuous meals are served, the main fare consisting of the fabulous mythical fish leviathan.[7]

According to legend, when God formed the world, He created a male and female leviathan. But they turned out to be so large that He feared they would have destroyed the whole world when they mated and bore offspring. God therefore emasculated the male and killed the female, preserving her flesh in brine so that it might be enjoyed in the hereafter.

Why did belief in the resurrection of the dead become a cardinal principle of Judaism?

Although belief in the resurrection of the dead (in Hebrew, *techiyat ha-metim*) first entered Jewish thought as early as the sixth century B.C.E. under the influence of the Persians who ruled Palestine, it took several centuries for the concept to take root among Jews.

In the Bible itself there are very few references to the resurrection of the dead. The most famous is the vision of the Prophet Ezekiel (37), which describes a valley of dry bones that will come to life again. The concept is also mentioned in the Book of Daniel (12:2):

> And many of those who that sleep in the dust of the earth shall awake, some to everlasting life, others to everlasting reproach and contempt. Then the knowledgeable shall shine like the brightness of the sky; those who lead the many to righteousness will be like the stars, forever and ever.

Not until the fourth century B.C.E., when the Greeks conquered Palestine and the influence of Plato and others began to be felt, did the doctrine of the resurrection emerge and become accepted by Jews. It was embraced and accepted by those who militantly opposed domination by the Syrian-Greeks in the second century B.C.E. Loss of life was so great during those battles that the survivors found it necessary to cling to a belief in a world-to-come where the righteous would be resurrected and rewarded.

At this point in Jewish history, the two major Jewish sects debated whether the doctrine of resurrection should be accepted as a basic article of Jewish faith. The Sadducees believed that only that which is explicitly commanded in the Bible should be accepted. Since belief in the resurrection of the dead is not specifically advocated in the Pentateuch, they denied the doctrine. The Pharisees, however, maintained that the words of the Torah are subject to interpretation, and they affirmed a belief in resurrection.

The Pharisaic view was adopted by the later Rabbis of the Talmud, who expressed their belief forcefully: "Anyone who denies acceptance of the doctrine of the resurrection of the dead as a Torah-based commandment excludes himself from the Jewish fold and will have no share in the world-to-come."[8]

Why is Abraham's purchase of a burial plot in Hebron, in the Land of Canaan, considered so important?

One of the earliest intimations that this world is but the precursor of a world-to-come is considered to be implicit in the story of Abraham's obsession with the idea of acquiring a family burial plot, the Me'arat (Cave) Hamachpela described in the Book of Genesis (23:3-20). Located in present-day Hebron, it is the burial place of the patriarchs and matriarchs (except for Rachel, who died on the road to Bethlehem and was buried there).

The acquisition of the Cave of Machpela as a permanent family resting place for Abraham and his descendants represented one link that would tie the Jewish people to the Holy Land, regardless of where they might reside. This connection was vital if revival of the dead in an afterlife was to be possible, for in Jewish tradition the resurrection can take place only in the Land of Israel. This association of the Land of Israel with the people of Israel and life eternal was well understood by Jacob, Abraham's grandson, for although he had already been settled in Egypt and had lived there for seventeen years, Jacob left instructions that upon his death he was to be taken to the Land of Israel (then known as Canaan) for burial.

Why was the view of Maimonides on resurrection considered revolutionary?

From the Maccabean period (second century B.C.E.) onward, the concept of heaven and hell was coupled with an evergrowing belief that not only does the soul survive death, but the body comes to life again and is reunited with the soul. One of the first to advance this idea was Gabicha ben Pasisa, the fourth-century B.C.E. spokesman of Palestinian Jewry during the reign of Alexander the Great. He said:

> If what never existed before now can exist, why cannot that which did once exist come to life again?[9]

Ben Pasisa's view of resurrection as a physical happening was the traditional Jewish view for many centuries.[10] However, later scholars—most notably the poet Yehuda Halevi (1075-1135) and the Spanish philosopher Moses Maimonides (1135-1204)—challenged it.

Maimonides' revolutionary idea of the nature of resurrection was first presented in his commentary on the first *mishna* of the tenth chapter of the tractate Sanhedrin, where he emphasizes that the concept of resurrection must be thought of as allegory and that the statements of the Rabbis regarding physical life in the hereafter must not be taken literally.

Therefore, says Maimonides, when one comes across a statement of the Rabbis that seems to conflict with reason, he must "surely understand that it is but a riddle or a parable." To illustrate the point, Maimonides reminds us of the oft-quoted comment of the Rabbis on the afterlife:[11]

> In the future world, there will be no eating, nor drinking, nor washing, nor anointing, nor marital intercourse, but the righteous will sit with their crowns on their heads enjoying the brilliance of the Divine presence.

To Maimonides, saying that the righteous will "sit with

their crowns on their heads" is but a dramatic way of affirming that the righteous will be rewarded by experiencing the heightened spiritual and intellectual pleasure of knowing and understanding God. Only the soul of man is capable of such experience; it is beyond the physical realm.[12]

Abraham Maimoni, the son of Maimonides, expanded upon his father's belief, noting that when philosophers speak of matter never being completely destroyed, they mean that it assumes new form. In like manner, he says, man's nature or spirit or soul is not propelled into oblivion when his body dies. It merely assumes new form, and that new form is pure intelligence. And, he adds, since we here on earth have no experience in such matters, it is difficult for us to grasp the concept of pure spirit or soul, totally independent of bodily form.[13]

Isaac Bashevis Singer (1904-1991), in his *Magician of Lublin,* declares through his hero, Yasha: "Only the body dies. The soul lives on. The body is like a garment. When a garment becomes soiled or threadbare, it is cast aside."

Today, the more liberal wings of Judaism (Reform, Reconstructionist, and part of the Conservative movement) do not believe in the physical resurrection of the dead, but do affirm the concept of immortality of the soul. The prayerbooks of these groups have been modified accordingly, and even those that have retained references to resurrection of the dead leave it to worshippers to apply their own interpretation and understanding of the concept.[14]

Why did some Rabbis believe that only the educated would enjoy immortality?

In the Talmud[15] Rabbi Elazar stated: "The ignorant will not be resurrected."

To scholars such as Maimonides this meant that for man to merit life in the hereafter he must nourish his soul in the here-and-now by serious and intensive study, for study leads to righteous living and righteous living leads to a healthy soul that will enjoy immortality.

The equation of study and learning with life in the hereafter was first suggested by Hillel the Great, who said: "An ignorant man cannot be truly pious."[16] And the idea was further emphasized by later Rabbis of the Talmud, who added:[17] "The righteous, even after death, are referred to as living."[18]

Why did our ancestors believe that the essence of a person is in his breath?

In biblical times and for centuries thereafter it was generally believed that a person was made of flesh *(basar)* and spirit or soul *(ruach)*. When God created man, the Bible (Genesis 2:7) says, "He [God] blew into his nostrils the breath of life, and he [man] became a living being." The seat of the soul is in man's breath.[19]

Elsewhere in Scripture, the soul is described as being located in the heart, the kidneys, the liver, and sometimes in the blood (Leviticus 17:11). But most often, the soul is associated with the breath of man. Once a person stops breathing, he is considered dead. His body becomes lifeless, at rest. In Exodus 31:17, the word for "[He] rested" is *va-yi-nafash,* the root of which is *nefesh,* meaning "soul." Of Rachel, the Bible (Genesis 35:18) says, "She breathed her last, for she was dying."

The Hebrew term *neshama,* which means "breath," is used interchangeably with *nefesh.* Such usage can be found in the Book of Joshua (11:11) and the Book of Psalms (150:6).

Why did the concept of Messiah become important in Jewish tradition?

Har Megiddo, "the Mountain of Megiddo," is a site in central Israel where decisive battles were fought in biblical times.[20]

In Jewish tradition, based upon a prophecy in Chapters 38 and 39 of the Book of Ezekiel, it is Har Megiddo (Armageddon in Greek) where a final, mammoth war will take place. The enemy will be Gog, ruler over the Land of Magog. His forces will be defeated and Israel's primacy will be established. The world stage will be set for the arrival of the Messiah (in Hebrew *Mashiach,* "Anointed One"), and he will prepare the world for an age of peace.

Belief in the coming of a Messiah is linked to the concept of resurrection of the dead. The term *gilgul mechilot* ("rolling through underground passages") is used to express the belief that when the Messiah comes, all the deserving Jewish dead in the Diaspora will roll through tunnels until they reach the Holy Land, where they will be resurrected.

Why was the prophet Elijah singled out to be the forerunner of the Messiah?

The charismatic prophet, Elijah, who burst upon the Jewish scene in the ninth century B.C.E. during the reign of King Ahab and Queen Jezebel, was said to be the forerunner of the Messiah because he, more than any other prophet, battled the pagan foes of Israel who sought to discredit God (I Kings 18:17ff.). For this reason Elijah became the "guardian angel" of the Jewish people. He insisted that Israel must not forsake God, so that the Covenant that was made between God and Abraham may endure.

In the Book of Malachi (3:1), the last of the prophets identified Elijah as "the messenger of the Covenant." Malachi prophesied that the Messianic Age would be heralded by a reappearance of Elijah: "Behold, I will, send you Elijah the Prophet before the coming of the great and awesome day of the Lord" (3:23).

The belief in Elijah as the forerunner of the Messiah has been kept alive over the centuries in the ritual of the Passover *seder.* Elijah is the expected guest in every Jewish home where a *seder* is held. Shortly after the meal, the outer door of the house is opened, and Elijah is greeted with a warm welcome.

According to tradition, one of the missions of the prophet Elijah is to protect every infant from danger. To symbolize Elijah's protective presence at the circumcision ceremony *(Brit)* of a Jewish boy, a chair reserved for the prophet is sometimes placed next to the seat reserved for the *sandek,* who holds the child during the ceremony.

Why is it believed that a *shofar* will be sounded to herald the coming of the Messiah?

Based upon the prophecy of Isaiah (27:13), "In that day a great horn shall be blown," it was commonly believed that a *shofar* (ram's horn) would be sounded to herald the coming of the Messiah.

Since the sounding of the *shofar* was a call to war, and since the final war (see the previous answers) was to be the prelude to the advent of the Messiah, the sounding of the ram's horn itself became identified with the Messiah's arrival. Some scholars contend that the loud blasts of the *shofar* will drive away evil spirits that might try to interfere with the mission of the Messiah.[21]

Where would this *shofar* come from? According to one legend, one of the two horns of the ram that Abraham used as a replacement for the sacrifice of Isaac was used as the *shofar* blown when the Torah was given to Israel at Sinai (Exodus 19:16,19). The other, somewhat larger horn was saved to herald the coming of the Messiah.[22]

Why are there conflicting views about the nature of the Messiah?

The word "Messiah" is used by some to refer to an actual person and by others to refer to a future time when a world of perfection will be established. The exact nature of the Messiah is not clarified in the Bible, the Talmud, or later rabbinic writings. In fact, these sources contain many vague and contradictory statements.

In the Bible, the Messiah idea is connected with the concept of the world-to-come *(olam ha-ba),* a time described by the prophets Isaiah (2:2-4) and Jeremiah (23:5-6; 30:3) as the "end of days." In the writings of these prophets the ideal condition of man is portrayed: God will redeem Israel and establish His kingship over all the earth. There will be no war and no want, no struggle and no strife. Righteousness will prevail and eternal peace and prosperity will be the lot of all good people, Jew and Gentile alike. Those who deny God—Jew and Gentile alike—will perish.

Beginning with the talmudic period (second century C.E.) there was a shift away from the concept of Messiah as a point in time to the concept of Messiah as an actual person who would proclaim himself or would be proclaimed by others to be the precursor of a golden age.

Maimonides speaks of the Messiah as both a person and an age. He refers to the person as King Messiah, *Melech Ha-mashiach,* a descendant of David, and he describes[23] the age as a time when a serene climate will exist. Jews will then be able to devote themselves undisturbed to the study of Torah in order to gain in wisdom and thus serve God better.

Today, many traditional Jews accept Maimonides' evaluation of the messianic concept. Less traditional Jews, however, tend to think of the Messiah only as an age in which perfect harmony will reign throughout the world.

Why did Rabbi Akiba hail Bar Kochba as the Messiah?

During the decades preceding and following the destruction of the Second Temple in 70 C.E., oppression of Jews by the Romans was intense, and every sign pointing toward redemption was cherished. In his *Antiquities,* which records the events of that period, the historian Josephus tells of the many people who came forward claiming to be the Messiah or suggesting the identity of the Messiah.

Bar Kochba, the Jewish general who in 132 C.E., during the reign of Hadrian, led an armed rebellion against the Romans, was one individual who proclaimed himself the Messiah. Rabbi Akiba accepted the general's claim, citing a verse in the Book of Numbers (24:17), "There shall come forth a star [kochav] out of [the house of] Jacob." This, he said, refers to Bar Kochba (also spelled Bar Kochva), who is destined to be the Messiah. Most of Akiba's colleagues ridiculed the idea. One of them, Rabbi Yochanan ben Torta, exclaimed, "Akiba, grass will grow from your cheeks [you will be long dead] and still the Messiah will not have come."[24]

Nevertheless, Akiba clung to his belief. He travelled from Palestine to distant Jewish communities in Babylonia, Egypt, North Africa, and Gaul in order to raise funds and rally support for the man he believed to be the Messiah. Akiba even permitted his thousands of students to join the army of Bar Kochba, most of whom were massacred by the Romans. In 135, at Betar, the rebellion against Rome was totally crushed, and Akiba abandoned his belief in Bar Kochba as the Messiah.

Why was it thought that the Messiah was destined to be a descendant of the family of David?

According to Jewish tradition, the Messiah will be a descendant of the House of David. In Jeremiah (23:5), the Messiah is called Mashiach ben David ("Anointed One, son of David") or Tzemach David ("Offshoot of David"). In the Book of Psalms (18:51), we find this identification once again: "He [God] gives deliverance to His king and shows kindness to His anointed [mashiach], to David, and to his seed forever."[25]

In his *Mishneh Torah*,[26] Maimonides says that the Messiah will restore the Davidic dynasty, will gather up the dispersed remnant of Jewry, will rebuild the Temple, and will reinstitute the sacrificial system. Anyone who does not believe this and does not look forward to its happening, says Maimonides, is a renegade (*kofer* in Hebrew), for he denies the truth of the Torah, which says, "And the Lord your God will restore your exiled people."

Why have Jews over the centuries fallen prey to the claims of false Messiahs?

There is a strong tradition noted in the Talmud[27] that the Messiah will appear only after the world has become engulfed in moral decay. The following are some of the striking views expressed by the Rabbis who lived during the years of oppressive Roman rule in Palestine:

- Rabbi Nehorai said: "The Messiah will appear in a generation when young men will insult old men, and old men will stand before the young [to show them honor]."
- Rabbi Nehemiah said: "The Messiah will appear in a generation when impudence is on the increase and no one will esteem a fellow man."
- Rabbi Isaac said: "The Messiah will appear when the world is converted to, and fully accepts, the belief of heretics."
- Rabbi Chanina said: "The son of David [the Messiah] will not come until [moral decay is so bad] that a fish needed for the cure of an invalid cannot be procured."

These sentiments of the Rabbis of talmudic times persisted throughout Jewish history, particularly in the Middle Ages, when Jewish communities regularly faced persecution. During these periods of crisis Jews often despaired and were thus vulnerable to the claims of charismatic individuals who promised them salvation. Thus, pseudo-Messiahs began to appear.

Among the more prominent of the false Messiahs were David Alroy, who appeared in Mesopotamia in 1147, and Abraham Abulafia, who was active in Sicily in the thirteenth century. In 1391, owing to persecution in Spain, Moses Botarel became a popular messianic figure. And following the expulsion of Jews from Spain in 1492, numerous pseudo-Messiahs surfaced, Shelomo Molcho (1500-1532) being the most famous. Best known and most charismatic of all false Messiahs was Shabbetai Zevi, of Smyrna, Turkey (1626-1676), who in the end converted to Islam. The most recent pseudo-Messiah was Loibele Prossnitz, who appeared in Yemen in 1889.

Why did the idea of reincarnation never take root in Jewish tradition?

The concept of transmigration of souls (in Hebrew, *gilgul neshamot* or *gilgul nefashot*), the doctrine which asserts that the soul reappears after death in another body —human or animal—was condemned by most Jewish authorities as heathen superstition. However, disciples of Rabbi Isaac Luria, the sixteenth-century Kabbalist of Safed, accepted it as a legitimate Jewish belief.[28]

READINGS FOR THE BEREAVED

PRECIOUS BEYOND PRICE

When Helen Hayes (1900–), the first lady of the American theater, lost her young child, Mary, she was inconsolable. Helen Hayes concealed her sorrow behind a facade of joy so that she might continue functioning. She felt, as did the author of the Book of Proverbs, that "the heart alone knows its bitterness, and no stranger can share its joy" (14:10). But that changed for Helen when she decided to open her heart to another grieving mother.

On each New Year's Eve the mail brings me a gift that is done up in ordinary brown paper, yet is precious to me beyond price. It is from Mr. and Mrs. Isaac Frantz of Brooklyn. To understand the value of this gift you must know something about the Frantzes.

They came into my life in 1949, just after my daughter, Mary, had died of polio and I was being tortured by the unanswerable question—Why? Mary had been so lovely and talented, so young and free from sin. Why had this happened to her? I could only feel that her death had been a cruel, senseless thing.

This was a self-destroying mood, for an artist needs the belief that life holds some beauty and meaning. I could not create beauty or meaning on the stage if there was none within me. So to save myself I began to search for God. I read St. Thomas Aquinas, explored the life and works of Ghandi, read the Bible. But the search failed. My daughter was dead! That brutal fact overwhelmed me, blinded my heart.

All during this time I accepted no professional or social engagements and saw only my family and most intimate friends. But, in this self-possessed isolation, I became aware that a Mr. Isaac Frantz was telephoning almost every day, trying to get through to me. My husband finally talked to him and reported: "He has just lost a little boy with polio and he seems to think it would help his wife if she could see you."

"Oh Charles—no! I have no strength to give her. I have barely enough for myself. I simply can't do it."

"Of course, darling. That's what I told him."

But Isaac Frantz kept telephoning and we finally agreed to let him bring his wife to our home.

I steeled myself for the ordeal.

When they arrived in their Sunday best, they were ill at ease, but they had a quiet dignity that surmounted their painful self-consciousness. Coming face to face with us was obviously something that demanded all their courage. Charles and I tried to put them at ease.

Now I discovered the truth about their visit. It had been the husband's idea entirely and he had arranged it without his wife's knowledge. But he was so sure that a meeting would bring some comfort to his wife that he forced himself to ask it. As for his wife, she was appalled when she heard of the completed arrangements, but knowing how difficult it had been for her husband, and how important to him, she consented to come. Each was doing this for the other—in the moment of great need.

The Frantzes owned a tiny stationery store and obviously had to struggle for the necessities of life. Charles and I had never known anything but success, fame, luxury. And yet the four of us suddenly had one thing to share, the tragic loss of our children.

Mrs. Frantz soon began talking about her son in a most natural manner, and, before I quite knew what was happening, I had plunged into a series of stories about Mary. Then a glance at Charles's surprised face made me realize that I was actually mentioning her name for the first time since her death. I had taken her memory out of hiding, and I felt better for it.

Then Mrs. Frantz told us of her plans to adopt an orphan from Israel, and for a moment I was shocked.

"You are thinking I am letting him take my little boy's place?" she asked gently, guessing my thoughts. "No one could ever do that. But in my heart there is still love and wisdom, too. Should I let these dry up and go to waste?"

"I–I don't know, Mrs. Frantz, "I said.

"No, my dear, we cannot die because our children die. I should not love less because the one I loved is gone— but more should I love because my heart knows the suffering of others."

While she talked, I thought about my child. Mary had been a big and wonderful part of my life. Even though that part had ended, I was a better human being for having had Mary, for having hoped and dreamed and worked for her. Tragic that it should have ended, but how much better than if it had never existed.

These were the things that Mrs. Frantz was saying, in her own way. These were the things that I now understood. Then I thought how ironic it was that I hadn't wanted Mrs. Frantz to come because I feared she would draw upon my feeble strength. It was I who drew upon hers!

When they finally rose to leave, I realized why my search for God had been fruitless. I had looked in the wrong places. He was not to be found between the covers of a book, but in the human heart.

We never met after that. Charles and I invited them back a couple of times, but they were always busy with their store and their new son. I think they understood that our worlds were meant to touch but briefly.

Every New Year's Eve since then I have received from them a box of candy wrapped in plain brown paper. Perhaps you can understand why it is so precious to me. For it was through these simple people that I learned humility, and God's pattern finally came clear. Now I know that when He afflicts the celebrated of the world, it is His way of saying, "None is privileged. In My eyes, all are equal."

DEATH AS A CELEBRATION OF LIFE

The eminent second-century mystic and scholar Rabbi Shimon bar Yochai instructed his disciples not to mourn on the anniversary of his death. That day, he said, should be celebrated with song and study. This positive attitude toward death was shared by other Rabbis of the Talmud. The Midrash (Ecclesiastes Rabba 7:4) relates the following.

When a person is born, all rejoice; when he dies, all weep. It should not be so. When a person is born, there should be no rejoicing over him, because it is not known how he will develop, whether righteous or wicked, good or bad. When he dies, however, there is cause for rejoicing if he departs with a good name and leaves the world in peace.

This may be compared to two oceangoing ships, one leaving the harbor, the other entering it. Everyone cheers the outgoing ship, but no one is exuberant over the incoming one.

One wise man witnessing the scene commented: "I see things differently. The opposite should be happening. There is no reason to cheer the passengers on the ship that is departing, for no one knows its fate; no one knows what storms or crises it will encounter. When it returns safely from its trip, that is the time for rejoicing."

"Similarly," continued the wise man, "when a person dies, all should rejoice and offer thanks that he has departed this world with a good name and in peace." That is what Solomon meant when he said, "Better is the day of death than the day of birth."

LIFE: A GIFT ON LOAN

Beruria bat Chanina ben Teradyon, the illustrious wife of Rabbi Meir, one of the prominent students of Rabbi Akiba, was highly respected for her talmudic learning. The story of Beruria's stoic and God-loving attitude is related in the *Yalkut Shimoni,* a thirteenth-century compilation of *midrashim.**

While Rabbi Meir was preaching in the synagogue one Sabbath afternoon, his wife Beruria was home with their two young sons, who were taking a Sabbath afternoon nap.

When Beruria went into the children's bedroom to awaken, she found them both dead. After recovering from the initial shock, she took a sheet and spread it over the lifeless bodies.

When the Sabbath was over and Rabbi Meir returned home after the evening synagogue service, he said to his wife, "Where are my boys?"

"They went to the synagogue," she replied.

"I didn't see them," said Meir.

Beruria didn't respond, but instead handed her husband a cup of wine so that he might recite the Sabbath night *Havdala* prayers to bring the Sabbath to an official close.

When he finished the *Havdala,* he turned to his wife and asked once again, "Where are my sons?"

"They'll be back soon," she answered. And then she brought him some food.

---

*This story appears in the midrashic commentary on the Book of Proverbs, section 964.

After Meir had finished eating, Beruria said to her husband, "I have a question for you, rabbi."

"Ask," he said.

"Rabbi," she began, "someone came to me recently and gave me an object to hold for him a while, and now he wants it back. Shall I return it to him?"

"Why, of course," he replied. "Anyone who has been given an object to be held in trust must return it when the owner asks for it."

She then took her husband by the hand and led him to the room where their sons lay. She removed the cover, and when Meir saw the lifeless bodies of his two children, he cried out bitterly: "O, my sons, my sons; my teachers, my teachers! They were my sons as all sons are sons to a father, but they were also my teachers, for they enlightened me with their knowledge of the Torah."

Beruria tried to console him: "Rabbi, did you not say that we are obligated to return a pledge to its rightful owner? And does it not say: 'The Lord gave, and the Lord has taken away?'"*

For easing her husband's grief, says the Rabbis, Beruria merited the appellation *eshet cha'yil,* "woman of valor." **

---

* Job 1:21.
**Proverbs 31:11.

A WOMAN OF VALOR
Proverbs 31:10-31
(Abbreviated)

A woman of valour, where is she to be found?
  Her value is far above rubies.
Her husband puts his trust in her,
  and he lacks nothing.
She is good to him, never disagreeable,
  all the days of her life.
She is like a merchant fleet,
  bringing food from afar.
She rises while it is still night,
  and provides food for her household.
She girds herself with strength,
  and performs her duties with vigor.
She gives generously to the poor,
  and stretches her hand out to the needy.
She is clothed with strength and splendor,
  and looks to the future hopefully.
Her mouth is full of wisdom,
  and the law of kindness is on her tongue.
She oversees the activities of her household,
  and never sits about idly.
Her children rise up and call her blessed;
  her husband sings her praises.
Many daughters have done valiantly,
  but you surpass them all.
Grace is deceptive;
Beauty is an illusion.
She fears the Lord,
  and is to be praised.
Extol the fruit of her hand,
  and let her works be praised in the gates.

A Daughter's Kaddish

In 1859, Benjamin Szold came to America from Hungary to assume the post of rabbi of Congregation Oheb Shalom in Baltimore, Maryland. In 1861, he was joined by his wife and one-year-old daughter, Henrietta, who in 1914 was to become the first president of Hadassah. Henrietta's father died in 1902, and, contrary to traditional Jewish practice, she and her sisters recited Kaddish for him. When Henrietta's mother died in 1916, Hayim Peretz, a close family friend offered to say Kaddish to honor her memory. This is Henrietta's Szold's reply, dated September 16, 1916.

It is impossible for me to find words in which to tell you how deeply I was touched by your offer to act as "Kaddish" for my dear mother. I cannot even thank you—it is something that goes beyond thanks. It is beautiful, what you have offered to do—I shall never forget it.

You will wonder, then, why I cannot accept your offer. Perhaps it would be best for me not to try to explain to you in writing, but to wait until I see you to tell you why it is so. I know well, and appreciate what you say about the Jewish custom; and Jewish custom is very dear and sacred to me. And yet I cannot ask you to say Kaddish after my mother. The Kaddish means to me that the survivor openly and markedly manifests his wish and intention to assume the same relation to the Jewish community as had his parent, so the chain of tradition remains unbroken. You can do that for the generations of your family. I must do that for the generations of my family.

I believe that the elimination of women from such duties was never intended by our law and custom—women were freed from positive duties when they could not perform them, but not when they could. It was never intended that if they could perform them, their performance of them should not be considered as valuable and valid as when one of the male sex performed them. And of the Kaddish I feel sure this is particularly true.

My mother had eight daughters and no sons and yet never did I hear a word of regret pass the lips of either my mother or my father that one of us was not a son. When my father died, my mother would not permit others to take her daughters' place in saying the Kaddish, and so I am sure I am acting in her spirit when I am moved to decline your offer. But beautiful your offer remains nevertheless.

KADDISH IN MANY PLACES

Seymour J. Cohen, the author of this moving piece, is rabbi emeritus of Anshe Emet Synagogue, Chicago, Illinois, and past president of the Rabbinical Assembly and the Synagogue Council of America. He is the author of a volume of sermons, *A Time to Speak,* and has edited and translated a number of works on Jewish ethics.

Thursday was a landmark date for me. It was the fifteenth day of Shevat, an easy day to remember, for it was the new year of the trees. Yesterday was the first day in eleven months that I was not required to recite the Kaddish—to join the row of mourners in remembering their sacred dead. Yesterday was the beginning of a new year in Israel and of a new stage in my life. In Israel little saplings were planted on this day. They will grow into beautiful trees, gracing the landscape of our Holy Land. In my life many memories were planted during this year that has now ended. Let me name some of them.

At times during this year I have said Kaddish in some most unusual places. A few weeks ago, waiting for the plane to Israel in the El Al terminal, I noticed a family in the corner of the waiting room who were quite bereft, and whose garments had been torn with the traditional *keriah.* I was asked, "Would you like to *daven* Minhah with us?" I joined them in Minhah, and then, after the service, I asked discreetly about the family. I learned that they were to fly on the same plane. They were like the family of our ancestors, Jacob and Joseph, who pleaded that they not be buried in Egypt, but that their remains be brought back to the land of their birth. They were bringing back the remains of a member of their family, born somewhere in Europe, but in the spiritual sense, born in the land of Israel three thousand years ago.

On the plane, we had another minyan in the morning. The sun was rising over the Mediterranean, or perhaps we were over the Italian peninsula, and we read from a small Torah scroll that was going to be presented by some congregation to Zahal, the Israeli defense forces. We had no table, so the Torah was held up by two men. A Bar Mitzvah boy read from the scroll, *"Bo el Pharaoh"*—"Go to Pharaoh and tell him to let my people go." I was deeply touched by this. The Bar Mitzvah boy's grandfather had been my teacher in high-school days and taught me Talmud years ago. It was so symbolic. In the hold of the plane were the remains of a Jew who had passed on, and above, in the passenger compartment, a vibrant dynamic *minyan* was reaffirming its continuity and its faith in God.

During the course of this last year I recited Kaddish many times in our own synagogue chapel. Day after day the *minyan* starts while it is still pitch-dark. It is an experience to come to this *bet hamidrash* and see how a handful of men make up this daily service and keep up the continuum of praise to God. The individual members of the minyan come and go but the *minyan* continues every single day of the year, every single year of the synagogue's life. It is touching to see how the members encourage each other, how their friendships develop, how concerned they become if one does not show up for a few days. They are truly a *havurah,* a fellowship, and they care for their *haverim.* In recent weeks, a fine woman has joined the minyan. She comes to pray for the well-being of her grown family and to recall the sacred memory of her mother. At first she seemed an outsider; now she is a part of the group.

During the course of the year I recited Kaddish at the *Kotel Maaravi,* the Western Wall. There the tears of Israel have been shed since the destruction of the Temple. I felt privileged saying the ancient words there, and I felt that in a sense I was saying them there as my father's representative, since he never had the privilege of being there.

But there were jollier settings in which I said the Kaddish. There was the Hasidic *shtiblach* to which I had been introduced by my friend, Rabbi Abraham Karp. I had been to Meah Shearim many, many times, but I never knew that just a few yards away from the din of the Meah Shearim marketplace there was another din, not of peddlers and housewives debating the price of fish, but of men raising their voices in prayer. I had been to Jerusalem many times. I didn't know about this particular little set of miniature synagogues, these little spiritual diamonds in the rough. What a charming atmosphere pervades them. "Minhah, Minhah, Minhah," was the cry as I walked in, "we need a tenth man for the minyan." I needed them for my Kaddish, and they needed me for their minyan and so we felt connected, these Hasidim and I, even though we had never met before. The service was the service of the Sephardic ritual. I noticed that the prayer books that they used were very, very torn. My book dealer, Mr. Schreiber, was there, and so I said, "Perhaps you ought to get them some new prayer books. Order them for the synagogue, will you please, and inscribe my father's name." I had never been there before, and I do not know when or whether I will be back there again, but meantime something of me and something of my father's memory is there in those books.

Once a week, on Thursdays, the eve of the eve of the Sabbath, the little people of Jerusalem, the humble beggars, come in to that synagogue. With great dignity they receive their offerings. I noticed one beggar giving a bit of charity to another. This is the custom among these people—even the poorest of men has to help others.

One day, after leaving the "Minhah, Minhah, Minhah" setting, I saw people running. They were loading on lorries, small trucks. "Where are you going?" I asked.

"Why it's the Yahrzeit of the Or Hahayim," the answer came. The Or Hahayim is the famous mystical commentator on the Bible whose works are beloved and revered by both the Ashkenazic and Sephardic communities. (I once met a cab driver in Jerusalem who goes up the grave of the Or Hahayim every morning at 4:00 A.M. to light an oil lamp at the grave of this great sage.) The old Yiddish expression has it that if the whole world runs, you should run too. So I went to my Hertz car and followed them up to the Mount of Olives. There in one of the oldest burial grounds of Jewish history I came to the grave of the Or Hahayim, where I found the Jews of my little synagogue praying and reciting the words of the Psalms. In one corner there was a Minhah service. A little while later, as twilight came to Jerusalem, which is a glorious experience in itself, as the blue skies turned gradually to purple and finally to black, there was an Ashkenazic service. For the first time in my life I did not worship in an easterly direction, toward Jerusalem, but instead I prayed toward the west, for the Mount of Olives is east of the Temple site. There I could see the massive walls of Herodian stone that have stood as silent witnesses for thousands of years, testifying to the love of the Jewish people for the city of Jerusalem. I was praying for the first time in a westerly direction, for I was on the other side of the wall, but I could see the Jews at the wall in mind from where I stood, and in my mind I could join my prayers to theirs.

On the way home from Jerusalem last summer, I stopped off in London. One morning I went to a small synagogue near my hotel for services and for Kaddish. I noticed that the leader of the service prayed with the tallit draped over his head. The voice sounded vaguely familiar, but it was not until the service was over and he doffed his tallit and turned around that I realized who it was. It was the Chief Rabbi of England, in mourning for his mother, who was leading us that day in the Kaddish. But until the service was over and he turned around I did not know that. It could have been any ordinary Jew leading the prayers or mourning for his parent. The words were the same and the service was the same and the grief was the same no matter who happened to be leading the prayers.

Yes, there were many, many places and many occasions when I said Kaddish during those eleven months. Of all of them, however, this is the one that means the most to me. A week ago I visited the soldiers at Hadassah Hospital. Those who are still there are the ones who are most difficult to treat. They have been there since the Yom Kippur War, and as I went from bed to bed shaking hands and mumbling a few inadequate words of encouragement to them I felt so feeble, so helpless, so unable to say what I wanted to to them. Finally, after I had spent some time with them, I broke away from the crowd and went to the synagogue of the hospital to get some emotional relief. I went in there and sat down to look at the Chagall windows that are so lovely and to be by myself for a few minutes just to think. As I sat studying the windows, I noticed a *mohel,* a circumcisor, come in. I asked him, "When will the Brith be?" "In a little while," he replied. Then a modest Sephardic family and their guests came in. Soon they were joined by the proud father, who was one of the soldiers from the ward upstairs, still in his bandages and still in his cast. Then they brought the little child in, and the Brith began.

At the end of the service, they recited the Kaddish. I don't know for whom but I was delighted to join their quorum. As I did, I sensed the whole cycle of life revolving before me. I had said the Kaddish once on a plane carrying a man to his last resting place. Now I was saying it again as a new life entered the Covenant of Abraham. I was reciting Kaddish for my father, surrounded by the majestic beauty of the Chagall windows, but more than the creation by man was the creation of God. I was thinking of my father, who lay many thousands of miles away, but I was in the company of new kinsmen with whose path mine had now crossed. Somehow, I had the feeling that there is a wondrous continuity, a never-ending flow of life, to death and through death, and that therefore, despite all its aches and all its pains, there is great beauty and great meaning in our lives.

I have said Kaddish in many places and with many different people during these eleven months. The Kaddish has brought me into contact with many Jews, and with my father and with myself. I think that he would be pleased.

My Greatest Misfortune

Moses Maimonides (1135-1204), perhaps the greatest Jewish philosopher and scholar of all times, and his younger
brother, David, were partners in the jewelry business.
During one of David's trips to India, the ship sank and
David lost his life. This was a loss from which Moses Maimonides never recovered. The following is excerpted
from a letter Maimonides wrote to Japhet ben Eliyahu of
Acco (1176).

The greatest misfortune that has befallen me during
my entire life—worse than anything else—was the passing of [my brother] the saint...who drowned in the Indian
Sea, carrying much money belonging to me, to him, and
to others. He left me with a little daughter and a widow.
On the day I received the news I fell ill and remained in
bed for about a year, suffering from a sore boil, fever,
and depression.

About eight years have since passed, but I am still
mourning and unable to accept consolation. And how
can I console myself? He grew up on my knees. He was
my brother. He was my student. He traded in the marketplace and earned money so I could sit safely at home.
He was well versed in the Talmud and the Bible, and
knew [Hebrew] grammar well. My great joy in life was to
gaze upon him.

Now, all joy has gone. He has passed away and left me
in a foreign country [Egypt], disturbed and upset. Whenever I see his handwriting or read one of his letters, my
heart turns somersaults and my grief is stirred up again.
In the words of Jacob (Genesis 37:35): "I shall go down
to the nether world...in mourning."

ACCEPTANCE:
The Epitome of Faith

The second-century scholar Nahum was a contemporary of Rabbi Yochanan ben Zakkai and one of Rabbi Akiba's teachers. This heroic and legendary Jewish historical figure was a native of Gimzo (or Gimzu), also known as Emmaus, a town situated three miles from Yavneh (Jamnia) in southwest Palestine. He acquired the name Gamzu (which was a play on the name Gimzu) because of the manner in which he reacted to the many tragedies that marked his life. The following is adapted from talmudic legends .*

The disciples of Rabbi Nachum of Gamzu said to him: "Master, you are such a righteous person, why have so many misfortunes befallen you?"

"I brought them on myself," he replied.

"How is that?" they asked.

"Once," said Nachum, "I was on the road heading for the house of my father-in-law. I had with me three donkeys, one laden with food, the second with drinks, and the third will all kinds of delicacies. Suddenly, a poor man stopped me and said: 'Master, give me something to eat.'

"I replied, 'Wait until I have unloaded the animals.' And before I even managed to open one of the packs, the man died [from hunger].

"I laid myself on top of his prone body and cried out, 'May my eyes which had no pity upon your eyes become blind; may my hands which had no pity upon your hands be cut off; may my legs which had no pity upon your legs be amputated; and may may mind never know peace until my whole body is covered with boils.'"

---

*Taanit 21a.

Whereupon his pupil exclaimed, "Alas, we are so sad to see you in such plight!"

To this Nachum replied: "Woe would it be to me if you did not see me in such a sorry state. [I deserved to be punished.]"

Why was he called Nachum of Gamzu?

Because no matter what tragedy befell him he would say: "This, too, is for the best *[Gam zu le-tova]*."

Once the Jews wished to send the Roman emperor a gift. After discussing who should be designated to carry the gift to the king, it was decided that Nachum of Gamzu should be the carrier because of his character and because he had experienced many miracles in his lifetime.

As a gift for the emperor, the townspeople filled a bag with precious stones and pearls, and they sent Rabbi Nachum to deliver it. Since the trip to the palace would require more than one day, Nachum had to spend one night at the inn. While he was asleep, burglars entered his room, emptied the bag that was carrying the gifts, and filled the bag with earth.

When Nachum arose in the morning and discovered what had happened, instead of cursing the day he was born, as Job did, he merely said, "*Gam zu le-tova* [This, too, is for the best]."

Several hours later, Nachum arrived at the palace and handed the bag to the king's courtiers. When the bag was opened and the king saw its contents, he said, "The Jews are mocking me," and he ordered that all Jews be put to death.

"This, too, is for the best," thought Nachum.

Suddenly, out of nowhere, Elijah the prophet appeared in the guise of a Roman courtier and said, "This is some of the [precious] earth of our ancestor Abraham. Whenever Abraham threw some earth against his enemies, it turned into swords; and when he threw stubble, it changed into arrows, for it is written (Isaiah 41:2):

"His sword maketh them as dust, his bow as the driven stubble."

Now, it so happened that there was one province which the emperor had hitherto not been able to conquer, so he threw some of this earth [against it], and they were able to conquer the province.

As a reward, Rabbi Nachum was taken to the royal treasury, where his bag was filled with precious stones and jewels, and he was sent home with great honor.

God Has Willed It for the Best

American poet Edgar A. Guest (1881-1959) captured the spirit of Nachum of Gamzu in the following sensitive poem.

When sorrow comes, as come it must,
In God a man must put his trust.
There is no power in mortal speech
The anguish of his soul to reach,
No voice, however sweet and low,
Can comfort him or ease the blow.

He cannot from his fellow men
Take strength that will sustain him then.
With all that kindly hands will do,
And all that love may offer, too.
He must believe throughout the test
That God has willed it for the best.

We who would be his friends are dumb;
Words from our lips but feebly come;
We feel, as we extend our hands,
That one Power only understands
And truly knows the reason why
So beautiful a soul must die.

We realize how helpless then
Are all the gifts of mortal men.
No words which we have the power to say
Can take the sting of grief away—
That Power which marks the sparrow's fall
Must comfort and sustain us all.

When sorrow comes, as come it must,

In God a man must place his trust.
With all the wealth which he may own,
He cannot meet the test alone,
And only he may stand serene
Who has a faith on which to lean.

THINGS ARE NOT WHAT THEY SEEM

Henry Wadsworth Longfellow (1807-1882) captured the spirit of the Hebrew *Elohai Neshama* prayer in his majestic poem "A Psalm of Life." Longfellow refused to accept death as the end of all existence.

> Tell me not, in mournful numbers,
> Life is but an empty dream,
> For the soul is dead that slumbers
> And things are not what they seem.
>
> Life is real! Life is earnest!
> And the grave is not its goal;
> Dust thou art, to dust returnest,
> Was not spoken of the soul."

THUS SPAKE ECCLESIASTES

According to Jewish tradition King Solomon was the author of three books of the Bible: Song of Songs, a book of life and love, composed when Solomon was a young man; Book of Proverbs, a book of commentary and wisdom, composed in his mature years; and Book of Ecclesiastes (Kohelet), written in Solomon's waning years when he had become somewhat disillusioned with life. The following excerpt is from Chapter 3 of Ecclesiastes.

> For everything there is a season,
>   and a time for every experience
>   under the sun;
> A time to be born,
>   and a time to die;
> A time to plant,
>   and a time to uproot that which has
>   been planted;
> A time to kill,
>   and a time to heal;
> A time to tear down,
>   and a time to rebuild;
> A time to weep,
>   and a time to laugh;
> A time to mourn,
>   and a time to dance;
> A time to throw stones,
>   and a time to gather stones;
> A time to embrace,
>   and a time to refrain from embracing;

A time to search for what is lost,
and a time to abandon the search;
A time to preserve,
and a time to discard;
A time to tear,
and a time to mend;
A time to be silent,
and a time to speak;
A time to love,
and a time to hate;
A time for war,
and a time for peace.

The Rabbis* make the following comment on some of the
thoughts expressed above:

As a man enters the world, so he departs.
He enters the world with a cry,
and departs with a cry.
He enters the world weeping,
and leaves it weeping.
He enters the world with love,
and leaves it with love.
He enters the world with a sigh,
and leaves it with a sigh.
He enters the world devoid of knowledge,
and leaves it devoid of knowledge.

---

*Ecclesiastes Rabba 5:14.

THE MAKING OF MAN

The English poet and critic Algernon Charles Swinburne (1837-1909) caught the spirit of Ecclesiastes in this revealing poem.

> Before the beginning of years,
> There came to the making of man:
> Time, with a gift of tears;
> Grief, with a glass that ran;
> Pleasure, with pain for leaven,
> Summer, with flowers that fell;
> Remembrance fallen from heaven,
> And madness risen from hell;
> Strength without hands to smite;
> Love that endures for a breath;
> Night, the shadow of light,
> And life, the shadow of death.

Letting Go of Grief

>‹-

Rabbi Yochanan ben Zakkai, head of the Sanhedrin during the first century C.E., had five famous disciples: Eliezer ben Hyrcanus, Joshua ben Chananya, Yosi the Priest,
Simon ben Nathaniel, and Elazar ben Arach. When Rabbi
Yochanan's beloved son died, he was so overcome with
grief that even when the Shiva period had ended, he continued to sit and mourn.

One by one, Rabbi Yochanan's disciples called upon him,
offering comfort and trying to influence him to accept his
fate.

This selection is condensed from *The Fathers According to
Rabbi Nathan.*

When Rabbi Yochanan ben Zakkai's son died, his disciples came to comfort him. Rabbi Eliezer entered first
and sat down before him and said, "With your permission, master, may I speak?"

"Speak," said Yochanan.

Rabbi Eliezer then said: "Adam [the first man on earth]
had a son who died, yet he allowed himself to be comforted. You, too should be comforted."

Rabbi Yochanan replied: "Is it not enough that I grieve
over my own that you remind me of Adam's grief?"

Rabbi Joshua then visited Yochanan and said: "With
your permission, master, may I speak?"

"Speak," said Yochanan.

Rabbi Joshua then said: "Job had sons and daughters, all of whom died in one day, and he permitted himself to be comforted. You, too, should be comforted."

Rabbi Yochanan replied: "Is it not enough that I grieve
over my own that you remind me of the grief of Job?"

Rabbi Yosi approached Yochanan next and sat down
before him and said: "May I speak, master?"

"Speak," said Yochanan.

"Aaron had two grown sons," said Yosi, "both of whom died on the same day, yet he allowed himself to be comforted. Therefore, you, too, should be comforted."

Rabbi Yochanan replied: "Is it not enough that I grieve over my son that you should remind me of the grief of Aaron?"

Rabbi Simon entered next and said: "With your permission, master, may I speak?"

"Speak," said Yochanan.

"King David had a son who died," said Simon, "yet he allowed himself to be comforted. Therefore, you, too, should be comforted."

Rabbi Yochanan replied: "Is it not enough that I grieve over my own loss that you must remind me of King David?"

Finally, the brilliant Rabbi Elazar, Yochanan's favorite disciple, entered. As soon as Rabbi Yochanan saw him, he knew that he would not be able to contest Elazar's argument easily, so he ordered his servant to gather his clothing and to be prepared to proceed after him to the bathhouse, a signal that his period of mourning had come to an end.

Rabbi Elazar sat down and said: "Master, I would like to recite a parable. To what may this [situation of yours] be compared? To a man with whom a king left a valuable object in his custody. Each day, that man [fearful that the object would be lost, stolen, or damaged] would cry and say: 'Woe is me. When will I be rid of the responsibility for this article placed in my trust!'"

Rabbi Elazar continued: "You, too, master, had a son [a valuable object in trust]. He studied Torah, the Prophets, the Holy Writings; he studied Mishnah, and Aggadah; and he departed from this world without sin. And you should be comforted for having returned your trust undamaged."

Rabbi Yochanan responded: "Elazar, my son, you have comforted me as one *should* comfort a person who is grieving."

THE RAINY DAY

Henry Wadsworth Longfellow

The day is cold, and dark, and dreary;
It rains, and the wind is never weary;
The vine still clings to the mouldering wall,
But at every gust the dead leaves fall,
    And the day is dark and dreary.

My life is cold, and dark, and dreary;
It rains, and the wind is never weary;
My thoughts still cling to the mouldering past,
But the hopes of youth fall thick in the blast,
    And the days are dark and dreary.

Be still, sad heart! and cease repining;
Behind the clouds is the sun still shining;
Thy fate is the common fate of all,
Into each life some rain must fall,
    Some days must be dark and dreary.

PSALM 23*
The Lord Is My Shepherd

The Lord is my shepherd, I shall not want;
He makes me lie down in green pastures;
He leads me beside still waters.

He guides me on the path of righteousness;
He revives my soul for the sake of His glory.

Though I walk in the valley of darkness,
I fear no harm, for You are beside me,
Your staff and Your rod they comfort me.

You set a table before me in the sight of my enemies;
You anoint my head with oil; my cup overflows.

Throughout the days of my life
Goodness and kindness shall be my portion;

Throughout the long years ahead
The Lord's house shall be my dwelling place.

---

*The psalms in this section are based on translations by the late
Rabbi Gershon Hadas that appeared in his *Book of Psalms*.

PSALM 49
Hear This, All You Peoples

Hear this, all you peoples;
Listen, everyone and everywhere,

The mighty as well as the lowly,
The rich as well as the poor.
My mouth will speak the wisdom,
The probings of a discerning heart.

I shall attune my ear to its teaching;
I shall reveal its mystery on the lyre.

Why should I be afraid in days of evil,
Even when surrounded by treacherous foes?
They put their trust in riches;
They boast of their great wealth.

But man cannot save even a brother from death;
There is no bribing God to recall His decree.

The most costly ransom cannot save a life;
There is no way to evade death forever.
There is no way to avoid the grave.
Man sees that wise men too must die,

Even as do the fools and the senseless,
All leaving their possessions to others.

They delude themselves in their hearts
That their homes will endure forever,
That their land will always be their own,
That their ownership will outlast time.

But man's vaunted glory is soon gone;
He dies even as do all creatures.

This is the fate of self-confident fools,
They who delight in their own blusterings. Selah!
Like sheep are they marked for death;
Like sheep are they herded to graves.

Straight down into their tombs they go;
There they remain to mold and waste away.

But God will ransom my soul from death;
When He takes me, He will save my soul.
Therefore, do not envy a man his riches,
Nor be jealous of his growing possessions.

Psalm 90
You Have Been Our Refuge

O Lord, You have been our refuge
From generation to generation.
Before the mountains were brought forth,
Before the earth was fashioned,
From eternity to eternity
You are everlastingly God.

You crush man to dust;
You say: "Return, O mortal man."
A thousand years are in Your sight
As a passing day, an hour of night.
You sweep men away and they sleep;
Like grass they flourish for a day.

In the morning they sprout afresh;
By nightfall they fade and wither.
In Your anger we are consumed;
In Your wrath we are overcome.
You set our sins before You,
Our secrets before Your presence.

Your wrath darkens our days;
Our lives expire like a sigh.
Three score and ten our years may number,
Four score years if granted the vigor.

Laden with trouble and travail,
Life quickly passes, and flies away.

Who can weigh the power of Your anger?
Who can measure the reverence due You?

Teach us to use all of our days
That we may attain a heart of wisdom.
Relent, O Lord! How long must we suffer?
Have compassion on Your servants.

Grant us Your love in the morning
That we may joyously sing all our days.
Match days of sorrow with days of joy
Equal to the years we have suffered.
Then Your servants will see Your power;
Then their children will know Your glory.

The favor of the Lord, our God, be upon us;
He will establish the work of our hands.
The work of our hands He will surely establish.

PSALM 91
The Antidemonic Psalm

(Yosher b'seter Elyon)

O You who dwell in the shelter of the Most High
    And abide in the shadow of the Almighty,
I call the Lord, my Refuge and my Fortress,
    He is my God in whom I trust.
He will save you from the fowler's snare,
    From deadly pestilence.
He will cover you with his wings,
    You will find safety in their shelter.
    His faithfulness is a protective shield.

You need not fear the terror that strikes at night,
    Nor the arrow that flies by day,
Nor the pestilence that stalks in the darkness,
    Nor the destruction that ravages at noon.
Though a thousand may fall as victims to your left,
    Ten thousands to your right,
    The plague shall not touch you.
You will see it with your eyes,
    You will be witness to the punishment of the
        wicked.

Because you have made the Lord your stronghold,
    The Most High your refuge,
No harm will befall you,
    No disease shall touch your tent.
For He will order His angels to
    guard you wherever you go.

What Is the Soul?

Isaac Leib Peretz (1852-1915) was one of the most prolific Yiddish writers—and one of the most accomplished. After completing his studies in Russian jurisprudence, he practiced law in Warsaw from 1877 to 1887. But his heart was in writing. Although he wrote in Hebrew and Polish, he preferred Yiddish because he felt he could reach the souls of the working masses best if he wrote in the language most familiar to them. They appreciated his writings because he was able to express their pain and anguish in a down-to-earth, realistic manner. Peretz's many stories about the soul are stirring and meaningful, as is the one presented here which he wrote in 1890 and is in abbreviated and slightly modified form.

I think back—it is like a dream now—and I can recall a short, thin man pacing the floor in our house. He had a pointed beard and he would hug me and kiss me all the time.

Then, some time later, I saw this same man lying in bed. He was very sick and he moaned and groaned a lot. My mother stood by the bedside, her head clasped tightly between her hands.

One night, I awakened suddenly and saw a room full of people. Some were wailing and crying. I was frightened and began to scream.

A man approached me, dressed me, and took me to a neighbor's house to sleep.

When I returned to my house the next day, I didn't recognize my home. The floor was strewn with straw, the mirror was turned to face the wall, the hanging lamp was covered with a tablecloth, and my mother was sitting on a low stool in her stocking feet.

When my mother saw me, she let out a piercing cry

and began to lament: "*Oy vay!* The orphan! The poor orphan!"

A light was burning in the window. A glass of water stood nearby, and a piece of cloth was hanging next to it.

I was told that my father had died, that his soul washed itself in the glass of water and dried itself on the cloth, and that if I did a good job of saying the Kaddish, his soul would fly straight up to heaven,.

I imagined that the soul was a little bird.

Once, when my teacher's assistant was taking me home, several birds flew quite low and near us. "Souls are flying, souls are flying!" I called out.

The assistant looked around, "You foolish boy," he said to me, "those are ordinary birds!"

Afterwards, I asked my mother: "How can you tell the difference between a soul and an ordinary bird?"

When I was fourteen years old, I was already studying the Talmud with commentaries at the home of Zorach Pinch.

To this day I don't know whether that was his real name, or whether his students gave him this nickname because he often pinched them until it hurt. He didn't even wait until you had done something wrong and deserved to be pinched—he paid in advance. "Remind me," he said. "I'll deduct it from the next time!"

Zorach Pinch hated his wife intensely, but his only daughter, Shprintze, was the apple of his eye. We boys hated Shprintze because she used to squeal on us to her father. But we loved Pinch's wife because she sold us beans and peas on credit, and more than once she saved us from her husband's wrath.

I was her favorite. I used to get the biggest portion, and when the teacher started up with me, she would shout: "Murderer, what do you want from an orphan? His father's soul will take vengeance on you!"

* * *

There were times when Zorach Pinch declared a holiday. He closed the Talmud and began to tell us stories. Then he was a different person. He would unbutton his coat and smooth his brow, and a smile would appear on his lips. His voice became more gentle.

"When God chooses a soul," said Zorach, "and orders it to enter the sinful world, it trembles and cries. Afterwards an angel comes to it inside the mother's belly and teaches it the entire Torah. But when it comes time for a child to be born, the angel taps it under the nose and it forgets everything it has learned. For this reason," said the teacher, "all Jewish children have a dimple above their upper lip."

That same evening we were skating in back of the town, and I looked at the Gentile boys Yantek, Voytek, and Yashek. They all had dimples above their upper lips, the same as we did.

"Yashek!" I risked my life and asked in Polish, "You have a soul, too?"

"And you, you with a dog's soul, what's that to you?" was his curt response.

Besides studying with my teacher, I also took writing lessons from a tutor.

This tutor was considered a freethinker in the town, and the neighbors didn't believe he kept the dietary laws religiously. He was a widower, and people didn't believe that his daughter, Gitele, a girl of my age, knew how to kosher meat.

But he was a talented man, and my mother wanted her only son to know how to write. "I beg of you," she said. "Do not teach him any freethinking things. Just teach him how to write a letter in Yiddish, a simple, ordinary letter!"

But I don't know if the tutor kept his promise.

When I raised with him the difficult question of the

depression above the upper lip, he became very angry. He stood up quickly, kicked the bench away with his foot and began pacing the room and shouting: "Boors, murderers!"

Gradually, he quieted down, sat down again, wiped his glasses, drew me to his side and said, "Don't believe such foolish things, my child. Did you take a good look at the Gentile boys who were skating? What are their names?"

I told him their names.

"Well," he asked me, "do any of them have eyes that are different from yours? Do they have hands and feet or other limbs that are different?

"Don't they laugh and cry the same way you do? Why shouldn't they have a soul the same as you do? All human beings are the same, children of the same God, inhabiting the same earth!"

"True, today the nations hate each other; each nation considers itself superior to all the others. But we hope that a time of better understanding will come when all men will acknowledge one God, one law...."

My tutor said quite a bit more, but I didn't understand very much of it; I couldn't believe that a Gentile also has brains, that all human beings are the same! I knew that my tutor was a freethinker; he didn't even believe in the transmigration of souls.

On the eve of Rosh Hashana I finished the chapter of the Talmud I had been studying with Zorach Pinch, and I was then assigned to a new teacher. I felt as though I had been liberated from Egyptian slavery.

I was told that Reb Yoyzl, my new teacher, did not pinch. He didn't even hit you just for the sake of hitting, He was our congregation's assistant rabbi.

Our rabbi was an old, sickly man, and it was expected that when he completed his alloted hundred and twenty years, Reb Yoyzl would take his place. Reb Yoyzl would preach the sermons on the Sabbath before Passover and on Rosh Hashana, and deliver the occasional eulogy.

I was glad to be one of Reb Yoyzl's students because I had a chance to talk to him about the soul. The soul had become a kind of fixation for me; it was never out of my thoughts for a minute.

Reb Yoyzl explained: "Even among us Jews, not all souls are the same. There are coarse, ordinary souls," he said, "like Zorach Pinch and your tutor, the freethinker. Then there are great souls, very great souls, that come from beneath the Throne of Glory. These are great and elevated souls—souls like the most refined flour."

I didn't understand too well about the different gradations of souls, and very little about the origin of souls that came from beneath the Throne of Glory; but I did know what the most refined flour meant, and I imagined the difference between the souls to be like the difference between rye flour, corn flour, wheat flour, and the flour that was used to make the Sabbath loaves. The greatest souls must be those that contain saffron and raisins!

"But the main thing," said Reb Yoyzl, "concerns suffering. No soul is ever lost; they must all return to their original state, as they were before they descended into this world. And souls are cleansed only through suffering. God in His great mercy sends us suffering so that we never forget that we are only flesh and blood, insignificant broken vessels. By a mere glance of God, we disintegrate and become as the dust of the earth. But in the next world the souls are cleansed."

Then he told me what is done to all the poor souls in the seven departments of hell.

One night, I dreamt that I was in the next world and I saw how the angels in heaven stretched their hands to receive the souls that were approaching from this world. The angels chose only souls that were pure, those as white as snow. The dirty souls were piled in a large heap and were thrown into a frozen sea where black angels with rolled-up sleeves stood and scrubbed them. Afterwards they were cooked in huge black pots kept boiling by the fires of hell. And as the dirt was squeezed out of them, and as they were pressed, you could hear the souls crying out from one end of the world to the other.

Among the dirty souls being washed, I saw my free-thinking tutor's soul. It had his long nose, his sunken cheeks, his pointed beard, and it was wearing his big blue glasses. But the more his soul was washed, the dirtier it became.

And an angel called out, "This is the soul of the tutor, the freethinker!" Afterwards, the same angel said angrily to me, "If you follow in his ways, your soul will become as dirty as his, and every night it will be washed until it is lost in the tortures of hell!"

"I won't follow in his ways!" I cried out in my sleep.

My mother woke me up. "What is it, darling?" she asked me, startled. "You're covered with sweat!" She spat three times to ward off the evil eye.

"Mother, I was in the next world!" I cried out.

In the morning my mother asked me, very seriously, if I had seen my father there. I said, "No."

"What a pity, what a pity!" she said, disappointed. "He surely would have given you a message for me."

When I was sixteen years old, matchmakers began to pressure my mother.

Gitele, the daughter of my freethinking tutor, was considered to be a very clever girl. Neighbors used to say that she was as bright as day, and if she were only as pious as she was smart, her mother would rejoice in paradise. My mother also praised her intellect and said she would make a perfect daughter-in-law—if only she were more trustworthy at koshering meat.

Once, when I didn't find the tutor at home and Gitele was alone, it occurred to me that I should talk to her about the soul.

My legs were trembling, my hands shaking, my heart palpitating, and my eyes penetrated the ground like a knife being koshered. I managed to say: "Gitele, you are smart. Please tell me, what sort of thing is a soul?"

She smiled and answered, "How would I know?"

But suddenly she became sad, and her eyes began to fill with tears. "I remember," she then said, "when my mother, may she rest in peace, was alive, my father always said that she was his soul...They loved each other so much!"

I don't know what came over me, but at that moment I took her hand, and said, "Gitele, would you be my soul?"

She answered very softly, "Yes!"

But my mother was unhappy over this. "If your father were to rise from the grave and see to whom I am giving you in marriage, he would return to his grave in shame."

That gave me an idea.

In the middle of the night I began crying.

"What is it?" said mother.

"I was once again in the world beyond," I told her, "but this time Father sent greetings to you, and said how much he approved of the match."

And that is how I acquired a new soul.

THE PURITY OF THE SOUL

The soul is the essence of man. This is acknowledged each morning in the very personal, powerful prayer that opens with the words *Elohai, neshama she-nata-ta bi tehora hi,* "O Lord, the soul which Thou hast given me is pure."

O my God, the soul which Thou hast given
   unto me is pure.
Thou hast created it; Thou hast formed it;
Thou hast breathed it into me;
   and Thou shieldest and protectest it.
I know that one day Thou wilt take it from me,
   but return it to me at some future time.

So long as the soul is within me,
I offer thanks to Thee, O Lord,
   my God and God of my fathers,
Master of Creation, Lord of all souls.
Praised be Thou, O Lord, restorer of all souls.

Appendices

Appendix I

Appendix II

Appendix III

Appendix IV

THE RABBIS' KADDISH

קַדִּישׁ דְּרַבָּנָן

KADDISH DE-RABBANAN

[The first three and last two paragraphs of this Kaddish are identical to those of the Complete Kaddish. See page 334.]

יִתְגַּדַּל וְיִתְקַדַּשׁ שְׁמֵהּ רַבָּא בְּעָלְמָא דִּי בְרָא כִרְעוּתֵהּ, וְיַמְלִיךְ מַלְכוּתֵהּ* בְּחַיֵּיכוֹן וּבְיוֹמֵיכוֹן וּבְחַיֵּי דְכָל־בֵּית יִשְׂרָאֵל, בַּעֲגָלָא וּבִזְמַן קָרִיב, וְאִמְרוּ אָמֵן.

יְהֵא שְׁמֵהּ רַבָּא מְבָרַךְ לְעָלַם וּלְעָלְמֵי עָלְמַיָּא.

יִתְבָּרַךְ וְיִשְׁתַּבַּח וְיִתְפָּאַר וְיִתְרוֹמַם וְיִתְנַשֵּׂא, וְיִתְהַדָּר וְיִתְעַלֶּה וְיִתְהַלָּל שְׁמֵהּ דְּקוּדְשָׁא. בְּרִיךְ הוּא לְעֵלָּא מִן** כָּל בִּרְכָתָא וְשִׁירָתָא, תֻּשְׁבְּחָתָא וְנֶחֱמָתָא דַּאֲמִירָן בְּעָלְמָא, וְאִמְרוּ אָמֵן.

עַל יִשְׂרָאֵל וְעַל רַבָּנָן וְעַל תַּלְמִידֵיהוֹן, וְעַל כָּל־תַּלְמִידֵי תַלְמִידֵיהוֹן, וְעַל כָּל־מָאן דְּעָסְקִין בְּאוֹרַיְתָא, דִּי בְאַתְרָא הָדֵין וְדִי בְכָל־אֲתַר וַאֲתַר, יְהֵא לְהוֹן וּלְכוֹן שְׁלָמָא

---

* Sephardim add here: וְיַצְמַח פּוּרְקָנֵהּ וִיקָרֵב מְשִׁיחֵהּ.

** From Rosh Hashana through Yom Kippur substitute the words לְעֵלָּא מִכָּל for לְעֵלָּא מִן כָּל. In some communities the words לְעֵלָּא וּלְעֵלָּא מִכָּל are substituted.

רַבָּא, חִנָּא וְחִסְדָּא וְרַחֲמִין, וְחַיִּין אֲרִיכִין וּמְזוֹנָא רְוִיחָא, וּפוּרְקָנָא מִן קֳדָם אֲבוּהוֹן דִי בִשְׁמַיָּא (וְאַרְעָא), וְאִמְרוּ אָמֵן.

יְהֵא שְׁלָמָא רַבָּא מִן שְׁמַיָּא וְחַיִּים (טוֹבִים) עָלֵינוּ וְעַל כָּל־יִשְׂרָאֵל, וְאִמְרוּ אָמֵן.

עוֹשֶׂה שָׁלוֹם בִּמְרוֹמָיו, הוּא (בְּרַחֲמָיו) יַעֲשֶׂה שָׁלוֹם עָלֵינוּ וְעַל כָּל־יִשְׂרָאֵל, וְאִמְרוּ אָמֵן.

TRANSLITERATION

Yit-gadal ve-yit-kadash shmay rabba be-alma di-vera chiru-tay, ve-yamlich malchutay* be-cha'yaychon u-ve-yomaychon u-ve-cha'yay de-chol bet Yisrael ba-agala u-vi-zeman kariv, ve-imru, Amen.

Y'hay shmay rabba me-vorach le-olam u-le-almay alma'ya.

Yit-barach ve-yishtabach, ve-yit-pa'ar ve'yit-romam, ve-yit-nasay, ve-yit-hadar, ve-yit-aleh ve-yit-halal shmay de-Kudesha. B'rich Hu le-ayla min** kol birchata ve-shirata tushbechata ve-nechemata, da-amiran be-alma, ve-imru, Amen.

Al Yisrael ve-al Rabbanan ve-al talmidayhon, ve-al kol talmiday talmidayhon, ve-al kol man de-askin be-ora'yeta, di ve-atra hadayn ve-di ve-chol atar va-atar, yehay le-hon u-le-chon shelama rabba, china ve-chisda ve-rachamin, ve-cha-yin arichin, u-mezona revicha, u-fur-

---

*Sephardim add here: ve-yitzmach purkanay vi-karev meshichay.

**From Rosh Hashana through Yom Kippur substitute the words le-ayla mi-kol for le-ayla min kol. In some communities the words le-ayla u-le-ayla mi-kol are substituted.

kana min kadam Avuhon de-viShema'ya (veara), ve-imru, Amen.

Y'hay shemala rabba min she-ma'ya ve-cha'yim (tovim) alaynu ve-al kol Yisrael, ve-imru, Amen.

Oseh shalom bi-meromav, Hu (be-rachamav) ya-aseh shalom alaynu ve-al kol Yisrael, ve-imru, Amen.

Translation

Glorified and sanctified be God's great name throughout the world, which He has created according to His will. May He establish His kingdom within your lifetime and within the lifetime of the whole house of Israel, speedily and soon, and let us say, Amen.

May His great name be praised unto all eternity.

Exalted and praised, glorified and adored, extolled and revered be the name of the Holy One. Blessed is He beyond all song and psalm, beyond all praise mortal man can bestow upon Him, and let us say, Amen.

We pray for the entire family of Israel, for our rabbis and their students; for all the students of their students, and for all who study Torah, here and everywhere. May they enjoy much peace, lovingkindness, longevity, and abundance of sustenance and salvation from their Father who is is heaven (and on earth), and let us say, Amen.

May life and abundant peace descend from heaven upon us and all Israel, and let us say, Amen.

May the Creator of heavenly peace bestow peace upon us and all Israel, and let us say, Amen.

→←

Mourner's Kaddish

קַדִּישׁ יָתוֹם

Kaddish Yatom

[This Kaddish is recited by all mourners as well as those observing Yahrzeit.]

יִתְגַּדַּל וְיִתְקַדַּשׁ שְׁמֵהּ רַבָּא בְּעָלְמָא דִּי בְרָא כִרְעוּתֵהּ,
וְיַמְלִיךְ מַלְכוּתֵהּ* בְּחַיֵּיכוֹן וּבְיוֹמֵיכוֹן וּבְחַיֵּי דְכָל־בֵּית
יִשְׂרָאֵל, בַּעֲגָלָא וּבִזְמַן קָרִיב, וְאִמְרוּ אָמֵן.

יְהֵא שְׁמֵהּ רַבָּא מְבָרַךְ לְעָלַם וּלְעָלְמֵי עָלְמַיָּא.

יִתְבָּרַךְ וְיִשְׁתַּבַּח וְיִתְפָּאַר וְיִתְרוֹמַם וְיִתְנַשֵּׂא, וְיִתְהַדָּר
וְיִתְעַלֶּה וְיִתְהַלָּל שְׁמֵהּ דְּקוּדְשָׁא. בְּרִיךְ הוּא לְעֵלָּא
מִן**־כָּל בִּרְכָתָא וְשִׁירָתָא, תֻּשְׁבְּחָתָא וְנֶחֱמָתָא דַּאֲמִירָן
בְּעָלְמָא, וְאִמְרוּ אָמֵן.

יְהֵא שְׁלָמָא רַבָּא מִן שְׁמַיָּא וְחַיִּים (טוֹבִים) עָלֵינוּ וְעַל
כָּל־יִשְׂרָאֵל, וְאִמְרוּ אָמֵן.

עוֹשֶׂה שָׁלוֹם בִּמְרוֹמָיו, הוּא (בְּרַחֲמָיו) יַעֲשֶׂה שָׁלוֹם
עָלֵינוּ וְעַל כָּל־יִשְׂרָאֵל, וְאִמְרוּ אָמֵן.

Transliteration

Yit-gadal ve-yit-kadash shmay rabba be-alma di-vera chiru-tay, ve-yamlich malchutay*** be-cha'yaychon u-ve-yomay-

---

* Sephardim add here: וְיַצְמַח פּוּרְקָנֵהּ וִיקָרֵב מְשִׁיחֵהּ.

** From Rosh Hashana through Yom Kippur substitute the words לְעֵלָּא מִכָּל for לְעֵלָּא מִן כָּל. In some communities the words לְעֵלָּא וּלְעֵלָּא מִכָּל are substituted.

***Sephardim add here: ve-yitzmach purkanay vi-karev meshichay.

chon u-ve-cha'yay de-chol bet Yisrael ba-agala u-vi-zeman kariv, ve-imru, Amen.

Y'hay shmay rabba me-vorach le-olam u-le-almay alma'ya.

Yit-barach ve-yishtabach, ve-yit-pa'ar ve-yit-romam, ve-yit-nasay ve-yit-hadar, ve-yit-aleh ve-yit-halal shmay de-Kudesha. Brich Hu le-ayla min* kol birchata ve-shirata tushbechata ve-nechemata, da-amiran be-alma, ve-imru, Amen.

Y'hay shelama rabba min She-ma'ya ve-cha'yim (tovim) alaynu ve-al kol Yisrael, ve-imru, Amen.

Oseh shalom bi-meramov, Hu (be-rachamav) ya-aseh shalom alaynu ve-al kol Yisrael, ve-imru, Amen.

TRANSLATION

Glorified and sanctified be God's great name throughout the world, which He has created according to His will. May he establish His kingdom within your lifetime and within the lifetime of the whole house of Israel, speedily and soon, and let us say, Amen.

May His great name be praised unto all eternity.

Exalted and praised, glorified and adored, extolled and revered be the name of the Holy One. Blessed is He beyond all song and psalm, beyond all praise mortal man can bestow upon Him, and let us say, Amen.

---

*From Rosh Hashana through Yom Kippur substitute the words *le-ayla mi-kol* for *le-ayla min kol*. In some communities the words *le-ayla u-le-ayla mi-kol* are substituted.

May life and abundant peace descend from heaven upon us and all Israel, and let us say, Amen.

May the Creator of heavenly peace bestow peace upon us and all Israel, and let us say, Amen.

THE FULL (COMPLETE) KADDISH

קַדִּישׁ שָׁלֵם

KADDISH SHALEM
[This Kaddish is also referred to as Kaddish Titkabel.]

יִתְגַּדַּל וְיִתְקַדַּשׁ שְׁמֵהּ רַבָּא בְּעָלְמָא דִּי בְרָא כִרְעוּתֵהּ,
וְיַמְלִיךְ מַלְכוּתֵהּ* בְּחַיֵּיכוֹן וּבְיוֹמֵיכוֹן וּבְחַיֵּי דְכָל־בֵּית
יִשְׂרָאֵל, בַּעֲגָלָא וּבִזְמַן קָרִיב, וְאִמְרוּ אָמֵן.

יְהֵא שְׁמֵהּ רַבָּא מְבָרַךְ לְעָלַם וּלְעָלְמֵי עָלְמַיָּא.

יִתְבָּרַךְ וְיִשְׁתַּבַּח וְיִתְפָּאַר וְיִתְרוֹמַם וְיִתְנַשֵּׂא, וְיִתְהַדָּר
וְיִתְעַלֶּה וְיִתְהַלָּל שְׁמֵהּ דְּקוּדְשָׁא. בְּרִיךְ הוּא לְעֵלָּא
מִן** כָּל בִּרְכָתָא וְשִׁירָתָא, תֻּשְׁבְּחָתָא וְנֶחֱמָתָא דַּאֲמִירָן
בְּעָלְמָא, וְאִמְרוּ אָמֵן.

תִּתְקַבֵּל*** צְלוֹתְהוֹן וּבָעוּתְהוֹן דְּכָל־בֵּית יִשְׂרָאֵל קֳדָם
אֲבוּהוֹן דִּי בִשְׁמַיָּא וְאִמְרוּ אָמֵן.

---

* Sephardim add here: וְיַצְמַח פּוּרְקָנֵהּ וִיקָרֵב מְשִׁיחֵהּ.

** From Rosh Hashana through Yom Kippur substitute the words לְעֵלָּא מִכָּל fo
לְעֵלָּא וּלְעֵלָּא מִכָּל. In some communities the words לְעֵלָּא מִן כָּל are substituted

*** Also vocalized תִּתְקַבַּל.

יְהֵא שְׁלָמָא רַבָּא מִן שְׁמַיָּא וְחַיִּים (טוֹבִים) עָלֵינוּ וְעַל
כָּל־יִשְׂרָאֵל, וְאִמְרוּ אָמֵן.
עוֹשֶׂה שָׁלוֹם בִּמְרוֹמָיו, הוּא (בְּרַחֲמָיו) יַעֲשֶׂה שָׁלוֹם
עָלֵינוּ וְעַל כָּל־יִשְׂרָאֵל, וְאִמְרוּ אָמֵן.

TRANSLITERATION

Yit-gadal ve-yit-kadash shmay rabba be-alma di-vera chi-ru-tay, ve-yamlich malchutay* be-cha'yaychon u-ve- yo-maychon u-ve-cha'yay de-chol bet Yisrael ba-agala u-vi-zeman kariv, ve-imru, Amen.

Y'hay shmay rabba me-vorach le-olam u-le-almay almaya.

Yit-barach ve-yishtabach, ve-yit-pa'ar ve-yit-romam, ve-yit-nasay ve-yit-hadar, ve-yit-aleh ve-yit-halal shmay de-Kudesha. Brich Hu le-ayla min** kol birchata ve-shirata tushbechata ve-nechemata, da-amiran be-alma, ve-imru, Amen.

Titkabel*** tzelot'hon u-va-ut'hon de-chol Yisrael kadam Avuhon di vi-Shema'ya, ve-imru, Amen.

Y'hay shelama rabba min She-ma'ya ve-cha'yim tovim alaynu ve-al kol Yisrael, ve'imru, Amen.

Oseh shalom bi-meromav, Hu (be-rachamav) ya-aseh shalom alaynu ve-al kol Yisrael, ve-imru, Amen.

---

*Sephardim add here: *ve-yitzmach purkanay vi-karev meshichay*.

From Rosh Hashana through Yom Kippur substitute the words *le-ayla mi-kol* for *le-ayla min kol*. In some communities the words *le-ayla u-le-ayla mi-kol* are substituted.

***Also vocalized *titkabal*.

TRANSLATION

Glorified and sanctified be God's great name throughout the world, which He has created according to His will. May He establish His kingdom within your lifetime and within the lifetime of the whole house of Israel, speedily and soon, and let us say, Amen.

May His great name be praised unto all eternity.

Exalted and praised, glorified and adored, extolled and revered be the name of the Holy One. Blessed is He beyond all song and psalm, beyond all praise mortal man can bestow upon Him, and let us say, Amen.

May the prayers and supplications of the whole house of Israel be accepted by their Father who is in heaven, and let us say, Amen.

May life and abundant peace descend from heaven upon us and all Israel, and let us say, Amen.

May the Creator of heavenly peace bestow peace upon us and all Israel, and let us say, Amen.

HALF KADDISH

חֲצִי קַדִּישׁ

CHATZI KADDISH

יִתְגַּדַּל וְיִתְקַדַּשׁ שְׁמֵהּ רַבָּא בְּעָלְמָא דִּי בְרָא כִרְעוּתֵהּ,
וְיַמְלִיךְ מַלְכוּתֵהּ* בְּחַיֵּיכוֹן וּבְיוֹמֵיכוֹן וּבְחַיֵּי דְכָל־בֵּית

---

* Sephardim add here: וְיַצְמַח פּוּרְקָנֵהּ וִיקָרֵב מְשִׁיחֵהּ.

יִשְׂרָאֵל, בַּעֲגָלָא וּבִזְמַן קָרִיב, וְאִמְרוּ אָמֵן.

יְהֵא שְׁמֵהּ רַבָּא מְבָרַךְ לְעָלַם וּלְעָלְמֵי עָלְמַיָּא.

יִתְבָּרַךְ וְיִשְׁתַּבַּח וְיִתְפָּאַר וְיִתְרוֹמַם וְיִתְנַשֵּׂא, וְיִתְהַדָּר וְיִתְעַלֶּה וְיִתְהַלָּל שְׁמֵהּ דְּקוּדְשָׁא. בְּרִיךְ הוּא לְעֵלָּא מִן* כָּל בִּרְכָתָא וְשִׁירָתָא, תֻּשְׁבְּחָתָא וְנֶחֱמָתָא דַּאֲמִירָן בְּעָלְמָא, וְאִמְרוּ אָמֵן.

TRANSLITERATION

Yit-gadal ve-yit kadash shmay rabba be-alma di-vera chi-ru-tay, ve-yamlich malchutay** be-cha'yaychon u-ve-yo-maychon u-ve-cha'yay de-chol bet Yisrael ba-agala u-vi-zeman kariv, ve-imru, Amen.

Y'hay shmay rabba me-vorach le-olam u-le-almay alma' ya.

Yit-barach ve-yishtabach, ve-yit-pa'ar ve-yit-romam, ve-yit-nasay ve-yit-hadar, ve-yit-aleh ve-yit-halal shmay de-Kudesha. Brich Hu le-ayla min*** kol birchata ve-shirata tushbechata ve-nechemata, da-amiran be-alma, ve-imru, Amen.

---

* From Rosh Hashana through Yom Kippur substitute the words לְעֵלָּא מִכָּל for לְעֵלָּא מִן כָּל. In some communities the words לְעֵלָּא וּלְעֵלָּא מִכָּל are substituted.

**Sephardim add here: ve-yitzmach purkanay vi-karev meshichay.

***From Rosh Hashana through Yom Kippur substitute the words le-ayla mi-kol for le-ayla min kol. In some communities the words le-ayla u-le-ayla mi-kol are substituted.

TRANSLATION

Glorified and sanctified be God's great name throughout
the world, which He has created according to His will.
May He establish His kingdom within your lifetime and
within the lifetime of the whole house of Israel, speedily
and soon, and let us say, Amen.

May His great name be praised unto all eternity.

Exalted and praised, glorified and adored, extolled and
revered be the name of the Holy One. Blessed is He
beyond all song and psalm, beyond all praise mortal man
can bestow upon Him, and let us say, Amen.

THE BURIAL KADDISH

קַדִּישׁ דְּאִתְחַדְתָּא

KADDISH DE-ITCHADETA

[The Burial Kaddish is not recited on days when
Tachanun is omitted from the morning prayer service
and the *Tziduk Ha-din* prayer is omitted from the
cemetery service. On those days the regular Mourners' Kaddish is recited at the cemetery.]

יִתְגַּדַּל וְיִתְקַדַּשׁ שְׁמֵהּ רַבָּא בְּעָלְמָא דְּהוּא עָתִיד
לְאִתְחַדְתָּא, וּלְאַחֲיָא מֵתַיָא, וּלְאַסָּקָא לְחַיֵּי עָלְמָא;
וּלְמִבְנֵי קַרְתָּא דִירוּשְׁלֵם, וּלְשַׁכְלֵל הֵיכָלֵהּ בְּגַוַּהּ,
וּלְמֶעֱקַר פּוּלְחָנָא נוּכְרָאָה מֵאַרְעָא, וּלְאָתָבָא פּוּלְחָנָא
דִשְׁמַיָּא לְאַתְרֵהּ, וְיַמְלִיךְ קוּדְשָׁא בְּרִיךְ הוּא בְּמַלְכוּתֵהּ

וִיקָרֵהּ, בְּחַיֵּיכוֹן וּבְיוֹמֵיכוֹן, וּבְחַיֵּי דְכָל־בֵּית יִשְׂרָאֵל,
בַּעֲגָלָא וּבִזְמַן קָרִיב, וְאִמְרוּ, אָמֵן.

יְהֵא שְׁמֵהּ רַבָּא מְבָרַךְ לְעָלַם וּלְעָלְמֵי עָלְמַיָּא.

יִתְבָּרַךְ וְיִשְׁתַּבַּח, וְיִתְפָּאַר וְיִתְרוֹמַם, וְיִתְנַשֵּׂא וְיִתְהַדָּר,
וְיִתְעַלֶּה וְיִתְהַלָּל שְׁמֵהּ דְּקוּדְשָׁא. בְּרִיךְ הוּא לְעֵלָּא
מִן* כָּל בִּרְכָתָא וְשִׁירָתָא, תֻּשְׁבְּחָתָא וְנֶחֱמָתָא, דַּאֲמִירָן
בְּעָלְמָא, וְאִמְרוּ אָמֵן.

יְהֵא שְׁלָמָא רַבָּא מִן שְׁמַיָּא וְחַיִּים (טוֹבִים) עָלֵינוּ וְעַל
כָּל־יִשְׂרָאֵל, וְאִמְרוּ אָמֵן.

עֹשֶׂה שָׁלוֹם בִּמְרוֹמָיו, הוּא (בְּרַחֲמָיו) יַעֲשֶׂה שָׁלוֹם
עָלֵינוּ וְעַל כָּל־יִשְׂרָאֵל, וְאִמְרוּ אָמֵן.

TRANSLITERATION

Yitgadal ve-yitkadash shmay rabba. Be-alma de-hu atid le-itchadeta, u-le-acha'ya meta'ya, u-le-asaka le-cha'yay al-ma; u-le-mivnay karta di-Yerushlem, u-le-shachlel he-cha-lay be-gava, u-le-me'ekar pulchana nuchra'a me-ar'a, u-le-atava pulchana di-Shema'ya le-atra, ve-yamlich Ku-desha, brich Hu be-malchutay vi-karay, be-cha'yaychon u-ve-yomaychon, u-ve-cha'yay de-chol bet Yisrael, ba-agala u-vi-zeman kariv, ve-imru, Amen.

Y'hay shmay rabba me-vorach le-olam u-le-almay alma-ya.

---

* From Rosh Hashana through Yom Kippur substitute the words לְעֵלָּא מִכָּל for לְעֵלָּא מִן כָּל. In some communities the words לְעֵלָּא וּלְעֵלָּא מִכָּל are substituted.

Yit-barach ve-yishtabach, ve-yit-pa'ar ve-yit-romam, ve-yit-nasay ve-yit-hadar, ve-yit-aleh ve-yit-halal shmay de-Kudesha. Brich Hu le-ayla min* kol birchata ve-shirata tushbechata ve-nechemata, da-amiran be-alma, ve-imru, Amen.

Y'hay shelama rabba min she-ma'ya ve-cha'yim (tovim) alaynu ve-al kol Yisrael, ve-imru, Amen.

Oseh shalom bi-meromav, Hu (be-rachamav) ya-aseh shalom alaynu ve-al kol Yisrael, ve-imru, Amen.

Translation

Glorified and sanctified be the great name of God in the world which He will create anew, and in which the dead will be revived and ushered into everlasting life. There, Jerusalem and the Temple will be rebuilt, the worship of idols will be eradicated, and true heavenly worship restored to its position of primacy. May this happen within your lifetime and within the lifetime of the whole house of Israel, speedily and soon, and let us say, Amen.

May His great name be praised unto all eternity.

Exalted and praised, glorified and adored, extolled and revered be the name of the Holy One. Blessed is He beyond all song and psalm, beyond all tributes mortal man can bestow upon Him.

May the prayers and supplications of the whole household of Israel be accepted by their Father who is in heaven, and let us say, Amen.

---

*From Rosh Hashana through Yom Kippur substitute the words *le-ayla-mi-kol* for *le-ayla min kol*. In some communities the words *le-ayla u-le-ayla mi-kol* are substituted.

May life and abundant peace descend from heaven upon us and all Israel, and let us say, Amen.

May the Creator of heavenly peace bestow peace upon us and all Israel, and let us say, Amen.

UNVEILING SERVICE

הֲקָמַת מַצֵּבָה

[A cloth covering is draped over the monument before the ceremony begins.]

Leader:

In solemn assembly we have gathered at the grave of our dear relative and friend _____, who within the year was summoned to his (her) heavenly abode. Though days and weeks and months have passed since he (she) was taken from our midst, the void in our lives has made us ever conscious of his (her) passing. As evidence of our devotion to his (her) memory, this monument, inscribed with his (her) name, has been erected, and is to be unveiled and consecrated after appropriate words of prayer and meditation.

Psalm I

(Responsive reading)

Leader:

אַשְׁרֵי הָאִישׁ אֲשֶׁר לֹא הָלַךְ בַּעֲצַת רְשָׁעִים, וּבְדֶרֶךְ
חַטָּאִים לֹא עָמָד, וּבְמוֹשַׁב לֵצִים לֹא יָשָׁב.

Assembly:

Fortunate are they who have not followed the
counsel of the wicked, nor followed in the ways
of sinners, nor dwelt in the midst of scoffers.

Leader:

כִּי אִם בְּתוֹרַת יהוה חֶפְצוֹ, וּבְתוֹרָתוֹ יֶהְגֶּה יוֹמָם
וָלָיְלָה.

Assembly:

Their delight has been to study the laws of the
Lord and to meditate on his teachings day and
night.

Leader:

וְהָיָה כְּעֵץ שָׁתוּל עַל פַּלְגֵי מָיִם, אֲשֶׁר פִּרְיוֹ יִתֵּן בְּעִתּוֹ,
וְעָלֵהוּ לֹא יִבּוֹל, וְכֹל אֲשֶׁר יַעֲשֶׂה יַצְלִיחַ.

Assembly:

They shall be like trees planted by streams of
water, that bring forth fruit in its season, and
whose leaf does not wither; and whatsoever
they undertake, they shall prosper.

Leader:

כִּי יוֹדֵעַ יהוה דֶּרֶךְ צַדִּיקִים, וְדֶרֶךְ רְשָׁעִים תֹּאבֵד.

Assembly:

For the Lord is pleased with the ways of the righteous, and the ways of the wicked shall not prosper.

[A family member removes the cloth covering from the monument.]

Leader:

In the presence of this assembly of devoted relatives and friends of our late departed _____ , we unveil and consecrate this monument to his (her) memory as a token of love and respect.

[The leader then reads the words inscribed on the monument.]

All recite in unison:

תְּהֵא נִשְׁמָתוֹ (נִשְׁמָתָהּ) צְרוּרָה בִּצְרוֹר הַחַיִּים.

Tehay nishmato (*for a woman say:* nishmata) tzerura bi-tzeror ha-cha'yim.

May his (her) soul be bound up in the bond of eternal life.

[At this point a eulogy may be spoken.]

El Malay Rachamim

(FOR A MALE)

אֵל מָלֵא רַחֲמִים, שׁוֹכֵן בַּמְּרוֹמִים, הַמְצֵא מְנוּחָה נְכוֹנָה
תַּחַת כַּנְפֵי הַשְּׁכִינָה, בְּמַעֲלוֹת קְדוֹשִׁים וּטְהוֹרִים כְּזֹהַר
הָרָקִיעַ מַזְהִירִים, אֶת־נִשְׁמַת _____ בֶּן _____ שֶׁהָלַךְ
לְעוֹלָמוֹ, בְּגַן עֵדֶן תְּהֵא מְנוּחָתוֹ.

אָנָּא, בַּעַל הָרַחֲמִים, הַסְתִּירֵהוּ בְּסֵתֶר כְּנָפֶיךָ לְעוֹלָמִים,
וּצְרוֹר בִּצְרוֹר הַחַיִּים אֶת־נִשְׁמָתוֹ, יהוה הוּא נַחֲלָתוֹ,
וְיָנוּחַ בְּשָׁלוֹם עַל מִשְׁכָּבוֹ, וְנֹאמַר אָמֵן.

El malay rachamim, shochen ba-meromim, hamtzay
menucha nechona tachat kanfay ha-Shechina, be-maalot
kedoshim u-tehorim ke-zohar ha-rakia mazhirim, et nishmat _____ ben _____ she-halach le-olamo. Be-
Gan Eden tehay menuchato.

Ana, Baal Ha-rachamim, hastirayhu be-seter kenafe-cha
le-olamim, u-tzeror bi-tzeror ha-cha'yím et nishmato,
Adonai Hu nachalato, ve-yanuach be-shalom al mishkavo, ve-nomar, Amen.

O God, full of compassion, who dwellest on high, grant
perfect peace to our dear departed _____ son
of _____. May his soul radiate splendor along with
the souls of all the righteous ones of this world. May his
eternal resting place be the Garden of Eden.

We beseech Thee, God of mercy, harbor him under Thy

protective wings, and may his soul be bound up with the souls of the living. May he rest in peace, and let us say, Amen.

El Malay Rachamim

(FOR A FEMALE)

אֵל מָלֵא רַחֲמִים, שׁוֹכֵן בַּמְּרוֹמִים, הַמְצֵא מְנוּחָה נְכוֹנָה תַּחַת כַּנְפֵי הַשְּׁכִינָה, בְּמַעֲלוֹת קְדוֹשִׁים וּטְהוֹרִים כְּזֹהַר הָרָקִיעַ מַזְהִירִים, אֶת־נִשְׁמַת _____ בַּת _____ שֶׁהָלְכָה לְעוֹלָמָהּ, בְּגַן עֵדֶן תְּהֵא מְנוּחָתָהּ.

אָנָּא, בַּעַל הָרַחֲמִים, הַסְתִּירֶהָ בְּסֵתֶר כְּנָפֶיךָ לְעוֹלָמִים, וּצְרוֹר בִּצְרוֹר הַחַיִּים אֶת־נִשְׁמָתָהּ, יהוה הוּא נַחֲלָתָהּ, וְתָנוּחַ בְּשָׁלוֹם עַל מִשְׁכָּבָהּ, וְנֹאמַר אָמֵן.

El malay rachamim, shochen ba-meromim, hamtzay menucha nechona tachat kanfay ha-Shechina, be-maalot kedoshim u-tehorim ke-zohar ha-rakia mazhirim, et nishmat _____ bat _____ she-halcha le-olama. Be-gan Eden tehay menuchata.

Ana, Baal Ha-rachamim, hastireha be-seter kenafecha le-olamim, u-tzeror bi-tzeror ha-cha'yim et nishmata, Adonai Hu nachalata, ve-tanuach be-shalom al mishkava, ve-nomar, Amen.

O God, full of compassion, who dwellest on high, grant perfect peace to our dear departed _____ daughter of _____. May her soul radiate splendor along with the souls of all the righteous ones of this world. May her eternal resting place be the Garden of Eden.

We beseech Thee, God of mercy, harbor her under Thy protective wings, and may her soul be bound up with the souls of the living. May she rest in peace, and let us say, Amen.

Concluding Prayer

All-merciful father, we have consecrated this monument to the memory of our dear departed _____. We have perfect faith in Thy judgement and Thy decree. We know, O Thou who givest and takest life, that in Thy infinite wisdom Thou doest what is best for the children of men.

In the midst of our grief, we raise our voices to Thee in prayer and thanksgiving for the pleasant years which it was our good fortune to share with our departed, and for the sweet and tender memories that those years have given unto us. We shall always guard them and cherish them.

Send, we pray Thee, of Thine abundant goodness and mercy upon the sorrowing (mate, children, brothers, sisters) relatives and friends who have assembled here to honor him (her) who has been taken from us. Make them steadfast in their faith in Thee, and in their future. Teach them to face the trying days ahead firmly and courageously, that by their living example they may do honor to him (her) who was so dear to them in life. Comfort them and sustain them and bless them. Amen.

Appendix III

Home Yizkor Memorial Service

[Yizkor is traditionally recited in the synagogue. However, if for any reason one cannot attend a synagogue service, he or she may recite the Yizkor prayers at home. Since a *minyan* (quorum) will not be present in the home, the Kaddish, which is often recited as part of the Yizkor service, is omitted.]

In this solemn hour, my thoughts turn to the memory of my dear and loving relatives who are no longer with me. Despite the passage of time and the absence of their physical form, I feel their presence, their love, and their influence. The power of their lives is still real, as real as when they were alive. They remain for me a tower of strength, a source of inspiration, and a constant influence for good. The values and lessons they transmitted to me and instilled within me still energize and motivate me. May they never lose their potency.

In this sacred hour of remembrance, I pray that these feelings of gratefulness never recede as I now recall those individuals who were closest and dearest to me. May their souls ever be linked with my soul, and may they rest in peace.

[Continue with this selection of verses from the Book of Psalms and the Book of Ecclesiastes.]

יהוה מָה־אָדָם וַתֵּדָעֵהוּ, בֶּן־אֱנוֹשׁ וַתְּחַשְּׁבֵהוּ.

Adonai ma adam va-tayda'ayhu, ben enosh va-te-chash-vayhu.

O Lord, what is a man that you are mindful of him.

אָדָם לַהֶבֶל דָּמָה, יָמָיו כְּצֵל עוֹבֵר.

Adam la-hevel dama, yamav ke-tzayl over.

Man is like a breath, his days like a passing shadow.

348

בַּבֹּקֶר יָצִיץ וְחָלָף, לָעֶרֶב יְמוֹלֵל וְיָבֵשׁ.

Ba-boker yatzitz ve-chalaf, la-erev yemolel ve-yavesh.

In the morning he flourishes and grows up like grass,
In the evening he is cut down and withers.

לִמְנוֹת יָמֵינוּ כֵּן הוֹדַע, וְנָבִיא לְבַב חָכְמָה.

Limnot yamenu ken hoda, ve-navi levav chochma.

So teach us to number our days,
That we may get us a heart of wisdom.

שְׁמָר־תָּם וּרְאֵה יָשָׁר, כִּי־אַחֲרִית לְאִישׁ שָׁלוֹם.

Shmor tam u-re'ay yashar, ki acharit le-ish shalom.

Mark the man of integrity, and behold the upright,
For there is a future for the man of peace.

> [Continue with the Yizkor prayer(s) that apply to your individual situation.]

Yizkor in memory of a father:

יִזְכֹּר אֱלֹהִים אֶת נִשְׁמַת אָבִי מוֹרִי _____ בֶּן _____ שֶׁהָלַךְ לְעוֹלָמוֹ. אֲנִי נוֹדֵר (נוֹדֶרֶת) צְדָקָה בְּעַד הַזְכָּרַת נִשְׁמָתוֹ. וּבִשְׂכַר זֶה, תְּהֵא נַפְשׁוֹ צְרוּרָה בִּצְרוֹר הַחַיִּים עִם נִשְׁמוֹת אַבְרָהָם, יִצְחָק, וְיַעֲקֹב, וְעִם שְׁאָר צַדִּיקִים שֶׁבְּגַן עֵדֶן. אָמֵן.

Yizkor Elohim et nishmat avi mori _____ ben _____ she-halach le-olamo. Ani noder (women say: noderet) tzedaka be-ad hazkarat nishmato. Bi-sechar zeh, tehay nafsho tzerura bi-tzeror ha-cha'yim im nishmot Avraham, Yitzchak ve-Yaakov, ve-im she'ar tzadikim she-b' Gan Eden. Amen.

May God remember the soul of my dear father _____

ben _____ who has gone to his eternal reward. In his memory I pledge charity to a worthy cause. As a reward for my charitable act, may his soul be bound up with the souls of the patriarchs Abraham, Isaac, and Jacob, along with all the other righteous men of all generations who have merited eternal life. May he rest in peace. Amen.

Yizkor in memory of a mother:

יִזְכֹּר אֱלֹהִים אֶת נִשְׁמַת אִמִּי מוֹרָתִי _____ בַּת _____ שֶׁהָלְכָה לְעוֹלָמָהּ. אֲנִי נוֹדֵר (נוֹדֶרֶת) צְדָקָה בְּעַד הַזְכָּרַת נִשְׁמָתָהּ. וּבִשְׂכַר זֶה, תְּהֵא נַפְשָׁהּ צְרוּרָה בִּצְרוֹר הַחַיִּים עִם נִשְׁמוֹת שָׂרָה, רִבְקָה, רָחֵל, וְלֵאָה וְעִם שְׁאָר צִדְקָנִיּוֹת שֶׁבְּגַן עֵדֶן. אָמֵן.

Yizkor Elohim et nishmat imi morati _____ bat _____ she-halcha le-olama. Ani noder (women say: noderet) tzedaka be-ad hazkarat nishmata. Bi-sechar zeh, tehay nafsha tzerura bi-tzeror ha-cha'yim im nishmot Sara, Rivka, Rachel, ve-Leah, ve-im she'ar tzidkaniyot she-b'Gan Eden. Amen

May God remember the soul of of my dear mother _____ bat _____ who has gone to her eternal reward. In her memory I pledge charity to a worthy cause. As a reward for my charitable act may her soul be bound up with the souls of our matriarchs Sarah, Rebecca, Rachel, and Leah, along with all the righteous women of all generations who have merited eternal life. May she rest in peace. Amen.

Yizkor in memory of a husband:

יִזְכֹּר אֱלֹהִים אֶת נִשְׁמַת בַּעֲלִי _____ בֶּן _____
שֶׁהָלַךְ לְעוֹלָמוֹ. אֲנִי נוֹדֶרֶת צְדָקָה בְּעַד הַזְכָּרַת נִשְׁמָתוֹ.
וּבִשְׂכַר זֶה, תְּהֵא נַפְשׁוֹ צְרוּרָה בִּצְרוֹר הַחַיִּים עִם נִשְׁמוֹת
אַבְרָהָם יִצְחָק וְיַעֲקֹב וְעִם שְׁאָר צַדִּיקִים שֶׁבְּגַן עֵדֶן. אָמֵן.

Yizkor Elohim et nishmat baali _____ ben _____
she-halach le-olomo. Ani noderet tzedaka be-ad haz-
karat nishmato. Bi-sechar zeh, tehay nafsho tzerura bi-
tzeror ha-cha'yim im nishmot Avraham, Yitzchak, ve-
Yaakov, ve-im she'ar tzadikim she-b'Gan Eden. Amen.

May God remember the soul of my dear husband
_____ ben _____ who has gone to his eternal
reward. In his memory I pledge charity to a worthy
cause. As a reward for my charitable act, may his soul be
bound up with the souls of our patriarchs Abraham,
Isaac, and Jacob, along with all the other righteous men
of all generations who have merited eternal life. May he
rest in peace. Amen.

Yizkor in memory of a wife:

יִזְכֹּר אֱלֹהִים אֶת נִשְׁמַת אִשְׁתִּי _____ בַּת _____
שֶׁהָלְכָה לְעוֹלָמָהּ. אֲנִי נוֹדֵר צְדָקָה בְּעַד הַזְכָּרַת נִשְׁמָתָהּ.
וּבִשְׂכַר זֶה, תְּהֵא נַפְשָׁהּ צְרוּרָה בִּצְרוֹר הַחַיִּים עִם
נִשְׁמוֹת שָׂרָה רִבְקָה רָחֵל וְלֵאָה וְעִם שְׁאָר צִדְקָנִיּוֹת
שֶׁבְּגַן עֵדֶן. אָמֵן.

Yizkor Elohim et nishmat ishti _____ bat _____
she-halcha le-olama. Ani noder tzedaka be-ad hazkarat
nishmata. Bi-sechar zeh, tehay nafsha tzerura bi-tzeror

ha-cha'yim im nishmot Sara, Rivka, Rachel, ve-Leah, ve-im she'ar tzidkaniyot she-b'Gan Eden. Amen.

May God remember the soul of my dear wife _____ bat _____ who has gone to her eternal reward. In mer memory I pledge charity to a worthy cause. As a reward for my charitable act, may her soul be bound up with the souls of our matriarchs Sarah, Rebecca, Rachel, and Leah, along with all the righteous women of all generations who have merited eternal life. May she rest in peace. Amen.

Yizkor in memory of a son:

יִזְכֹּר אֱלֹהִים אֶת נִשְׁמַת בְּנִי _____ בֶּן _____ שֶׁהָלַךְ לְעוֹלָמוֹ. אֲנִי נוֹדֵר (נוֹדֶרֶת) צְדָקָה בְּעַד הַזְכָּרַת נִשְׁמָתוֹ. וּבִשְׂכַר זֶה, תְּהֵא נַפְשׁוֹ צְרוּרָה בִּצְרוֹר הַחַיִּים עִם נִשְׁמוֹת אַבְרָהָם יִצְחָק וְיַעֲקֹב, וְעִם שְׁאָר צַדִּיקִים שֶׁבְּגַן עֵדֶן. אָמֵן.

Yizkor Elohim et nishmat b'ni _____ ben _____ she-halach le-olamo. Ani noder (women say: noderet) tzedaka be-ad hazkarat nishmato. Bi-sechar zeh, tehay nafsho tzerura bi-tzeror ha-cha-yim im nishmot Avraham, Yitzchak, ve-Yaakov, ve-im she'ar tzadikim she-b'Gan Eden. Amen.

May God remember the soul of my dear son _____ ben _____ who has gone to his eternal reward. In his memory I pledge charity to a worthy cause. As a reward for my charitable act, may his soul be bound up with the souls of our patriarchs Abraham, Isaac, and Jacob, along with all other righteous men of all generations who have merited eternal life. May he rest in peace. Amen.

Yizkor in memory of a daughter:

יִזְכֹּר אֱלֹהִים אֶת נִשְׁמַת בִּתִּי _____ בַּת
_____שֶׁהָלְכָה לְעוֹלָמָהּ. אֲנִי נוֹדֵר (נוֹדֶרֶת) צְדָקָה
בְּעַד הַזְכָּרַת נִשְׁמָתָהּ. וּבִשְׂכַר זֶה, תְּהֵא נַפְשָׁהּ צְרוּרָה
בִּצְרוֹר הַחַיִּים עִם נִשְׁמוֹת שָׂרָה, רִבְקָה, רָחֵל, וְלֵאָה
וְעִם שְׁאָר צִדְקָנִיּוֹת שֶׁבְּגַן עֵדֶן. אָמֵן.

Yizkor Elohim et nishmat biti _____ bat _____
she-halcha le-olama. Ani noder (women say: *noderet*)
tzedaka be-ad hazkarat nishmata. Bi-sechar zeh, tehay
nafsha tzerura bi-tzeror ha-cha'yim im nishmot Sara,
Rivka, Rachel, ve-Leah, ve-im she'ar tzidkaniyot she-
b'Gan Eden. Amen.

May God remember the soul of my dear daughter _____
daughter _____ of who has gone to her eternal reward.
In her memory I pledge charity to a worthy cause. As a
reward for my charitable act, may her soul be bound up
with the souls of our matriarchs Sarah, Rebecca, Rachel,
and Leah, along with all the righteous women of all generations who have merited eternal life. May she rest in
peace. Amen.

Yizkor in memory of relatives and friends:

יִזְכֹּר אֱלֹהִים אֶת נִשְׁמוֹת _____ שֶׁהָלְכוּ לְעוֹלָמָם. אֲנִי
נוֹדֵר (נוֹדֶרֶת) צְדָקָה בְּעַד הַזְכָּרַת נִשְׁמוֹתֵיהֶם. לָכֵן בַּעַל
הָרַחֲמִים יַסְתִּירֵם בְּסֵתֶר כְּנָפָיו לְעוֹלָמִים, וְיִצְרוֹר בִּצְרוֹר
הַחַיִּים אֶת נִשְׁמוֹתֵיהֶם, וְיָנוּחוּ בְּשָׁלוֹם עַל מִשְׁכְּבוֹתָם.
אָמֵן.

Yizkor Elohim et nishmot _____ she-halchu le-ola-
mam. Ani noder (women say: *noderet*) *tzedaka be-ad*

*hazkarat nishmotayhem. Lachen Baal Ha-rachamim yas-
tiraym be-seter kenafav le-olamim, ve-yitzror bi-tzeror
ha-cha'yim et nishmotayhem, ve-yanuchu be-shalom al
mishkevotam. Amen.*

May God remember the souls of my friends and relatives
_____ who have gone to their eternal reward. In
their memory I pledge charity to a worthy cause. As a reward for my charitable act, may their souls be bound up
with the souls of the living, and may they rest in peace.
Amen.

EL MALAY RACHAMIM

(FOR A MALE)

אֵל מָלֵא רַחֲמִים, שׁוֹכֵן בַּמְּרוֹמִים, הַמְצֵא מְנוּחָה נְכוֹנָה
תַּחַת כַּנְפֵי הַשְּׁכִינָה, בְּמַעֲלוֹת קְדוֹשִׁים וּטְהוֹרִים כְּזֹהַר
הָרָקִיעַ מַזְהִירִים, אֶת־נִשְׁמַת _____ בֶּן _____ שֶׁהָלַךְ
לְעוֹלָמוֹ, בְּגַן עֵדֶן תְּהֵא מְנוּחָתוֹ.

אָנָּא, בַּעַל הָרַחֲמִים, הַסְתִּירֵהוּ בְּסֵתֶר כְּנָפֶיךָ לְעוֹלָמִים,
וּצְרוֹר בִּצְרוֹר הַחַיִּים אֶת־נִשְׁמָתוֹ, יהוה הוּא נַחֲלָתוֹ,
וְיָנוּחַ בְּשָׁלוֹם עַל מִשְׁכָּבוֹ, וְנֹאמַר אָמֵן.

*El malay rachamim, shochen ba-meromim, hamtzay
menucha nechona tachat kanfay ha-Shechina, be-ma-
alot kedoshim u-tehorim ke-zohar ha-rakia mazhirim, et
nishmat _____ ben _____ she-halach le-olamo.
Be-Gan Eden tehay menuchato.*

Ana, Baal Ha-rachamim, hastirayhu be-seter kenafecha le-olamim, u-tzeror bi-tzeror ha-cha'yim et nishmato, Adonai Hu nachalato, ve-yanuach be-shalom al mishkavo, ve-nomar, Amen.

O God, full of compassion, who dwellest on high, grant perfect peace to our dear departed _____ son of _____ . May his soul radiate splendor along with the souls of all the righteous ones of this world. May his eternal resting place be the Garden of Eden. We beseech Thee, God of mercy, harbor him under Thy protective wings, and may his soul be bound up with the souls of the living. May he rest in peace, And let us say, Amen.

EL MALAY RACHAMIM

(FOR A FEMALE)

אֵל מָלֵא רַחֲמִים, שׁוֹכֵן בַּמְּרוֹמִים, הַמְצֵא מְנוּחָה
נְכוֹנָה תַּחַת כַּנְפֵי הַשְּׁכִינָה, בְּמַעֲלוֹת קְדוֹשִׁים וּטְהוֹרִים
כְּזֹהַר הָרָקִיעַ מַזְהִירִים, אֶת־נִשְׁמַת _____ בַּת _____
שֶׁהָלְכָה לְעוֹלָמָהּ, בְּגַן עֵדֶן תְּהֵא מְנוּחָתָהּ.
אָנָּא, בַּעַל הָרַחֲמִים, הַסְתִּירֶהָ בְּסֵתֶר כְּנָפֶיךָ לְעוֹלָמִים,
וּצְרוֹר בִּצְרוֹר הַחַיִּים אֶת־נִשְׁמָתָהּ, יהוה הוּא נַחֲלָתָהּ,
וְתָנוּחַ בְּשָׁלוֹם עַל מִשְׁכָּבָהּ, וְנֹאמַר אָמֵן.

El malay rachamim, shochen ba-meromim, hamtzay menucha nechona tachat kanfay ha-Schechina, be-ma-alot kedoshim u-tehorim ke-zohar ha-rakia mazhirim, et

nishmat _____ *bat* _____ *she-halcha le-olama.*
Be-Gan Eden tehay menuchata.

Ana, Baal Ha-rachamim, hastireha be-seter kenafecha
le-olamim, u-tzeror bi-tzeror ha-cha'yim et nishmata,
Adonai Hu nachalata, ve-tanuach be-shalom al mishka-
va, ve-nomar, Amen.

O God, full of compassion, who dwellest on high, grant
perfect peace to our dear departed _____ daughter
of _____ . May her soul radiate splendor along with
the souls of all the righteous ones of this world. May her
eternal resting place be the Garden of Eden. We beseech
Thee, God of mercy, harbor her under Thy protective
wings, and may her soul be bound up with the souls of
the living. May she rest in peace, and let us say, Amen.

[Conclude the Yizkor service with the recitation of
Psalm 23.]

מִזְמוֹר לְדָוִד:

יהוה רֹעִי לֹא אֶחְסָר.

בִּנְאוֹת דֶּשֶׁא יַרְבִּיצֵנִי, עַל־מֵי מְנָחוֹת יְנַהֲלֵנִי.

נַפְשִׁי יְשׁוֹבֵב, יַנְחֵנִי בְמַעְגְּלֵי־צֶדֶק לְמַעַן שְׁמוֹ.

גַּם כִּי אֵלֵךְ בְּגֵיא צַלְמָוֶת, לֹא אִירָא רָע

כִּי אַתָּה עִמָּדִי.

שִׁבְטְךָ וּמִשְׁעַנְתֶּךָ הֵמָּה יְנַחֲמֻנִי.

תַּעֲרֹךְ לְפָנַי שֻׁלְחָן נֶגֶד צֹרְרָי.

דִּשַּׁנְתָּ בַשֶּׁמֶן רֹאשִׁי כּוֹסִי רְוָיָה.

אַךְ טוֹב וָחֶסֶד יִרְדְּפוּנִי כָּל־יְמֵי חַיָּי,

וְשַׁבְתִּי בְּבֵית־יהוה לְאֹרֶךְ יָמִים.

Mizmor le-David.
Adonai ro'i lo echsar.
Bi-n'eot desheh yarbitzeni, al may
    menuchot ye-nahaleni.
Nafshi yeshovev, yancheni be-ma'aglay tzedek
    le-ma'an Shemo.
Gam ki aylaych b'gay tzalmavet, lo
    ira ra, ki ata imadi.
Shivtecha u-mishantecha hayma ye-nachamuni.
Ta'aroch lefanai shulchan neged tzorerai.
Dishanta va-shemen roshi, kosi reva'ya.
Ach tov va-chesed yirdefuni kol yemay cha'yai,
Ve-shavti be-vet Adonai le-orech yamim.

PSALM 23

The Lord is my shepherd; I shall not want.
    He maketh me to lie down in green pastures;
    He leadeth me beside the still waters.
He renews my life.
He guideth me in straight paths for His name's sake.
    Yea, though I walk through the valley of the shadow
        of death,
    I will fear no evil, for Thou art with me;
    Thy rod and Thy staff, they comfort me.
Thou preparest a table before me in the presence of
    mine enemies;
Thou hast anointed my head with oil; my cup runneth
    over.
Surely goodness and mercy shall follow me all the days
    of my life;
And I shall dwell in the house of the Lord forever.

APPENDIX IV

FAMILY YAHRZEIT RECORD

English name of deceased _____

Hebrew name of deceased _____

Family relationship _____

English date of death _____ Hebrew date of death _____

English date of burial _____ Hebrew date of burial _____

Name of cemetery _____ Plot no. _____

Names of immediate relatives:

       Father _____

       Mother _____

       Sons _____

       Daughters _____

       Brothers _____

       Sisters _____

➤❖➤

English name of deceased _____

Hebrew name of deceased _____

Family relationship _____

English date of death _____ Hebrew date of death _____

English date of burial _____ Hebrew date of burial _____

Name of cemetery _____ Plot no. _____

Names of immediate relatives:

       Father _____

       Mother _____

       Sons _____

       Daughters _____

       Brothers _____

       Sisters _____

Family Yahrzeit Record

English name of deceased _____

Hebrew name of deceased _____

Family relationship _____

English date of death _____ Hebrew date of death _____

English date of burial _____ Hebrew date of burial _____

Name of cemetery _____ Plot no. _____

Names of immediate relatives:

      Father _____

      Mother _____

      Sons _____

      Daughters _____

      Brothers _____

      Sisters _____

><

English name of deceased _____

Hebrew name of deceased _____

Family relationship _____

English date of death _____ Hebrew date of death _____

English date of burial _____ Hebrew date of burial _____

Name of cemetery _____ Plot no. _____

Names of immediate relatives:

      Father _____

      Mother _____

      Sons _____

      Daughters _____

      Brothers _____

      Sisters _____

Notes to Chapter 1

FROM LIFE TO DEATH
Pages 5 to 25

1. Nedarim 39b.
2. Ibid. 40a.
3. Hilchot Avel 14:5.
4. Ibid. See also the Jerusalem Talmud, Peah 3:9.
5. Shabbat 127a; Yoreh Deah 335:1; *Chochmat Adam* 151:1.
6. See Nidda 44b, comment of Tosafot, which says that despite the reality that most individuals characterized as *gossesim* ("terminally ill persons") die, violating the Sabbath for their benefit is permitted. See also *Kol Bo Al Avelut,* p.22.
7. Yoreh Deah 337:1.
8. See the responsum of Rabbi Solomon B. Freehof in *Reform Responsa and Recent Reform Responsa,* pp.122ff., for a full discussion.
9. Yoreh Deah 339:4.
10. See Joshua Trachtenberg's *Jewish Magic and Superstition,* p.49.
11. Rabbi Aaron Berechia ben Moses of Modena, an Italian Kabbalist who died in 1639, composed the classic *Ma-avar Yabok,* which details all the laws and customs of mourning.
12. Mishna Sanhedrin 6:2.
13. Yoreh Deah 338:1.
14. Yoreh Deah 338:2.
15. Moed Katan 28a.
16. Shabbat 55a.
17. See Exodus Rabba 32:1.
18. Romans 5:12 says: "Sin came into the world through one man [Adam] and death through [his] sin, and so death spread tc all men because all men sinned."
19. Tanchuma on Va-yeshev 4, Chorev edition.
20. Yoreh Deah 339:1.
21. See Isserles on Yoreh Deah 339:1. See also Maimonides' *Mishneh Torah,* Hilchot Avel 4:5, where the point is made that the terminally ill may not be touched if this might hasten death.
22. Nedarim 40a.
23. Ketubot 104a.

24. See *Theology in Responsa,* by Louis Jacobs, pp. 314-15, and *A Treasury of Responsa,* by Solomon B. Freehof, pp. 220-22.
25. See *What Does Judaism Say About...?,* by Rabbi Louis Jacobs, pp. 128 ff. See also *Jewish Medical Ethics,* by Rabbi Immanuel Jakobovitz, pp. 123ff. and 275ff.
26. Bava Batra 17a.
27. Deuteronomy Rabba 11:10.
28. Moed Katan 28a.
29. See *The Tractate Mourning,* by Dov Zlotnick, p. 19.
30. Yoreh Deah 339:1.
31. Shabbat 23:5.
32. See Zlotnick's *Tractate Mourning.* See also Yoreh Deah 339:1-5.
33. See Hayyim Schauss's *Lifetime of a Jew,* p. 230, and the Shach on Yoreh Deah 339:1.
34. Moed Katan 25a and Yoreh Deah 339:3.
35. See Trachtenberg's *Jewish Magic and Superstition,* p. 177.
36. See Yoreh Deah 339:5; Chochmat Adam 151:17; and *Jewish Magic and Superstition,* pp. 57 and 176.
37. See Greenwald's *Kol Bo Al Avelut,* pp. 24-25.
38. In the Middle Ages it was common for people to avoid walking in the dark without a candle or lantern for fear that evil spirits would pounce upon them. The famous scholar Rabbi Jacob Levi Mollin, better known as the Ma-haril (died 1427), warned: "One should not walk through his yard without a light. God forbid!" (See Trachtenberg's *Jewish Magic and Superstition,* p. 46.)
39. Berachot 8:6.
40. Yoma 85a.
41. *Igrot Moshe,* Yoreh Deah II, responsum 174. Later, in Yoreh Deah III, responsum 140, Rabbi Feinstein reverses himself and says, "Parts of a person's body may not be used for any purpose. They are not his to dispose of. Nor may his heirs grant such permission."
42. See Klein's *Responsa and Halakhic Studies,* pp. 34ff., and his essay "Teshuvah on Autopsy," *Conservative Judaism,* Fall 1958, pp. 52-58.
43. See Tuktzinsky's *Gesher Ha-cha'yim* I, p. 70.
44. See Landau's *Noda Bi-yehuda* II, Yoreh Deah 210.
45. See Chatam Sofer, Yoreh Deah 336.
46. Volume 35, pp. 130-34. Quoted on p. 278 of Walter Jacob's *American Reform Responsa.*
47. See *Responsa and Studies in Jewish Law,* by Isaac Klein, pp. 38ff., for a detailed description of the terms of the agreement.
48. See Ettlinger's *Binyan Tziyon* 170-71.
49. See Bleich's *Contemporary Halakhic Problems,* Volume I, pp. 125-26, for a more detailed discussion.
50. See Josephus's *Antiquities of the Jews* XIV 7:4.
51. See Tuktzinsky's *Gesher Ha-cha'yim,* Volume I, p. 73, and

Lamm's *Jewish Way in Death and Mourning,* pp. 8-12, for more detailed information.

52. Yoreh Deah 341:1.
53. Avot 4:23.
54. Semachot 10:1 and Yoreh Deah 341:1.
55. See Sukka 52b, Moed Katan 21a, and Yoreh Deah 388:1.
56. See p. 274.
57. Moed Katan 15b.
58. Yoreh Deah 341:1.
59. Semachot 10:15.

Notes to Chapter 2

PREPARING THE DECEASED FOR BURIAL
Pages 26 to 43

1. Bava Batra 100b and Sanhedrin 46b. Along these lines, owing to modesty considerations the *Code of Jewish Law* (Yoreh Deah 352:3) notes that women may dress a man in burial clothes if need be, but a man may not dress a woman.
2. Sanhedrin 46b and 47a.
3. Sota 14a.
4. See Moed Katan 25a and Yoreh Deah 373:5.
5. For a detailed account of the *tohora* procedure among Ashkenazim, see Maurice Lamm's *Jewish Way in Death and Mourning,* pp. 242ff. For the procedure followed by Sephardim, see Herbert C. Dobrinsky's *Treasury of Sephardic Laws and Customs,* pp. 399 ff.
6. See Tuktzinsky's *Gesher Ha-cha'yim* I, pp. 95-96.
7. See *The Falasha Anthology,* by Wolf Leslau, p. xviii.
8. See *Melamed Le-ho'il* II:122. Quoted in Isaac Klein's *Guide to Jewish Religious Practice,* p. 227.
9. Leviticus Rabba 26:7.
10. Genesis Rabba 100:2.
11. See Ketubot 8b and Yoreh Deah 352:1.
12. Moed Katan 27b.
13. See the Siftay Kohen commentary on Yoreh Deah 352:1. See also the Be'er Hetev commentary ad loc.
14. Moed Katan 27b.
15. Sanhedrin 90b.
16. See Be'er Hetev on Yoreh Deah 301:7.
17. See *Patrimony,* p. 234.
18. Genesis Rabba 100:2.
19. Genesis Rabba 100:2.
20. Yoreh Deah 352:2.

21. Some of the garments have names akin to the priestly garments.
22. In *Patrimony,* author Philip Roth recounts that when his father died in 1989, he and his brother found in his father's bureau a box containing two neatly folded prayershawls. Philip set aside one to be used to enwrap his father's body before it was placed in the coffin. Depite Roth's secularist posture, he could not deny his father the age-old practice of burying a man in the *talit* he wore during his lifetime.
23. See H. Rabinowicz, *A Guide to Life,* p.40.
24. See *Ma-avar Yabok,* by Aaron Berechya, of Modena, Italy, ed., Landshuth, no. 23, p. xxxviii.
25. Yoreh Deah 301:7 and 351:1.
26. Kila'yim 41b.
27. See Yoreh Deah 301:7, 351:1. See also *The Jewish Book of Why,* by Alfred J. Kolatch, p.104, for a fuller discussion of *shaatnez.*
28. See the analysis of Leon Wieseltier in *Congregation: Contemporary Writers Read the Bible,* p.36.
29. See Trachtenberg's *Jewish Magic and Superstition,* p. 127.
30. See Isserles on Orach Cha'yim 610:4 and 664:1.
31. Shabbat 77b.
32. Pirkay Avot 6:9.
33. Yoreh Deah 351:2.
34. See Danzig's *Chochmat Adam* 157:1.
35. Genesis Rabba 100:2.
36. See Trachtenberg's *Jewish Magic and Superstition,* pp.161ff. and 175.
37. Ecclesiastes Rabba 5:14.
38. Yoreh Deah 352:4.
39. See Dobrinsky's *Treasury of Sephardic Laws and Customs,* p.88.
40. Genesis Rabba 19:8.
41. Moed Katan 27a and Ketubot 8b.
42. Ketubot 111a.
43. S. Y. Agnon wrote a moving story on this subject, entitled "Earth From the Land of Israel." The story, translated from the Hebrew by Leah Ain Globe, appears in *A Treasury of Jewish Literature,* edited by Gloria Goldreich.

    Artist Frederick Terna, a survivor of Terezin now living in Brooklyn, New York, includes some Jerusalem soil in the paint he uses for his oils. He says that this ensures that his paintings will go to Jerusalem in the end of days.
44. See Genesis Rabba 100:2 and the Matnot Kehuna commentary.
45. Semachot 9:23 and Sanhedrin 48a.

Notes to Chapter 3
RENDING THE GARMENT
Pages 44 to 62

1. II Samuel 1:11.
2. Moed Katan 15a.
3. See Hayyim Schauss's *Lifetime of a Jew,* pp. 223-24.
4. See Moed Katan 25a and Yoreh Deah 340:5.
5. See Danzig's *Chochmat Adam* 152:4.
6. See Goldberg's *P'nay Baruch* 6:6 and Tuktzinsky's *Gesher Ha-cha'yim* I, p. 58
7. See Greenwald's *Ach Le-tzara,* p. 21.
8. Yoreh Deah 340:1.
9. See Freehof's *Reform Jewish Practice,* p. 168.
10. The Keria blessing appears in the *Rabbi's Manual* of the Central Conference of American Rabbis, edited by David Polish.
11. Semachot 9:5.
12. Yoreh Deah 340:1.
13. The Siftay Kohen (Yoreh Deah 340, note 19) remarks that the sixteenth-century Polish authority Rabbi Solomon Luria (the Maharshal) was unaware of the practice of tearing the garment on the left side for a parent. The Siftay Kohen points out that this is not a legal requirement.
14. Semachot 9:17.
15. See Yoreh Deah 340:23. See also *Ach Le-tzara,* p. 22, and *P'nay Baruch* 6:15.
16. Ibid.
17. Yoreh Deah 340:23 and Moed Katan 26b.
18. Ibid.
19. Yoreh Deah 340:30. See also Semachot 3:1-2.
20. Moed Katan 24a.
21. Yoreh Deah 340:18.
22. Moed Katan 25a.
23. See the Pitchay Teshuvah commentary on Yoreh Deah 340:2.
24. Moed Katan 26b.
25. *Ach Le-tzara,* p. 21.
26. See Yoma 39a and 44b.
27. See Greenwald's *Kol Bo Al Avelut,* p. 28.
28. Yoreh Deah 340:34.
29. Moed Katan 26b.
30. Yoreh Deah 340:29. The Taz and Shach and other commentators point out that although a Keria performed on the Sabbath is considered valid even though it violates the Sabbath, Keria performed on a stolen garment on the Sabbath is considered invalid. This is based not on the fact that the tear was made on the

Sabbath but on the fact that the garment was not owned by the mourner. The *Chochmat Adam* (152:18) reminds us of the principle involved: the mourner performed a *mitzva* through the transgression of a law *(mitzva haba'a ba-avera)*—in this case the law against stealing—and that is not acceptable.

31. See Moed Katan 14b, Semachot 9:6, Yoreh Deah 340:27 plus commentaries, and *Gesher Ha-cha'yim*, p. 61.
32. See Maurice Lamm's *Jewish Way in Death and Mourning*, p. 40.
33. Moed Katan 25a and Yoreh Deah 340:1.
34. See *Ach Le-tzara*, p. 20.
35. Semachot 9:4.
36. Yoreh Deah 340:14.
37. *Gesher Ha-cha'yim* I, pp. 55-63.
38. Moed Katan 20b.
39. Yoreh Deah 340:1.
40. See also *Ach Le-tzara*, p. 21, and *P'nay Baruch* 6:8.
41. Book I, p. 58.
42. See Dobrinsky's *Treasury of Sephardic Laws and Customs*, pp. 72, 83, and 91.
43. Ibid., p. 99.
44. Mishna Shabbat 7:2.
45. Moed Katan 25b.
46. See Isserles on Yoreh Deah 340:31.
47. Yoreh Deah 340:28.
48. *Gesher Ha-cha'yim* I, p. 61.
49. Semachot 9:8 and Moed Katan 26a.
50. See Epstein's *Aruch Ha-shulchan* 340:14 and Tuktzinsky's *Gesher Ha-cha'yim*, p. 60.
51. Moed Katan 22b; Yoreh Deah 340:15.

Notes to Chapter 4

THE CHAPEL SERVICE
Pages 63 to 84

1. Sota 14a.
2. See Berachot 19b and Nazir 47b.
3. See *Jewish Reflections on Death*, by Jack Riemer, pp. 47ff.
4. Yoreh Deah 357:1.
5. See Schauss's *Lifetime of a Jew*, p. 288.
6. Yoreh Deah 357:1.
7. Yoreh Deah 357:1.
8. Sanhedrin 44a.
9. 3b.
10. p. 137.

11. When the first-century historian Flavius Josephus refers to night burials, he is speaking only of burials for executed criminals. See Josephus's *Antiquities of the Jews* 4:8.
12. Semachot 9:9 and Moed Katan 22a.
13. Mishna Shabbat 7:2.
14. Orach Cha'yim 526:1-4. See also the note of Isserles.
15. See Harry Rabinowicz's *Guide to Life,* p.43.
16. Megilla 28b and Yoreh Deah 344:19-20.
17. Yoreh Deah 344:20.
18. Adas Israel Congregation, Washington, DC, and Temple Beth El, Poughkeepsie, NY, are two examples of synagogues that hold the funerals of members in their sanctuaries.
19. Moed Katan 27a, b and Ketubot 8b.
20. Berachot 53a and Bava Kama 16b.
21. Moed Katan 27a.
22. Yoreh Deah 344:1 and Shabbat 105a and 153a.
23. See Saperstein's *Jewish Preaching,* p.37. See also Dov Zlotnick's introduction to *The Tractate Mourning,* p. 19.
24. The remark was made in a eulogy delivered for the Talne Rebbetzin Rebecca Twersky, January 30, 1977. Quoted in Francine Klagsbrun's *Voices of Wisdom,* p.511.
25. Orach Chayim 670:13 and 697:1. See also Goldberg's *P'nay Baruch,* p. 317.
26. Moed Katan 27b.
27. Semachot 3:5 and Shabbat 153a.
28. Yoreh Deah 344:1.
29. 62a.
30. Yoreh Deah 344:5.
31. Semachot 2:1.
32. Yoreh Deah 345:1.
33. Shabbat 105b.
34. Yoreh Deah 344:10. Sanhedrin 47a states that "funeral rites are in honor of the dead." See also *Shulchan Aruch,* Yoreh Deah 344:10, and the notes of Isserles on this citation.
35. Shabbat 127a.
36. Ketubot 17a.
37. See Trachtenberg's *Jewish Magic and Superstition,* p.177.
    See also Isserles on Yoreh Deah 358:3 and the seventeenth-century Siftay Kohen commentary of Shabbetai ben Meir Ha-Kohen (the Shach), rabbi of Moravia (later part of Austria and Czechoslovakia) on Yoreh Deah 359:1. The Siftay Kohen notes that there are places where mourners *precede* the bier. Joel Serkes (Sirkes) (1561-1640), rabbi of communities in Poland and Lithuania, known as the Bach for his Ba'yit Chadash commentary on Yoreh Deah, says that in his time there was no such custom as mourners walking in front of the coffin.
38. Moed Katan 22b and Yoreh Deah 340:16.

39. Bava Kama 17a.
40. Semachot 9:2.
41. Semachot 9:3.
42. Moed Katan 22a and Semachot 9:9.
43. Yoreh Deah 357:2.
44. See Moed Katan 20b and Yoreh Deah 373:4. See also Yevamot 22b, where the Rabbis interpret the word *lishe'ero* in Leviticus 21:2 as meaning "his wife."
45. Yoreh Deah 371:1 and 373. See also *Mishneh Torah,* Hilchot Ha-met 1:10-15, where Maimonides discusses impurity as it relates to a Kohen.
46. See Isserles on Yoreh Deah 372:2. See also Greenwald's *Kol Bo Al Avelut,* p. 72, paragraph 6.
47. Hilchot Avel 3:11.
48. Semachot 2:6.
49. Many Rabbis of the Talmud were not in favor of capital punishment. The Talmud calls a court that executed a criminal even once in seven years "a wicked Sanhedrin [court]." Rabbi Eliazar ben Azariah says that such a court deserved that appellation if it executes a criminal even once in seventy years. Rabbis Tarfon and Akiba said, "Had we been in the Sanhedrin, no one would have ever been put to death" (Makkot 1:10).

    See *The Second Jewish Book of Why,* by Alfred J. Kolatch, pp. 282-83, for more on the attitude of the Rabbis toward capital punishment.
50. See Louis Jacobs' *Theology in the Responsa,* p. 313, for more on this subject.
51. See Dobrinsky's *Treasury of Sephardic Laws and Customs,* p. 74.

Notes to Chapter 5

The Cemetery Service
Pages 85 to 118

1. Sanhedrin 6:5.
2. Ecclesiastes Rabba 10:9.
3. Sanhedrin 96b.
4. Berachot 55a.
5. Bava Metzia 107a.
6. Bava Batra 112a.
7. Sanhedrin 47a.
8. Sanhedrin 46a.
9. Ach Le-tzara, p. 34.
10. *Kol Bo Al Avelut,* p. 163.

11. See Solomon Freehof's *Reform Jewish Practice*, pp. 137-38.
12. See the Rabbinical Assembly Law Committee's *Statement on the Laws of Avelut*, p. 16.
13. See Siftay Kohen on Yoreh Deah 362:4.
14. See I Samuel 31:12ff., where the bodies of King Saul and his sons who fell in the battle of Gilboa were cremated. See also Amos 6:10.
15. See Jacobs' *Theology in the Responsa*, p. 323.
16. See Yoreh Deah 282:10.

In his *Guide to Life*, Rabbi H. Rabinowicz of London, England, writes that when the wife of Dr. Maurice Davis was cremated (September 27, 1891), Chief Rabbi Hermann Adler was asked whether her ashes could be buried in the Jewish cemetery. He wrote, quoting from *The Jewish Chronicle*, October 2, 1891:

> I have given this request my full consideration in concert with the members of the Beth Din. We subscribe to the opinion stated by my venerated predecessor that there does not exist any precept prohibiting the interment in a Jewish cemetery of the ashes of a person who has already been cremated, an opinion supported by other eminent Rabbis including the Chief Rabbi of Kovno [Rabbi Isaac Elchanan Spektor, 1817-1896]. We accordingly permit such a burial. At the same time we earnestly beg you and the members of the community not to construe this permission into a sanction of the practice of cremation. We ardently hope that no brother or sister in faith will make a similar testamentary disposition, involving, as it does, a grave breach of Jewish law.

As an expression of respect and adoration for Jewish learning, worn-out Torah scrolls as well as sacred printed books and other religious articles are not discarded unceremoniously. They are brought to the cemetery for burial in a grave alongside a pious individual.

In ancient times, religious books and articles that were no longer usable were stored in the back room of the synagogue until such time as they could be taken to the cemetery. The storage room was called the *geniza*, "hiding place." The most famous *geniza*, in the synagogue of Fostat, Cairo (Egypt), was built in the year 882. Its large store of manuscripts was first discovered in 1763. At the end of the nineteenth century, Solomon Schechter acquired about 100,000 manuscript leaves and fragments from the Cairo *geniza*, and he brought them back to Cambridge University, England, on whose faculty he served.

17. Sanhedrin 47a.
18. Ibid. 46a. See also Mishna Sanhedrin 6:5.
19. Ketubot 111a.
20. Ibid. 111a.
21. Shulchan Aruch, Yoreh Deah 371:1 and 373.

22. Yevamot 22b; Yoreh Deah 373:3.

    So that a Kohen may visit patients in the Hadassah Hospital in Jerusalem, where Jewish corpses usually are to be found, double doors were installed to seal off certain areas so that the whole hospital is no longer considered a complete unit, thus enabling Kohanim to visit the sick in the hospital without violating the law of *Ohel.*

    See also *Mishneh Torah,* Hilchot Hamet 1:10-15, where Maimonides points out that one becomes "impure by enclosure *[ohel]*" even if he pokes his hand or a finger into the enclosure. The reason why a Gentile corpse (actually the word *akum,* meaning "idol worshipper," is used) does not cause a Kohen to become impure by enclosure is not explained. Maimonides simply says that this is a tradition *(kabbala)* that has been transmitted to us from the past.

23. Hilchot Avel 3:11.

24. See *Shulchan Aruch,* Yoreh Deah 371:5. Some Orthodox and Conservative authorities consider four *amot* to be equal to seven feet. *See A Guide to Jewish Religious Practice,* by Isaac Klein, p. 82. Generally, an *amah* (cubit) is the distance from the elbow to the tip of one's fingers, approximately eighteen inches.

25. Sanhedrin 44a.

26. See Dobrinsky's *Treasury of Sephardic Laws and Customs,* p. 103.

27. See Leslau's *Falasha Anthology,* p. xix.

28. Moed Katan 24a-b and Semachot 3:2.

29. In a responsum, Rashi (eleventh century) said that a father is exempt from sitting Shiva for a child who died four days after circumcision *(brit).* See *Sefer Teshuvot Rashi,* by Israel Elfenbein, p. 297. See also Goldberg's *P'nay Baruch,* pp. 103-104.

30. Yoreh Deah 353:6 and 374:8.

31. p. 426.

32. See Sanhedrin 22a. Rabbi Alexandri adds: "The world becomes dark for him whose wife died in his lifetime."

    The Talmud (Berachot 32b) observes: "When a man takes a second wife after his first, he continues to think of the deeds of the first."

33. See *Chochmat Adam* 158:21.

34. See Greenwald's *Ach Le-tzara,* p. 145:38, and Freehof's *Reform Jewish Practice,* pp. 146ff., for the divergent views on this subject.

35. See Alfred J. Kolatch's *Second Jewish Book of Why,* pp. 36-37, for a discussion of the origins of Sephardic Jewry.

36. p. 71.

37. p. 82.

38. p. 90. See Hayyim Schauss's *Lifetime of a Jew* for more information on this subject.

39. Berachot 51a.

   Joshua ben Levi was not only reputed to be a great scholar, but also to have a vivid, hallucinatory imagination. He claimed to have intimate knowledge of what transpires in heaven (paradise) and hell *(gehinnom)* and provided many details. "I measured the area of *gehinnom* and found it to be 100 miles long and 50 miles wide," he said. "Fiery lions are stationed everywhere, and they devour the inhabitants..." In paradise he found "80,000 trees in every corner...with 6,000 angels in each corner singing the praises of Creation..."

40. See Yoreh Deah 359:2 and the Shach on this.
41. See Trachtenberg's *Jewish Magic and Superstition.* p. 178.
42. Yoreh Deah 367:2-3.
43. Berachot 18a.
44. Moed Katan 27a, b.
45. Dobrinsky's *Treasury of Sephardic Laws and Customs,* p. 89.
46. Ibid., p. 100.
47. See Saperstein's *Jewish Preaching,* p. 326.
48. Talmud Yerushalmi Kila'yim 9:4. See also Genesis Rabba 100:7.
49. Shabbat 127a.
50. See Genesis 47:29 and Rashi's comment.
51. Berachot 18a.
52. See *The Second Jewish Book of Why,* by Alfred J. Kolatch, pp. 236-37, for a discussion of the significance of these numbers.
53. Bava Batra 100b.
54. Ecclesiastes Rabba 1:2.
55. See *Ma-avar Yabok,* edition Landshuth, p. 97, where the practice of making seven stops upon leaving the grave is mentioned.
56. Joshua Trachtenberg, in his *Jewish Magic and Superstition* (p. 178), reminds us of the instructions of Shabbetai, son of the mystic Isaiah Horowitz (died 1630), to his son. He wrote in his testament: "While my body is being lowered into the grave, have seven pious and learned men repeat Psalm 91 seven times."
57. See also *The Jewish Book of Why,* by Alfred J. Kolatch, pp., 149-50.
58. Numbers Rabba 12:3.
59. See Trachtenberg's *Jewish Magic and Superstition,* p. 47. This book contains a great number of examples of magical formulas designed to drive off demons and counteract magical spells. On pages 112-13, he tells about a *shofar* that refused to function in a Frankfurt synagogue one Rosh Hashana in the thirteenth century. Psalm 91 was recited to dislodge Satan, who it was believed had settled in the *shofar* and blocked the sound from coming out.

   See also Israel Abraham's *Jewish Life in the Middle Ages,* p. 391, for a description of the prevalence of the belief in evil spirits in the thirteenth century.

See also Irving Agus's *Rabbi Meir of Rothenburg,* p. 265, where the thirteenth-century scholar exhorts people to fasten *mezuzot* to their doors. He says, "I am convinced that no demon can harm a house properly provided with a *mezuza.*"

60. See Morgenstern's *Rites of Birth, Marriage and Death Among the Semites,* p. 249, note 66.
61. Shabbat 152b.
62. Betza 6a.
63. Moed Katan 27b.
64. Avoda Zara 17b-18a.
65. Yoreh Deah 344:4.
66. See Yoreh Deah 401:6, particularly the notes of Isserles. See also Greenwald's *Ach Le-tzara,* pp. 168-69.
67. See Greenwald's *Kol Bo Al Avelut,* p. 215, par. 20, regarding the custom in Jerusalem.
68. In his notes to the *Code of Jewish Law* (Orach Chayim 401:6 and 420:2), Moses Isserles comments that "some authorities are of the opinion that when a burial takes place at night, neither the *Kaddish* nor *Tziduk Ha-din* is recited.
69. Semachot 10:9. See also the commentary of Rambam on Berachot 3:2.
70. Sanhedrin 19a.
71. Berachot 43b and Rashi on Bava Batra 100b make the point that a man who walks alone is in danger of attack from demons, while two persons walking together are safe.
72. See Midrash Rabba, Genesis 100:13.
73. See Trachtenberg's *Jewish Magic and Superstition,* p. 178.
74. See also *Theology in the Responsa,* by Louis Jacobs, p. 136.
75. See Yoreh Deah 376:4 and the note of Isserles on this.
76. See *Jewish Magic and Superstition,* p. 178.
77. Ibid., p. 2.
78. Pesachim 102b. See also Berachot 49a, where it says, "We do not perform religious commandments in bundles."
79. See Freehof's *Reform Jewish Practice,* p. 132.
80. *Teshuvot Maharil,* no. 23.
81. See *Jewish Magic and Superstition,* p. 179.
82. See *Theology in the Responsa,* p. 136.

Notes to Chapter 6
KADDISH
Pages 119 to 139

1. Max Lerner's essay appears in Jack Riemer's *Jewish Reflections on Death,* pp. 155ff.
2. See Berachot 3a and especially the comment of the Tosafot.
3. This response was used in the Temple ritual, especially on Yom Kippur, in a slightly variant Hebrew version. When the High Priest uttered the name of God (the Tetragrammaton), the people would cry out: "Blessed be His name whose glorious kingdom is forever and ever." A similar response is found in the *Hallel* (Psalms 113:2).
4. In order to discourage people from riding to the synagogue on the Sabbath and holidays, some few Orthodox congregations omit the recitation of the Mourners' Kaddish on those days. They do not consider the recitation of the Kaddish to be of sufficient importance to warrant violation of the Sabbath. See Lamm's *Jewish Way of Death and Mourning,* p. 162, for more on this.
5. See Dobrinsky's *Treasury of Sephardic Laws and Customs,* p. 6.
6. See Greenwald's *Kol Bo Al Avelut,* p. 280; Tuktzinsky's *Gesher Ha-cha'yim* I, p. 208:8; and Goldberg's *P'nay Baruch* 16:23.
7. Maimonides, in his *Mishneh Torah* (Hilchot Tefila 12:20), points out: "In some communities it is customary to recite the Half-Kaddish before the person being honored with *maftir* is called to the Torah, while in others it is customary to recite it after the *maftir* portion has been read."
8. Rabbi Joseph B. Soloveitchik underscores the point when he asks, "What is the relationship of the solemn Doxology [Kaddish] to the burial?" (See his 1972 lecture entitled "The Halakhah of the First Day," which was printed in *The Jewish Advocate* and reprinted in *Jewish Reflections on Death,* p. 76.) His response is that through the Kaddish "we hurl defiance at death and its fiendish conspiracy against man...We profess publicly and solemnly that we are not giving up, that we are not surrendering, that we will carry on the work of our ancestors."
9. Philip Birnbaum, in his *Ha-siddur Ha-shalem,* p. 48, points out that in Deuteronomy 28:43 the Targum renders the words *mala mala,* "above and beyond," as *le-ayla le-ayla.*
10. See Orach Chayim 55:1.

Many theories have been advanced to explain why ten persons constitute a *minyan.* Philo believed that ten was decided upon because it is the most perfect number. The Rabbis of the Talmud (Megilla 23b and Berachot 21b) explain that because ten (evil) spies in Numbers 14:26 are referred to as an *ayda,* a "congregation," ten is the number that constitutes a *minyan.* The Rabbis base this conclusion on a similarity *(gezera shava)* that exists between a verse in Leviticus (22:32) and a verse in Numbers (16:21), both of which employ the word *betoch,* meaning "in the midst of." Leviticus says, "I will be sanctified in the midst of the Children of Israel." Numbers says, "Separate yourself from the midst of this congregation." Since this latter group consisting of the ten "evil" spies are called a congregation, so must every group that is to be called a congregation consist of ten people. See also Berachot 21b.

Other scholars find a basis for requiring ten people to a *minyan* in the verse in the Book of Genesis (42:5), "Thus, the sons of Israel were among those who came [to Egypt] to procure rations." Since the number of Jacob's sons who went down to Egypt was ten, it is inferred that a quorum must always consist of ten.

Only the Orthodox community demands that the ten persons that constitute a *minyan* be male.

In 1973, the Rabbinical Assembly Committee on Law and Standards (Conservative) voted that the decision on whether to count women as part of a *minyan* should be made by the individual congregational rabbi. Many Conservative rabbis prefer to follow the law as enunciated in the *Shulchan Aruch,* which states that a *minyan* for a prayer service must consist of ten adult males (Orach Chayim 55:1). Other Conservative rabbis favor counting women as part of a *minyan* and base their attitude on another passage in the same code, where it is stated, "All are to be counted in the *minyan* of seven [who may be called up to read the Torah on Sabbath], even a woman and a minor..." (Ibid. 282:3).

Although liberal rabbis acknowledge that this statement refers only to the *minyan* (quorum) required for the Sabbath Torah reading, they emphasize that the reading is an essential part of the synagogue service; and since women once enjoyed the honor of receiving *aliyot* and reading from the Torah, this privilege of being counted as equals with men should be restored and should even be extended to include women as equals when counting individuals as part of a *minyan* for a prayer service.

A recent responsum on the question of whether daughters *may* or *must* go to the synagogue to say Kaddish for a parent states that daughters are not permitted to do so, for if they were, people might mistakenly believe that women can also be counted to a *minyan.* See *The Israeli Responsa Yearbook,* 1965 edition, pp. 289-90.

11. Sanhedrin 104a.
12. See Moed Katan 20b and Yoreh Deah 374:4, 6-7.
13. Berachot 20 a-b.
14. Yoreh Deah 376:4.

15. A responsum (*Chavot Yair,* no. 222) by a German talmudic scholar and Kabbalist, Rabbi Yair Chayim Bachrach (1638-1702), addresses the question of whether a man's will can be honored if the will stipulates that upon the individual's death a quorum *(minyan)* should be paid to assemble in his house for one year to study and pray so that the deceased's daughter can say Kaddish. Bachrach explains that while he can see no legal objection, because everyone is obligated to honor parents and sanctify God's name, the wish of the deceased should not be carried out because it is contrary to established custom for women to recite the Kaddish.
16. See the magazine *Noam,* volume 8, pp. 291-96.
17. See the note of Isserles on Yoreh Deah 376:3. See also Greenwald's *Kol Bo Al Avelut,* p. 373, note 29, and Goldberg's *P'nay Baruch* 39:22.
18. Sanhedrin 19b.
19. Choshen Mishpat 42:15.
20. Yoreh Deah 340:5.
21. Sanhedrin 44a. See also *The Second Jewish Book of Why,* by Alfred J. Kolatch, p. 35.
22. *Shulchan Aruch,* Yoreh Deah 241:9. In a later section (Yoreh Deah 374:5), Caro adds that when authorities say that a convert does not have to mourn his parents, it only means that he is not *obligated* to do so, but *may* do so.
23. *Zekan Aharon,* no. 87. This responsum is noted by Rabbi Solomon Freehof in the *Central Conference of American Rabbis Yearbook,* LXVII (1957), pp. 82-85. Rabbi Maurice Lamm, in his *Jewish Way in Death and Mourning,* p. 170, indicates current Orthodox opinion as permitting the recital of Kaddish at graveside "for a close friend and also for a worthy Gentile, providing a duly constituted *minyan* is present."
24. Yoreh Deah 340:30.
25. See Greenwald's *Gesher Ha-cha'yim* 30:8-9 for more on this subject.
26. Pitchay Teshuva 3 on Yoreh Deah 375.
27. See Goldberg's *P'nay Baruch* 362:26.
28. See Jacobs' *Theology in the Responsa,* p. 271.
29. See Feinstein's *Igrot Moshe,* Yoreh Deah 254.
30. Berachot 58b. See also Eduyot II:10.
31. Yoreh Deah 376:4.
32. See Dobrinsky's *Treasury of Sephardic Laws and Customs,* pp. 86 and 107.

     Joshua Trachtenberg, in his *Jewish Magic and Superstition,* p. 223, recalls the belief current in the Middle Ages that during the first year after death bodies remain intact in their graves, during which time their souls ascend to heaven and return to the body. (Only on the Sabbath do the spirits of the dead rest.)

33. See *P'nay Baruch,* 39:2-3.
34. Ibid. 39:2.
35. See *A Treasury of Sephardic Laws and Customs,* pp. 93 and 107.
36. See Isserles and Pitchay Teshuva 9 on Yoreh Deah 376:4.
37. See Goldberg's *P'nay Baruch* 39:36.

Notes to Chapter 7

THE SHIVA PERIOD
Pages 140 to 187

1. See Moed Katan 27b.
2. Genesis Rabba 100:7. See also Yoreh Deah 398:1, where it is pointed out that only the first day of mourning is considered biblically mandated *[avelut de-oraita].*
3. Moed Katan 20a and Genesis Rabba 100:7.
4. Ketubot 2b.
5. See Ephraim Urbach's *Halakha,* p. 25, where he writes: "These were ancient customs which are nowhere explicitly enjoined in the Torah but arise out of biblical narratives."
6. Yoreh Deah 374:4. Here, the wife is one of the original seven. See also Greenwald's *Kol Bo Al Avelut,* p. 259.
7. Yoreh Deah 396:3.
8. See Goldberg's *P'nay Baruch* 30:5. See also *Death and Bereavement,* by Abner Weiss, p. 97.
9. Ketubot 103a.
10. See Greenwald's *Kol Bo Al Avelut,* p. 66:5.
11. Sanhedrin 46b.
12. Semachot 2.
13. Shulchan Aruch, Yoreh Deah 345:3.
14. See Greenwald's *Gesher Ha-cha'yim* 1:71-73. Rabbi Moses Sofer (1762-1832), the Hungarian authority on Jewish law, was particularly lenient in this regard.
15. See *American Reform Responsa,* edited by Walter Jacob, pp. 301-307. Taking a life—whether another person's or one's own—is a heinous crime in Jewish law. Rabbi Ishmael ben Elisha, the famous talmudic scholar of the first century, referred to one who commits suicide as "a misguided fool" who may be mourned. His celebrated contemporary, Rabbi Akiba ben Joseph, said: "Neither bless him nor curse him! Let him disappear!" (Semachot 2:1)

Rabbi Tarphon, the scholar sometimes referred to by the Greek name Tryphon, differed with his two colleagues and followed a middle course. He drew a distinction between planned suicides and suicides that were beyond the control of the individual. In a case where a boy, afraid of being beaten by his father, ran away and killed himself by jumping into a deep well, Tarphon ruled that this type of suicide was excusable.

16. Semachot 2:8.
17. Hilchot Avel 1:10.
18. Sanhedrin 44a.
19. Yoreh Deah 345:5.
20. See *The Jewish Way in Death and Mourning,* by Maurice Lamm, p. 83.

    The Rabbis were serious when they said, "Once a Jew, always a Jew." The door remains open for an apostate's return to the fold.

    The life of Heinrich Heine (1797-1856) illustrates the reasoning behind this talmudic view. This German-Jewish poet underwent baptism, but in the eyes of Jewish law he never ceased being a Jew. Heine explained his action as merely a way of seeking "an entrance ticket" to European culture, but in later years he expressed remorse for his action. Although never formally renouncing his baptism, the poet spoke of the Torah as "the portable fatherland of a Jew." And he wrote a beautiful, moving poem entitled *The Sabbath Jew.* This was Heine's way of doing *teshuva* (repenting). It is because cases such as this do occur that Judaism never writes off any Jew, even an apostate.

21. See *Theology in the Responsa,* by Louis Jacobs, p. 91.
22. The *Shulchan Aruch,* Yoreh Deah 345:5, states that "[one] does not mourn for an apostate." See also *Chochmat Adam* 156:6.
23. See Greenwald's *Ach Le-tzara,* p. 238, for opinions of various authorities. See also Freehof's *Recent Reform Responsa,* pp. 132ff., for a wide-ranging discussion on the subject.
24. See Yoreh Deah 344:10, including the comment of Moses Isserles.
25. See also Yoreh Deah 375:2-4.
26. Moed Katan 27b and Yoreh Deah 394:4.
27. See Genesis Rabba 100:7.
28. Yoreh Deah 375:10.
29. Moed Katan 21b.
30. Moed Katan 20a.
31. Yoreh Deah 402:1-4.
32. Yoreh Deah 402: 5, 6.
33. Pesachim 4a and Moed Katan 19b.
34. Yoreh Deah 395:1.
35. See Moed Katan 23a and 23b.
36. Moed Katan 24a.
37. Keeping one's head covered, even by the pious, was not the norm until a much later date. See *The Second Jewish Book of Why,* by Alfred J. Kolatch, pp. 48-51 and 184.
38. Moed Katan 19a and Semachot 7:1.

39. Yoreh Deah 399:1.
40. Orach Cha'yim 548:2.
41. Ibid. 548:2.
    The deeply ingrained attitude of Jews towards celebrating their holidays joyfully is depicted in one of the writings of Elie Wiesel. The Nobel Prize-winner describes what took place in a boxcar carrying hundreds of Jews to the death camps. The prisoners were pressed together so tightly, they could hardly move.
    Suddenly, an old rabbi shouted: "It's Simchat Torah today, have we forgotten what Jews are ordered to do on Simchat Torah?" Amazingly somebody had managed to smuggle a small Torah scroll aboard the train, and he handed it to the rabbi. The rabbi held it high in the air and began to move slowly, gracefully. Then they all began to sing, to dance in place; and they went on singing and dancing and celebrating the Torah, all the while knowing that every passing moment was bringing them closer to their end.
42. Shabbat 152 a-b.
43. See Isserles on Yoreh Deah 376:3 and 384:3.
44. See Danzig's *Chochmat Adam* 165:11.
45. Yoreh Deah 384:3.
46. *Chochmat Adam* 165:11.
47. *Igrot Moshe,* Yoreh Deah II:172.
48. See Alfred J. Kolatch's *Second Jewish Book of Why,* pp. 13-14, for a discussion of the *marit a'yin* principle.
49. See Dobrinsky's *Treasury of Sephardic Laws and Customs,* p. 83.
50. See Greenwald's *Kol Bo Al Avelut,* p. 272:14.
51. See Isserles on Yoreh Deah 393:2.
52. Moed Katan 15b and Yoreh Deah 380:1, 3.
53. *Chochmat Adam* 164:2.
54. Midrash Genesis Rabba 100:7. See also the comments of Isserles on Yoreh Deah 380:5.
55. Rabbi Joseph Telushkin recalls this incident in his book *Jewish Literacy,* p. 629.
56. See *Kol Bo Al Avelut,* p. 291, paragraph 36. See also Yoreh Deah 380 in Pitchay Teshuva, note 1.
57. Yoreh Deah 393:3.
58. *Igrot Moshe,* Yoreh Deah II:169.
59. See Alfred J. Kolatch's *Jewish Book of Why,* pp. 43-46, and *The Second Jewish Book of Why,* pp. 236 and 361, for more on the *Sheva Berachot.*
60. Ketubot 3b-4a.
61. Yoreh Deah 392:1.
62. Ketubot 103a.
63. Such superstitions were widely held among Jews in early times. The Talmud (Ketubot 8b) describes how fearful was the fabulous third-century Palestinian scholar Simon ben Lakish, noted for

his brute strength. He said: "One should never open his mouth [and utter ominous words] to [provoke] Satan." The Hebrew expression is *al tiftach peh lesatan.*

64. See Goldberg's *P'nay Baruch* 16:4.
65. See Dobrinsky's *Treasury of Sephardic Laws and Customs,* pp. 73, 83, 91.
66. Moed Katan 15a-b and Semachot 6:1. In Genesis Rabba 100:7, Rav says: "The overturned bed must be set aright on the Sabbath, for if it is not done, it would constitute public mourning on the Sabbath. People coming to visit would see the overturned bed."
67. See Trachtenberg's *Jewish Magic and Superstition,* p. 2; Yoreh Deah 387:1-2; and Goldberg's *P'nay Baruch* 17:2.
68. Moed Katan 3:5; 83a.
69. See Bader's *Jewish Spiritual Heroes,* p. 52.
70. Shabbat 114a.
71. Yoreh Deah 345:5. See the Shach on this.
72. Ibid.
73. See also *Chochmat Adam* 156:6.
74. Israel Abrahams, in his *Jewish Life in the Middle Ages* (p. 315), writes: "The Jews of all countries wore black; in Spain, Germany, and Italy the phenomenon was equally marked. Black being the color of grief of the Jews [who were in a constant state of mourning for the loss of Zion]." In Bava Kama 59b, one Rabbi, in response to the question "Why do you always wear black shoes?" said, "I am mourning for Jerusalem."
75. Moed Katan 15a and 24a.
76. See Maimonides' *Book of Judges,* Hilchot Avel 5:19.
77. Moed Katan 24a.
78. See the comments of Isserles and the Shach on Yoreh Deah 386:1.
79. *Sefer Teshuvot Rashi,* by Israel Elfenbein, Bnai Brak, Israel, 1980.
80. *Shulchan Aruch,* Yoreh Deah 386:1.
81. For more about covering the head in Jewish tradition, see Alfred J. Kolatch's *Jewish Book of Why,* pp. 120-22, and *Second Jewish Book of Why,* pp. 49-53 and 99-100.
82. See the tractate Semachot, p. 13, of the Zlotnick edition.
83. See Yoreh Deah 380:1 and 382:1. See also Ezekiel 24:17.
84. Yoreh Deah 382:2-4.
85. See Moed Katan 15b and 19b. See also Yoreh Deah 381:1-5.
86. See Yoreh Deah 383:1.
87. Moed Katan 15b.
88. For further information on this subject see *Mourning in Halachah,* by Chaim Goldberg, p. 209.
89. Yoreh Deah 390:6.
90. See Yoreh Deah 390:1.
91. Moed Katan 22b.

92. Yoreh Deah 393:2.
93. See Dobrinsky's *Treasury of Sephardic Laws and Customs,* pp. 83 and 91.
94. Bava Batra 60b.
95. Rabbi Solomon Freehof, in his *Reform Jewish Practice,* pp. 164-65, calls attention to the fact that there is no evidence that this was a practice current in talmudic times, although tractate Shabbat 152 a-b and Yoreh Deah 376:3 state that if a man dies and leaves no mourners, ten men should dwell in the house of the deceased for the Shiva period and conduct religious services.
96. Yoreh Deah 384:3.
97. Semachot 6:3 and Moed Katan 21a. See also *Chochmat Adam* 164:1 and 165:18, where it is noted that only on the first day of Shiva one may not don *tefilin.* See also Genesis Rabba 100:7.
98. See *Death and Bereavement,* by Abner Weiss, p. 49.
99. See Greenwald's *Kol Bo Al Avelut,* p. 277.
100. See *Aruch Ha-shulchan,* Orach Chayim 135:32. See also J.D. Bleich's *Contemporary Halakhic Problems,* Volume I, pp. 67ff., for a wide-ranging discussion of this matter.
101. See Dobrinsky's *Treasury of Sephardic Laws and Customs,* p.73.
102. Yoreh Deah 393:3.
103. *Aruch Ha-shulchan* 393:1.
104. Ibid.
105. For more about *Tachanun* see Alfred J. Kolatch's *Jewish Book of Why,* pp. 149-50, and Hayyim H. Donin's *To Pray as a Jew,* pp. 202-210.
106. See Goldberg's *P'nay Baruch* 34:15.
107. See Tuktzinsky's *Gesher Ha-cha'yim* 1:207.
108. See Greenwald's *Kol Bo Al Avelut,* pp. 285ff.
109. Orach Chayim 559:6.
110. Yoreh Deah 401:7.
111. *P'nay Baruch,* p. 317.
112. *Shulchan Aruch,* Yoreh Deah 393:4.
113. Yoreh Deah 393:4.
114. See *A Treasury of Sephardic Laws and Customs,* pp. 74, 93.
115. Yoreh Deah 384:2.
116. See the Siftay Kohen commentary on Yoreh Deah 384:2.
117. Yoreh Deah 400:1.
118. Ibid. 384:3 and *P'nay Baruch* 16:19.
119. Yoreh Deah 384:1 and Yoreh Deah Chidushim 16.
120. *P'nay Baruch* 28:23.
121. Ibid.
122. Yoreh Deah 384:4 and Orach Cha'yim 554:1-4.
123. Moed Katan 19b.

Notes to Chapter 8

COMFORTING THE MOURNER
Pages 188 to 201

1. See Greenberg's *Inner Eye*, Volume I, published posthumously by the Jewish Frontier Publishing Association.
2. See Ethics of the Fathers 4:23.
3. Moed Katan 21b.
4. Sota 14a.
5. Genesis 25:11.
6. Ketubot 8b and Eruvin 5a.
7. Yalkut Shimoni on Proverbs, Section 964.
8. Yoreh Deah 375:1.
9. See Danzig's *Chochmat Adam* 163:5.
10. Moed Katan 27b.
11. See Dobrinsky's *Treasury of Sephardic Laws and Customs*, p.27.
12. Yoreh Deah 378:9.
13. Bava Batra 16b.
14. Ibid.
15. *A Treasury of Sephardic Laws and Customs*, p. 91.
16. See Wolf Leslau's *Falasha Anthology: Black Jews of Ethiopia*, p. xviii.
17. Moed Katan 27a.
18. Yoreh Deah II:168.
19. Moed Katan 27a.
20. Tosefot on Nidda 9:17 comments on the use of white and colored glasses.
21. See Goldberg's *P'nay Baruch* 17:6.
22. Ibid. 17:12.
23. See Feinstein's *Igrot Moshe*, Orach Chayim IV 40:11.
24. Moed Katan 24a. see also note 7 in the Soncino translation of the Talmud.
25. Moed Katan 27b.
26. Ecclesiastes Rabba 3:9.
27. Semachot 6:2.
28. See also Yoreh Deah 385:1.
29. *Chochmat Adam* 165:14.
30. See Yoreh Deah 376:2 and Berachot 19a.
31. See *The ArtScroll Siddur*, p. 802, for additional information. See also *Death and Bereavement*, by Abner Weiss, pp. 280ff., which has over one hundred pages of selections from the Mishna, with commentary, that can be studied in a house of mourning.

Notes to Chapter 9

THE POST-SHIVA PERIOD
Pages 202 to 218

1. See the note of Isserles on Yoreh Deah 389:1.
2. Yoreh Deah 395:1.
3. Yoreh Deah 399:7.
4. Moed Katan 24b and Yoreh Deah 399:8.
5. See Moed Katan 24b and Yoreh Deah 399: 3, 6, 9.
6. 22b.
7. The Rabbis (Ibid. 14b) based this rule on the caution addressed to the sons of Aaron after two of their brothers, Nadav and Avihu, had met an untimely death for offering an unauthorized sacrifice on the altar. They were warned by Moses (Leviticus 10:6) not to let the hair on their heads grow long, as one does in mourning. Since Nadav and Avihu had violated the law, they were not to be mourned.

   From the verse in Leviticus, the Rabbis inferred, mourners should allow their hair to grow long during the Sheloshim period. That this prohibition against haircutting should last thirty days was derived by the Rabbis (Moed Katan 19b) from the parallel phrasing *(gezera shava)* of two biblical verses pertaining to the cutting of hair: the verse in Leviticus 10:6, just mentioned, and the verse in the Book of Numbers (6:5) where a nazirite is prohibited from cutting his hair. In both instances the Hebrew text uses the root word *paroa* for haircutting. The Rabbis concluded that since the standard period of time a nazirite was to remain loyal to his vow is thirty days, so must a mourner not cut his hair for thirty days.

   See Moed Katan 19b, where Rabbi Mattena asks:"Why is a nazirite's vow binding for thirty days?" He explains: "The text uses the Hebrew word *yi-he'yeh*, 'he shall be,' which is spelled *yud, hay, yud, hay* and has a numerical value of thirty [10 + 5 + 10 + 5]."

8. Yoreh Deah 390:4.
9. Moed Katan 22b.
10. See Greenwald's *Kol Bo Al Avelut,* p. 352.
11. Semachot 9:10 and Yoreh Deah 389:5.
12. Moed Katan 23a.
13. Moed Katan 22b.
14. See Yoreh Deah 391:1-3.
15. For a detailed analysis of the views and attitudes of various authorities, see *Death and Bereavement* by Abner Weiss, pp. 129-47, and *The Jewish Way in Death and Mourning,* by Maurice Lamm, pp. 175-82.

    In *Igrot Moshe,* Yoreh Deah I:255, Rabbi Moshe Feinstein

is asked whether a woman in mourning for her father may attend a synagogue dinner for the benefit of the congregation. Her husband insists that he will not attend the dinner alone; and if his wife does not accompany him, family harmony *(shelom ba'yit)* will be affected. Feinstein permits the woman to attend the function with her husband.

16. Moed Katan 22b.
17. See *The Jewish Way in Death and Mourning,* p. 179, and Emanuel Rackman's article in *The Jewish Week,* October 15, 1982.

   The ultra-Orthodox would not agree with this position. They even oppose a mourner's attending a gala function where music is not played.
18. *Kol Bo Al Avelut,* p. 361.
19. Yoreh Deah 392:1.
20. Ibid. 342:1.
21. Yoreh Deah 392:2.
22. Ibid. See also Moed Katan 23a.
23. Yoreh Deah 392:2. See the comment of the Shach.
24. Orach Cha'yim 128:44.
25. Yoreh Deah 344:20.
26. Greenwald's *Ach Le-tzara,* p. 137.
27. See Michael Higger's edition of the tractate Semachot, p. 79.

Notes to Chapter 10

GRAVES AND MONUMENTS
Pages 219 to 239

1. "Sof-Shavua," magazine section of *Maariv,* February 8, 1991.
2. Taanit 16a.
3. See Goldberg's *P'nay Baruch* 41:1.
4. Moed Katan 2a. The Mishna (1:1) indicates that grave sites were marked with white lime as a warning to passersby.
5. See Yerushalmi Shekalim 2:5.
6. Ibid. 11a.
7. See *Theology in the Responsa,* by Louis Jacobs, p. 305.
8. See Moed Katan 5a.
9. Yerushalmi Shekalim 2:5.
10. See *P'nay Baruch* 41:1, note 2.
    In Hebrew the term *olam ha-nefashim* is a poetic synonym for the "world-to-come," used by Moses ibn Ezra. See *P'nay Baruch,* p. 388.
11. Yoreh Deah 362:1. See also Eruvin 53a.
12. See Freehof's *Reform Jewish Practice,* pp. 123-24, for more on this subject.

13. Eruvin 55b.
14. See *Theology in the Responsa,* by Louis Jacobs, p.276.
15. See *P'nay Baruch* 41:7, note 12.
16. *Jewish Encyclopedia,* Volume XII, p. 193.
17. See Tuktzinsky's *Gesher Ha-cha'yim* 28:3 and Goldberg's *P'nay Baruch* 41:3-5.
18. In the Jewish literary tradition it is customary to substitute more delicate terminology for harsh or negative words and expressions. Thus, for example, the talmudic tractate that deals with death is euphemistically referred to as *Semachot,* meaning "Rejoicings," rather than by its original name, *Evel Rabbati,* meaning "The Great [Treatise on] Mourning."

    Similarly, page numbers in major Jewish classics are often changed because of their negative meaning. The page number 270 is *resh a'yin* in Hebrew, which spells out the word *ra,* meaning "evil," and the letters were therefore rearranged in many Jewish classics and appear as *a'yin resh,* which has no particular meaning. There are many such changes in page numbering, especially in *halachic* (legal) literature.

    For other examples of delicate language being substituted for harsher language, consult the masoretic text on Deuteronomy 28:27 and 28:30. See also Berachot 58a, where a blind man is referred to by the Aramaic expression *sagi-nahor,* literally meaning "one who sees much light."
19. See *Encyclopedia Judaica,* Volume VI, pp. 818-22.
20. This issue was the subject of a lawsuit in San Francisco, CA, in which Sinai Memorial Chapel objected to the erection in their cemetery of a stone engraved with a human likeness. On June 14, 1991, the San Francisco Appellate Court agreed with Sinai, which contended that it was a violation of Jewish law and that it offended many of its clients.
21. See Greenwald's *Kol Bo Al Avelut,* p. 380.
22. See Trachtenberg's *Jewish Magic and Superstition,* p. 190.
23. See Goldberg's *P'nay Baruch.* 41:10.
24. See Pesikta Rabbati, Piska 12:1, and *Jewish Magic and Superstition,* p. 64.
25. See the Be'er Hetev commentary on the *Code of the Jewish Law,* Orach Cha'yim 224, note 8.

    The Falashas of Ethiopia were known to have a unique practice of heaping stones over a grave and sometimes planting a young tree nearby. See Leslau's *Falasha Anthology,* p. xix.
26. See Freehof's *Reform Jewish Practice,* p. 176.
27. Orach Cha'yim 581:4.
28. Taanit 16a.
29. Exodus Rabba 44:1.
30. Taanit 16a.
31. See Tuktzinsky's *Gesher Ha-cha'yim* 1:307 and Goldberg's *P'nay*

Baruch, 42:8-9.

32. Reported in *The Jewish Week,* March 6-12, 1992.
33. Yoreh Deah 367:2-4.
34. See Isserles on Yoreh Deah 368:1, who calls it *kalut rosh,* "frivolity."
35. See *Jewish Magic and Superstition,* pp. 46, 130, 160.
36. Bava Batra 10a.
37. See Isserles on *Shulchan Aruch,* Orach Cha'yim 581:4, where giving charity in a cemetery is discussed.
38. The custom is mentioned in the commentary of Rashbam (Samuel ben Meir, grandson of Rashi) on Bava Batra 100b.
39. Yoreh Deah 363.
40. See Moshe Feinstein's *Igrot Moshe,* Yoreh Deah II:162.

Notes to Chapter 11

MEMORIALIZING THE DEAD
Pages 240 to 266

1. Orach Cha'yim 621:6.
2. Sifre, Shoftim, 209.
3. See Schauss's *Lifetime of a Jew,* pp. 299-300.
4. Nedarim 12a.
5. See Freehof's *Reform Jewish Practice,* p. 171.
6. See the Be'er Hetev on Orach Cha'yim 132, note 5, and also on Orach Cha'yim 568:8.
7. See Yoreh Deah 402:12 and Goldberg's *P'nay Baruch* 44:35.
8. See *P'nay Baruch* 44:37-38 for a detailed discussion of the views of various authorities and a listing of sources.
9. *P'nay Baruch* 44:11.
10. See pp. 297-98.
11. See the note of Isserles on Yoreh Deah 376:4.
12. See Dobrinsky's *Treasury of Sephardic Laws and Customs,* p. 75.
    Moses Isserles, in his notes to the *Code of Jewish Law* (Yoreh Deah 376:4), comments that a son should lead the Saturday night *Maariv* service and should recite the Kaddish. When the Sabbath is over, he explains, the souls that have not yet been permitted to enter paradise return to their place in *gehinnom* (hell). By leading the service and reciting the Kaddish, the son is "redeeming" his parents and forestalling their return to the netherworld. Isserles makes the point that it is customary to recite Kaddish for one's mother as well as one's father.
13. See Jacob's *Theology in the Responsa,* pp. 273-74.
14. Nedarim 12a.
15. See Orach Cha'yim 568:7 and *P'nay Baruch* 44:24.

16. Ibid. 44:28.
17. See Orach Cha'yim 581:4. Isserles notes: "There are some places where it is customary to visit graves, to pray there, and to give charity to the poor."
18. See *P'nay Baruch* 44:10.
19. Ibid. 44:12.
20. See *This Is the Torah,* by Alfred J. Kolatch, pp. 196-97, and Dobrinsky's *Treasury of Sephardic Laws and Customs,* p. 86.
21. See *P'nay Baruch* 44:8.
22. See Yoreh Deah 340:30.
23. Yevamot 122a and Nedarim 12a.
24. See *Yalkut Shimoni,* Tehilim 735.
25. See *P'nay Baruch* 44:16.
26. See Bleich's *Contemporary Halakhic Problems* I, pp. 221-24, for more on the use of electric lamps on the Sabbath and on Chanuka.
27. See Tuktzinsky's *Gesher Ha-cha'yim* 1:343.
28. See *P'nay Baruch* 44:15, 20.
29. Some scholars believe that the Yizkor service is much older. It was first introduced, they believe, in 165 B.C.E. in the Maccabean period, when Judah Maccabee and his soldiers prayed for their fallen comrades and brought sacrifices to the Temple in Jerusalem to atone for the sins of the dead (II Maccabees 12:39-43).
30. Orach Cha'yim 621:6.
31. The early Reform prayerbooks included the Yizkor only as part of the liturgy for the Day of Atonement. Later editions of the Union Prayerbook added the memorial prayers to the service of the seventh day of Passover. Today, in many Reform synagogues a Yizkor service is conducted on the other major festivals as well. See *Reform Jewish Practice,* by Solomon Freehof, p. 30.
32. The Rabbis refer to Shemini Atzeret as *regel bifnay atzma,* a separate holiday, and require that the *She-hecheyanu* prayer be recited when the candles are lighted and when the *Kiddush* is recited. This would not be required were Shemini Atzeret not an independent holiday.
33. See *P'nay Baruch* 43:7.
34. Ibid. 43:14.
35. Ibid. 43:9.
36. Ibid. 43:8.
37. Ibid. 43:10.
38. See Maurice Lamm's *Becoming a Jew,* pp. 247-53.
39. Parashat Lech Lecha. See also the Babylonian Talmud, Shabbat 66b.

Notes to Chapter 12
THE AFTERLIFE
Pages 267 to 282

1. See Moore's *Judaism,* Volume II, p. 380.
2. Ketubot 111b.
3. Sota 22a.
4. Berachot 28b.
5. In his *Judaism: Profile of a Faith,* p. 132, Rabbi Ben Zion Bokser notes that a survey of classic Jewish writers on the subject of heaven and hell reveals that this doctrine is subject to two interpretations. He writes: "The exponents of conventional Jewish piety who remained untouched by philosophical thought tended to interpret this doctrine literally." They understood the rewards and punishments associated with heaven and hell to be real and physical. On the other hand, the idea of a physical heaven and a physical hell where rewards and punishments were assigned and carried out "has seemed repugnant to many people in modern no less than in ancient times."
6. Throughout the Talmud there are references to *Gan Eden* and *gehinnom* as actual terrestrial places. See Taanit 10a; Bava Kama 84a; and Eruvin 19a.
7. Bava Batra 75a.
8. Sanhedrin 90a.
9. Gabicha ben Pasisa was the spokesman of the Jewish community in their dispute with the Samaritans. The Samaritans claimed that the Temple they had built on Mount Gerizim (near Shechem/Nablus), and not the one in Jerusalem, should be recognized as *the* Jewish Temple. See Bader's *Jewish Spiritual Heroes,* Volume I, p. 51.
10. One Rabbi of the Talmud (Taanit 31) visualized heaven as a place in which God sits surrounded by a chorus of righteous people who will dance all around Him, and with fingers pointed toward God will sing His praises, such as those written in the Book of Isaiah (25:9):

> In that day they shall say:
> This is our God;
> We trusted in Him, and He delivered us.
> This is the Lord in whom we trusted,
> Let us rejoice and revel in His deliverance.

11. Berachot 17a.
12. See Misneh Torah: Hilchot Teshuva 8:2.
13. See *Theology in the Responsa,* by Louis Jacobs, p. 53. Scholars of the post-talmudic era were less inclined to characterize life in the hereafter in physical terms. *Gan Eden* to Rabbi Moses ben

Nachman (Nachmanides, 1194-1270) was a "world of souls" (*olam ha-neshamot* in Hebrew), a place where only the souls, not the bodies, of the departed would enter after death.

14. One of the most ardent present-day disciples of Maimonides is the prominent Orthodox Israeli scientist, philosopher, and historian Yeshayahu Leibowitz. He shares many but not all of Maimonides' ideas on the afterlife and has expressed them forth rightly, even though they do not meet with the approval of the Orthodox establishment generally. In an interview with Israeli students (reported in the February 8, 1991 edition of "*Sof Shavua,*" the weekend supplement of the *Maariv* newspaper), the renowned Hebrew University professor was asked about his personal view of the afterlife.

    "Death has no significance,'" he said. "Only life matters."

    One student then asked: "What is Judaism's attitude toward death?"

    Leibowitz replied: "In the entire Torah there is not the slightest suggestion that anything happens after death. All the ideas and theories articulated on the subject of a world-to-come and the resurrection of the dead have no relationship to religious faith. It is sheer folklore. After you die, you simply do not exist." (See also *Conflicting Visions,* by David Hartman, for important essays on the philosophy of Yeshayahu Leibowitz.)

15. Ketubot 111b.
16. Ethics of the Fathers 2:6.
17. Berachot 18 a-b.
18. See also Fred Rosner's *Maimonides' Commentary on the Mishna,* pp. 144, 172-73.
19. Our ancestors believed that the nostrils are the apertures through which life enters and leaves man's body.

    Jewish legend tells that until the time of the patriarch Jacob, people did not become ill before dying. They simply sneezed, then died immediately. Sneezing was believed to signal approaching death.

    In early times, Jews as well as other peoples believed that sneezing was the work of evil spirits determined to take a man's life, and that their plan could be frustrated by uttering biblical quotations or other expressions. Jews have been known to respond to a sneeze with the verse uttered by Jacob on his deathbed, "For thy salvation have I hoped, O Lord" (Genesis 49:18), or by exclamations such as "God bless you" and *"Gezundheit"* ("to your health").
20. See Judges 5:19 and II Kings 23:29, where reference is made to two such conflicts.
21. See Trachtenberg's *Jewish Magic and Superstition,* p. 154.
22. See Louis Ginzberg's *Legends of the Jews,* Volume I., pp. 282-86, for detailed information on this subject.

Among the Jews of Tangiers, it is customary to blow the *shofar* (ram's horn) when a religious leader (*chacham,* literally "wise one") is being buried. See Dobrinsky's *Treasury of Sephardic Laws and Customs,* p. 82. This practice is linked to the traditional concept that when the Messiah comes in the end of days, his appearance will be heralded by blasts of the *shofar.*

23. *Mishneh Torah,* Hilchot Teshuva 9:2.
24. Yerushalmi Taanit 4:3.
25. See the Book of Ruth 4:18-22 for David's lineage.
26. Hilchot Teshuva 11:1.
27. Sanhedrin 97a, 98a.
28. In fact, Rabbi Chayim Vital, the famous disciple of Rabbi Isaac Luria, wrote a whole book on this theme, *Sefer Ha-gilgulim (Book of the Transmigration of Souls).* See *Jewish Magic and Superstition,* by Joshua Trachtenberg, p. 50.

Bibliography

Abrahams, Israel. *Jewish Life in the Middle Ages*. London: Edward Goldston Ltd., 1932.

Agus, Irving. *Rabbi Meir of Rothenburg*. New York: Ktav Publishing House, 1970.

Arzt, Max. *Justice and Mercy*. New York: Holt, Rinehart, and Winston, 1963.

Asheri, Michael. *Living Jewish*. New York: Everest House, 1978.

The Babylonian Talmud (Hebrew). Twenty volumes. Vilna: Romm, 1922.

The Babylonian Talmud (English). Thirty-five volumes. London: Soncino Press, 1935.

Bader, Gershom. *Jewish Spiritual Heroes*. Three volumes. New York: Pardes Publishing House, n.d.

Birnbaum, Philip. *Ha-siddur Ha-shalem*. New York: Hebrew Publishing Co., 1949.

Bleich, David J. *Contemporary Halakhic Problems*. Volume I. New York: Ktav Publishing House, 1977.

Bloch, Abraham P. *The Biblical and Historical Background of Jewish Customs and Ceremonies*. New York: Ktav Publishing House, 1980.

Bokser, Ben Zion. *Judaism: Profile of a Faith*. New York: Knopf, 1963.

Braude, William G. *Pesikta Rabbati*. Two volumes. New Haven: Yale University Press, 1968.

Caro, Joseph. *Code of Jewish Law (Shulchan Aruch)*. Eight volumes. Vilna edition. New York: Abraham Isaac Friedman, n.d.

Cohen, A. *Everyman's Talmud*. New York: E.P. Dutton, 1949.

The Complete ArtScroll Siddur. New York: Mesorah Publications, 1985.

Danby, Herbert. *The Mishna*. Oxford, England: Clarendon Press, 1933.

Danzig, Abraham ben Jechiel Michal. *Chochmat Adam.* Vilna, 1812.

Denburg, Chaim R. *Code of Jewish Law: Yoreh Deah.* Montreal, Canada: Jurisprudence Press, 1954.

Dobrinsky, Herbert A. *A Treasury of Sephardic Laws and Customs.* New York: Yeshiva University Press/Ktav Publishing House, 1986.

Donin, Hayim H. *To Be a Jew.* New York: Basic Books, 1972.

———. *To Pray as a Jew.* New York: Basic Books, 1980.

Eichhorn, David Max, *Musings of the Old Professor.* New York: Jonathan David Publishers, 1963.

Elfenbein, Israel. *Sefer Teshuvot Rashi.* Bnai Brak, Israel: Yahadut Publishers, 1980.

Encyclopedia Judaica. Seventeen volumes. Jerusalem: Keter Publishing House Ltd., 1971.

Epstein, Yechiel. *Aruch Ha-shulchan.* Eight volumes. Warsaw, 1900-1912.

Ettlinger, Yaakov. *Binyan Tziyon.* Germany, 1868.

Even-Shoshan, Abraham. *Milon Chadash.* Four volumes. Jerusalem: Kiryat Sepher, 1964.

———. *A New Concordance of the Bible.* Four volumes. Jerusalem: Kiryat Sepher, 1980.

Fackenheim, Emil L. *What Is Judaism?* New York: Summit Books, 1987.

Freehof, Solomon B. *Contemporary Reform Responsa.* Cincinnati: Hebrew Union College Press, 1974.

———. *Current Reform Responsa.* Cincinnati: Hebrew Union College Press, 1969.

———. *Modern Reform Responsa.* Cincinnati: Hebrew Union College Press, 1971.

———. *Reform Jewish Practice,* Volumes I and II. Augmented edition. This is a revised and enlarged edition of *Reform Jewish Practice* with material from *Reform Responsa.* Ktav Publishing House, 1976.

———. *Reform Responsa and Recent Reform Responsa.* Two volumes in one. New York: Ktav Publishing House, 1973.

Ginzberg, Louis. *The Legends of the Jews.* Seven volumes. Philadelphia: Jewish Publication Society, 1956.

Goldberg, Chayim Binyamin. *P'nay Baruch.* Jerusalem: Published privately, 1946.

———. *Mourning in Halachah.* New York: Mesorah Publications, 1991.

Goldreich, Gloria. *A Treasury of Jewish Literature*. New York: Holt, Rinehart and Winston, 1982.

Graetz, Heinrich. *History of the Jews*. Six volumes. Philadelphia: Jewish Publication Society, 1891.

Graves, Robert, and Patai, Raphael. *Hebrew Myths: The Book of Genesis*. New York: Greenwich House, 1983.

Grayzel, Solomon. *A History of the Jews*. Philadelphia: Jewish Publication Society, 1969.

Greenberg, Blu. *How to Run a Traditional Jewish Household*. New York: Simon and Schuster, 1983.

Greenberg, Sidney. *A Treasury of Comfort*. New York: Crown Publishers, 1954.

Greenwald, Yekutiel. *Ach Le-tzara*. St. Louis: Quality Printing and Publishing Co., 1939.

———. *Kol Bo Al Avelut*. New York: Printed privately, 1947.

Guttmann, Alexander. *The Struggle Over Reform in Rabbinic Literature*. New York: World Union for Progressive Judaism, 1977.

Hadas, Gershon. *The Book of Psalms*. New York: Jonathan David Publishers, 1964.

Hartman, David. *Conflicting Visions*. New York: Schocken Books, 1990.

Hertz, Joseph H. *Daily Prayer Book*. New York: Bloch Publishing Co., 1948.

The Interpreter's Bible. Twelve volumes. Nashville: Abingdon Press, 1957.

Jacob, Walter, editor. *American Reform Responsa*. New York: Central Conference of American Rabbis, 1983.

Jacobs, Louis. *Theology in the Responsa*. London: Routledge & Kegan Paul, 1975.

The Jewish Encyclopedia. Twelve volumes. New York: Funk and Wagnalls, 1912.

Josephus, Flavius. *The Antiquities of the Jews*. Grand Rapids, Michigan: Kregel Publications, 1960.

Kahn, Lothar. *God: What People Have Said About Him*. New York: Jonathan David Publishers, 1980.

Klagsbrun, Francine. *Voices of Wisdom*. New York: Jonathan David Publishers, 1986.

Klein, Isaac. *Responsa and Halakhic Studies*. New York: Ktav, 1975.

———. *A Guide to Jewish Religious Practice*. New York: Jewish Theological Seminary of America, 1979.

Kolatch, Alfred J. *The Jewish Book of Why*. New York: Jonathan David Publishers, 1981.

————. *The Second Jewish Book of Why.* New York: Jonathan David Publishers, 1985.

————. *This Is the Torah.* New York: Jonathan David Publishers, 1988.

————. *Who's Who in the Talmud.* New York: Jonathan David Publishers, 1964.

Lamm, Maurice. *The Jewish Way in Death and Mourning.* New York: Jonathan David Publishers, 1969.

————. *Becoming a Jew.* New York: Jonathan David Publishers, 1991.

Landau, Ezekiel. *Noda Biyehuda.* Two volumes. Jerusalem: Books Export Enterprises Ltd., n.d.

Leslau, Wolf. *Falasha Anthology: Black Jews of Ethiopia.* New Haven: Yale University Press, 1951.

Maimonides, Moses. *The Mishneh Torah.* Five volumes. Warsaw, 1881.

Millgram, Abraham. *Jewish Worship.* Philadelphia: Jewish Publication Society, 1971.

Moore, George Foot. *Judaism.* Three volumes. Cambridge, Massachusetts: Harvard University Press, 1954.

Morgenstern, Julian. *Rites of Birth, Marriage and Death Among the Semites.* Chicago: Quadrangle Books, 1966.

Polish, David, editor. *Rabbis's Manual.* New York: Central Conference of American Rabbis, 1988.

Rabinowicz, Harry M. *A Guide to Life: Jewish Laws and Customs of Mourning.* London: Jewish Chronicle Publications, 1964.

Riemer, Jack. *Jewish Reflections on Death.* New York: Schocken Books, 1974.

Rosner, Fred. *Maimonides Commentary on the Mishna: Tractate Sanhedrin.* New York: Sepher-Hermon Press, 1981.

Rosenberg, David. *Congregation: Contemporary Writers Read the Bible.* New York: Harcourt Brace Jovanovich, 1987.

Roth, Cecil, and Wigoder, Geoffrey. *The New Standard Jewish Encyclopedia.* New York: Doubleday & Co., 1977.

Roth, Philip. *Patrimony.* New York: Simon and Schuster, 1991.

Saperstein, Marc. *Jewish Preaching: 1200-1800.* New York: Yale University Press, 1989.

Schauss, Hayyim. *The Lifetime of a Jew.* New York: Union of American Hebrew Congregations, 1950.

Singer, Isaac Bashevis. *The Magician of Lublin.* New York: Noonday Press, 1960.

Sofian, Simone Lotven. *Taharat Ha-metim*. New York: Journal of Reform Judaism, 1991.

Svara: A Journal of Philosophy and Judaism. Vol. 1, no. 1. New York: Columbia University School of Law, 1990.

Telushkin, Joseph. *Jewish Literacy*. New York: William Morrow & Co., 1991.

Trachtenberg, Joshua. *Jewish Magic and Superstition*. New York: Behrman House, 1939.

Trepp, Leo. *The Complete Book of Jewish Observance*. New York: Behrman House, 1980.

Tuktzinsky, Yechiel. *Gesher Ha-cha'yim*. Three volumes. Jerusalem: Solomon Printers, 1960.

Urbach, Ephraim E. *The Halakhah: Its Source and Development*. Jerusalem: Massada Ltd., 1986.

Weiss, Abner. *Death and Bereavement*. Hoboken, New Jersey: Ktav Publishing House, 1991.

Wolfson, Harry A. *Philo*. Cambridge, Massachusetts: Harvard University Press, 1947.

Zlotnick, Dov. *The Tractate Mourning (Semachot)*. New Haven: Yale University Press, 1966.

Index

About the Author

ALFRED J. KOLATCH, a graduate of the Teacher's Institute of Yeshiva University and its College of Liberal Arts, was ordained by the Jewish Theological Seminary of America, which subsequently awarded him the Doctor of Divinity degree, *honoris causa*. From 1941 to 1948 he served as rabbi of congregations in Columbia, South Carolina, and Kew Gardens, New York, and as a chaplain in the United States Army. In 1948 he founded Jonathan David Publishers, of which he has since been president and editor-in-chief.

Rabbi Kolatch has authored more than a dozen books, the most popular of which are *The Jewish Home Advisor, This Is the Torah,* and the best-selling *Jewish Book of Why* and its sequel, *The Second Jewish Book of Why.* Several of the author's works deal with nomenclature, about which he is an acknowledged authority. *The New Name Dictionary* and *The Complete Dictionary of English and Hebrew First Names* are his most recent books on the subject. Other books by the author include *Our Religion: The Torah, Jewish Information Quiz Book, Who's Who in the Talmud,* and *The Family Seder.*

In addition to his scholarly work, Rabbi Kolatch is interested in the work of the military chaplaincy and has served as president of the Association of Jewish Chaplains of the Armed Forces and as vice-president of the interdenominational Military Chaplains Association of the United States.